The Futures of Old Age

The Futures of Old Age

edited by
John A. Vincent
Chris Phillipson
and
Murna Downs

 SAGE Publications

London ● Thousand Oaks ● New Delhi

published in association with

Editorial arrangement and Introductions
© British Society of Gerontology, 2006
Chapter 1 © Sage Publications, 2006
Chapter 2 © Sage Publications, 2006
Chapter 3 © Sage Publications, 2006
Chapter 4 © Sage Publications, 2006
Chapter 5 © Sage Publications, 2006
Chapter 6 © Sage Publications, 2006
Chapter 7 © Sage Publications, 2006
Chapter 8 © Sage Publications, 2006
Chapter 9 © Sage Publications, 2006
Chapter 10 © Sage Publications, 2006

Chapter 11 © Sage Publications, 2006
Chapter 12 © Sage Publications, 2006
Chapter 13 © Sage Publications, 2006
Chapter 14 © Sage Publications, 2006
Chapter 15 © Sage Publications, 2006
Chapter 16 © Sage Publications, 2006
Chapter 17 © Sage Publications, 2006
Chapter 18 © Sage Publications, 2006
Chapter 19 © Sage Publications, 2006
Chapter 20 © Sage Publications, 2006
Chapter 21 © Sage Publications, 2006

First published 2006

SAGE Publications Ltd
1 Oliver's Yard
55 City Road
London EC1Y 1SP

SAGE Publications Inc.
2455 Teller Road
Thousand Oaks, California 91320

SAGE Publications India Pvt Ltd
B-42, Panchsheel Enclave
Post Box 4109
New Delhi 110 017   Aug2017

British Library Cataloguing in Publication data

A catalogue record for this book is available
from the British Library

ISBN-10 1-4129-0107-3   ISBN-13 978-1-4129-0107-9
ISBN-10 1-4129-0108-1 (pbk)   ISBN-13 978-1-4129-0108-6 (pbk)

Library of Congress Control Number: 2005934447

Typeset by C&M Digitals (P) Ltd., Chennai, India
Printed on paper from sustainable resources

Contents

List of Figures and Tables

Figures

Tables

List of Contributors

Sara Arber is Professor of Sociology and Co-Director of the Centre for Research on Ageing and Gender (CRAG) at the University of Surrey, Guildford, UK. She was President of the British Sociological Association (1999–2001).

Vern Bengtson holds the AARP/University Chair in Gerontology and is Professor of Sociology at the University of Southern California, USA.

Simon Biggs has a background in social psychology and social policy and is Professor of Gerontology and Director of the Institute of Gerontology at King's College London, UK.

Andrew Blaikie is Professor of Historical Sociology in the School of Social Science at the University of Aberdeen, UK. He is co-editor of the journal *Cultural Sociology*.

John Bond was trained as a sociologist. He is Professor of Social Gerontology and Health Services Research at the Centre for Health Services Research, and an Associate Director of the Institute for Ageing and Health, based at the University of Newcastle upon Tyne, UK. He is senior editor of the BSG introductory textbook *Ageing in Society*.

Errollyn Bruce is Lecturer in Dementia Studies with the Bradford Dementia Group, the Division of Dementia Studies at the University of Bradford, UK.

Peter Coleman is Professor of Psychogerontology at the University of Southampton, and was editor of the BSG's journal *Ageing and Society* 1992–96 and co-editor of the first two editions of its textbook *Ageing in Society: An Introduction to Social Gerontology*, 1990 and 1993.

Lynne Corner is Research Associate at the Centre for Health Services Research and Institute for Aging and Health at the University of Newcastle upon Tyne, UK. She is also coordinator for Years Ahead – the North East Forum on Aging.

Dale Dannefer is Professor of Sociology, Case Western Reserve University, Cleveland, USA.

Kate Davidson was originally a nurse and health visitor before under-taking a degree in Social Policy as a mature student. She is a Senior Lecturer in the Department of Sociology at the University of Surrey, UK and Co-Director of the Centre for Research on Ageing and Gender (CRAG). She was BSG Secretary 1996–2002 and is currently President Elect taking office 2006–2008.

Murna Downs is Professor of Dementia Studies and Head of the Bradford Dementia Group, the Division of Dementia Studies at the University of Bradford, UK. She is a member of the Executive Committee of the British Society of Gerontology.

Maria Evandrou is Professor of Gerontology and Director of the Centre for Research on Ageing in the School of Social Sciences at the University of Southampton, UK. She was Honorary Secretary of the BSG and is currently a member.

Jane Falkingham is Professor of Demography and International Social Policy in the Division of Social Statistics at the University of Southampton, UK. She is a member of the BSG.

Liam Foster is a doctoral student, in the Department of Sociological Studies, University of Sheffield, UK, specializing in pensions and gender.

Jay Ginn is a Visiting Professor in the Sociology Department at Surrey University, UK. She has researched and published widely on gender inequalities in pensions including two recent books (Ginn, 2003; Ginn et al., 2001). She has also researched older workers' attitudes to retirement timing. She contributes to the work of the National Pensioners Convention (NPC), the Women's Budget Group, the Fawcett Society and the Independent Pensions Research Group.

Jaber F. Gubrium is Professor and Chair of Sociology at the University of Missouri-Columbia. He is the editor of the *Journal of Aging Studies*.

Sarah Harper is Director of the Oxford Institute of Ageing at the University of Oxford.

James A. Holstein is Professor of Sociology in the Department of Social and Cultural Sciences at Marquette University, USA. He is editor of the journal *Social Problems*.

Casey M. Miklowski is a graduate student in the Department of Sociology of Case Western Reserve University, Cleveland, USA.

Dr Marie Mills is both a practising psychotherapist and a researcher in the School of Psychology, University of Southampton, UK, with a background in residential and particularly dementia care practice.

Richard Minns is an independent researcher on economic development and pensions with degrees in politics and economics, political science, and social administration, and is a Visiting Fellow at Sheffield University, UK.

James Nazroo has qualifications in medicine and sociology, and is Professor of Medical Sociology in the International Institute for Society and Health, UCL, UK.

Sheila Peace was trained as a human geographer and is Professor of Social Gerontology and Associate Dean (Research) in the Faculty of Health and Social Care at The Open University, UK. She is currently a member of the Executive Committee of the BSG and is co-editor of the second and third editions of the textbook *Ageing in Society*.

Chris Phillipson was trained as a sociologist, is a Professor of Applied Social Studies and Social Gerontology at Keele University, UK, and is President of the British Society of Gerontology.

Debora Price is a lecturer in the Social Policy of Ageing at the Institute of Gerontology, King's College London, having previously practised law as a barrister in London.

Norella M. Putney has a doctorate in Sociology from the University of Southern California and teaches there in the Leonard Davis School of Gerontology.

Revd Prebendary Peter Speck trained in zoology and biochemistry before studying theology, has spent most of his ministry in health care chaplaincy, and is currently Visiting Fellow both at King's College London and the University of Southampton, UK.

Christina Victor is Professor of Social Gerontology and Health Services Research and Head of the School of Health and Social Care at the University of Reading, UK.

John A. Vincent was trained as a Social Anthropologist and is a Senior Lecturer in the Department of Sociology at the University of Exeter, UK. He is the BSG publications officer.

Alan Walker is Professor of Social Policy and Social Gerontology at the University of Sheffield, UK and Director of the UK New Dynamics of Ageing Programme and of the European Research Area in Ageing.

Tony Warnes trained in human geography and economic history. He is Professor of Social Gerontology at the Sheffield Institute for Studies on Ageing, University of Sheffield, UK. He was formerly Secretary (1984–90) and Chair (1994–2000) of the BSG, and is currently Editor of *Ageing and Society*, the CUP journal which the BSG co-sponsors with the Centre for Policy on Ageing.

Foreword

More people are living into old age than at any time in the past and this observation is true over much of the world. But old age is often seen as a problem. Many people are searching to find better ways of living a good old age. There are social movements striving to produce a more positive social attitude to old age and elderly people. Population ageing is seen as a major force transforming relationships at various levels – in the health and social care system, in the economy, and in society as a whole. As a result the future of old age has become an important and controversial issue in the contemporary world.

The British Society of Gerontology (BSG) commissioned this book to provide a major assessment of the different changes involved in the future of old age and to reflect upon options for key areas affecting older people. The Society itself was founded in 1971 to provide a multidisciplinary forum for researchers and practitioners involved in the field of ageing. The strength of the BSG has been its commitment to working across a broad area of the social and behavioural sciences, together with the humanities, to further understanding of the possibilities as well as the challenges introduced by population ageing. This volume provides an illustration of this approach, drawing on essays from a broad array of disciplines, and from researchers who have made major contributions to the development of social gerontology.

The book is an attempt to stand outside of immediate commercial and political pressures and to use the best of current research-informed insights to enable us to look into the futures of old age over the next generation. As well as illustrating a range of key issues arising from population ageing, this book also demonstrates the complexities of many of the questions involved, but at the same time the rewards that come from analysing both the options for social ageing as well as future scenarios. Social gerontology is currently a challenging and exciting endeavour and the purpose of this book is to provide readers with a grounding in the variety of current debates – theoretical and empirical as well as practitioner-based. The book should also be seen as demonstrating the value of expanding research into ageing, and bringing the full range of academic disciplines to explore what will be one of the critical issues for global society in the twenty-first century. The BSG is proud to be associated with this volume, is very grateful to its contributors, and hopes that it will provide a stimulus for further research and investigation in the years ahead.

Chris Phillipson
President, British Society of Gerontology

Acknowledgements

Figure 4.1 is reproduced with the kind permission of The Open University Press/McGraw-Hill Publishing Company.

We thank the Institute of Fiscal Studies for permission to use their copyright material in Table 4.2.

We acknowledge with thanks the use of Table 9.3 from P. Concialdi.

Figure 15.1 is reproduced with the kind permission of the Open University Press/McGraw-Hill Publishing Company.

Introduction

The purpose of this book is to examine the likely futures of old age over the next 30 years. The plural, 'futures', indicates the diversity and uncertainty of what lies ahead. The possibility of living a dignified fulfilled old age depends on both the numbers of older people and societal attitudes towards them. The twentieth century has seen dramatic changes to the way old age is experienced, driven in part by the unprecedented rise in the numbers of older people and the proportion of society they represent. It is anticipated that the changes that will occur in the present century will be no less dramatic. The various social, cultural, political and policy developments associated with demographic change are the key concerns addressed in this book. In this introduction we first consider the future of old age by looking at the demographic background and changes to the personal and social transitions associated with old age, and then introduce each section of the book with a brief overview of each of the contributions to the volume.

Population ageing and social change

The ageing of populations was one of the most important developments of the twentieth century and will raise major challenges for life in the twenty-first. The 2001 Census showed that for the first time the number of people in England and Wales aged 60 and over was greater than the number below age 16. The figures among the 'oldest old' illustrate the extent of change. In 1951 there were 0.2 million people aged 85 and over; by 2001 there were over 1.1 million. Populations across most of the world are ageing: the proportion of the global population aged 65 and over in 1900 was 1 per cent (UK 5 per cent); in 2000 it was 7 per cent (UK 16 per cent); and by 2050 it is estimated that it will be 20 per cent, a figure that the UK is likely to reach in 2020 (House of Lords, 2003). In general, population ageing reflects long-term declines in fertility and mortality rates. Parents are having on average fewer children, slowing the growth and even diminishing the size of successive generations. Improvements in health, hygiene and food supply mean that infant mortality has declined dramatically and many people who would have died in infancy now survive their full span of life to reach old age.

The past 100 years have seen major changes to the experiences and meanings associated with growing old. The conventional definition of chronological old age as starting at 60 or 65 is a modern phenomenon arising from the bureaucratization of the life course around the adminis-tration of retirement pensions. Historical work has identified the estab-lishment of retirement as a key marker of old age at 60 or 65 (Thane, 2000). In many western societies chronological age is symbolized through the cultural significance of birthdays (Bytheway, 2005). Landmark birth-days have come to include not only 21 and 100 but also the passing of decades. Bodily transitions such as greying hair, skin tone and acquisition of glasses, hearing aid or walking stick have meaning for the user but also act as signs to observers indicating membership of particular age cate-gories. The balance between chronological, bodily, social, spiritual, med-ical and other means of understanding old age have changed, and will continue to do so.

Cultural and behavioural as well as demographic changes form a sig-nificant background to debates about the shape of the institutions and social policies through which the future of old age will be worked out. There are a variety of debates across the world about the relationship between demographic change and its resulting impact on health, pensions and social welfare. This volume does not assume that greater numbers of older people automatically constitute a social problem. Rather, it seeks to explore, through the research evidence, possibilities for the future on the basis of what is currently known about economic, social and demo-graphic trends.

The structure of the book

The book is organized into seven parts, each of which has an introduc-tion and three contributions. The various sections deal with different kinds of futures which face older people: those relating to the life course and generational relations, social divisions in old age, retirement and pen-sions, the 'self' in old age, health issues, family and living arrangements for older people, and the impact of globalization on old age.

The first part assesses changes in the life course and the relationships between generations. In Chapter 1, Andrew Blaikie, examines generational issues from the perspective of cultural sociology. He suggests that people have contrasting views about fundamental issues such as the values attached to life and death, and that these to some degree reflect different generational locations. Blaikie goes on to highlight differences between 'baby-boomers' and 'Generation X' and explores the way in which the 'baby-boom generation' has attempted to sustain its orientation to youthfulness even into old age. Vern Bengtson and Norella Putney in Chapter 2 suggest that while relationships between people on the basis of age have become more problematic, family relations across the generations are crucial to the resolution of these 'intergenerational' issues. They argue that relatedness, interdependence and solidarity, which are essential parts of the multigenerational family, can mitigate potential conflicts between age groups and that there is a viable social contract between generations that will remain a characteristic of human society in the future. In Chapter 3, Dale Dannefer and Casey Miklowski take up the issue of the various ways in which the life course can be understood, exploring different levels of analysis – individual, collective and socio-cultural. After exploring each of these, they consider influences on the future of life course, notably in terms of the risks associated with late modernity, and the impact of globalization in creating new forms of inequality.

Part II examines the impact of social divisions in later life. Alan Walker and Liam Foster argue in Chapter 4 for the continued salience of class in understanding the experience of old age. The authors demonstrate the extent to which areas such as health, education and pensions continue to be structured by social class, influencing as a result a range of experiences throughout later life. In Chapter 5, Sara Arber examines the relationship between population change and gender, exploring in particular how the development of extended life expectancy combined with a narrowing in life-expectancy differences between men and women results in decreased rates of widowhood on the one hand and longer marriage on the other. In Chapter 6, James Nazroo focuses on issues facing ethnic minority groups. Nazroo emphasizes the extent of inequalities when different groups are compared, with those from Bangladesh and Pakistan facing particular problems in respect of health and income. Against this, the attachment to neighbourhoods and the availability of strong family and social networks appear important for a number of groups. The author also emphasizes the importance of generation and period for understanding changes affecting minority ethnic groups.

Part III examines a number of issues relating to income and pensions in later life. In Chapter 7, Debora Price and Jay Ginn examine some of the problems associated with pension provision, focusing in particular on the role of pensions in sustaining social inequality. The authors demonstrate that this issue has been especially acute for women, given their responsibilities for unpaid care within the home. Price and Ginn outline a number of policy options, arguing for a strengthening of the state system, with the retention of national insurance on top of substantial improvements to basic provision. Maria Evandrou and Jane Falkingham review likely scenarios for the 1960s baby-boom cohort in Chapter 8. They ask whether this cohort will fare better than their parents in retirement, especially as regards access to secure occupational pensions. A major finding from their study is that although many of the baby-boomers are indeed better off than their parents, this masks significant variation within the cohort. To redress these inequalities they propose, among other measures, restoring the link between the Basic State Pension and earnings and providing more generous credits to carers. Finally, in Chapter 9, Richard Minns examines the crisis affecting private pension provision, reflected in the shift from 'defined benefit' to 'defined contribution' schemes. He summarizes recent developments in pension policy, taking in Europe, Latin America and the Middle East. He notes that the pension reforms under way in most regions of the world have failed to justify the case for switching from state to privately financed support. He criticizes what he terms 'the stock-market model of social welfare', suggesting that this will almost certainly generate increased social divisions and inequalities.

Part IV examines the subjective dimension to growing old. In Chapter 10, Simon Biggs describes the 'self' of old age in relation to other, particularly younger, age groups, speculating how these relationships might change over time and their implications for sense of self and identity in old age. He describes the phenomena of age distinctiveness, in which there is a clear demarcation between young and old, and age blurring, in which such differences begin to disappear. He argues that while age blurring offers increased opportunities for more flexible identities in old age, at the same time it may lead to the neglect of the distinct developmental and existential tasks that need to be faced in this period of life. In Chapter 11, Jaber Gubrium and James Holstein discuss different ways of conceptualizing the future of the ageing self. One approach is to view the self as following a relatively fixed pathway through old age, determined either by developmental tasks or by specific historical experiences. Such options are, however, viewed by the authors as reducing the self to an appendage of other processes, related to stages in the life cycle or prior life experiences. An alternative model put forward is to consider the self as a product of ongoing 'biographical work', with individuals engaged in a process of assigning meaning to actions and experience over time. With this approach, the future of the ageing self is left open, dependent upon the interpretive possibilities available as individuals undertake the process of self-constructing their lives. In Chapter 12, Peter Coleman, Marie Mills and Peter Speck question whether conservatism and religiosity are 'natural' personality traits of the old. They ask whether personality, expressed in terms of religiosity, changes over time. Based on extensive empirical research they argue that a significant percentage of older people appear to become disenchanted with organized religion. Older people's view of themselves as religious may also be challenged by the contemporary climate of organized religion, which may fail to recognize the distinctive needs of an ageing congregation. The authors point to a number of possible futures in this area, with the possibility of a trend away from secularization, as evidenced by the significance of religious identity for many ethnic minority groups. At the same time, they note the importance of engaging with Church organizations with respect to the implications of demographic change, especially given their tendency to hold ageist assumptions about the spiritual needs of older people.

Part V examines a range of health issues arising from demographic change. In Chapter 13 Christina Victor addresses the extent to which our longevity will be linked to extended years of health or to longer periods of sickness. She provides three possible scenarios: the compression of morbidity, the expansion of morbidity, and the dynamic equilibrium between decreases in mortality and increases in life expectancy on the one hand and risk factors for disease on the other. Victor also highlights evidence for inequalities in the experience of chronic health conditions and associated morbidities, particularly with respect to gender, social class and ethnicity, and concludes that there is insufficient research on the diversity within the ageing population to understand who will have a healthy old age in future. In Chapter 14, Murna Downs and Errollyn Bruce consider the extent to which quality of life will be both maintained and improved for future cohorts of people with dementia and their families. They argue for the need for services and support for older people that promote health and well-being rather than exacerbate existing ill health or compromise well-being. Emotional well-being, particularly in care for people with dementia and for those at the end of life, has become a legitimate goal in and of itself. In Chapter 15 John Bond and Lynne Corner provide a critique of quality-of-life measurement and propose a more comprehensive approach to the idea of 'well-being'. They argue that our understanding has been hampered by a conceptual framework that places undue emphasis on health-related quality of life. The authors make a distinction between objective measures of quality of life and subjective accounts of how older people experience life, pointing out that such objective measures and subjective accounts are often at odds with one another. They argue that until we adequately conceptualize the meaning of life for an individual, including life with chronic conditions, measurements of quality of life will remain of questionable validity.

Part VI examines the family life and living arrangements of older people. In Chapter 16, Sarah Harper examines what she sees as the ageing of family life transitions, underpinned by changes to the 'demographic foundations of later life', notably with the delaying of key life events and the lengthening of life-stage durations. Harper reviews the impact of these developments on kinship roles and relationships, highlighting the importance of linking macro- and micro-levels of analysis in the study of contact and ties between generations. Chapter 17, by Kate Davidson, provides an account of the changing patterns of gender, family and intimate relationships in later life and their implications for the future. Her phrase 'flying solo again' captures the experience of many older people who face the prospect of living without their partners for the final period of their lives. In Chapter 18, Sheila Peace looks forward to the future of family relationships in terms of where and how people will live. She points to changing options for older people linked to the housing market, technological change and a variety of cultural and institutional changes. Peace points to the need for clarification and change in the current approach to social housing if the future is not to bring highly unequal possibilities of obtaining a decent old age.

The final part of the book considers the impact of globalization on the lives of older people. In Chapter 19 John Vincent looks at the way the global culture of science has brought significant changes to the way in which we think about growing old. The goals of anti-ageing science are widely popular, but they open the door to both commercial exploitation and bogus anti-ageing medicine. He concludes that a positive cultural evaluation of old age in the future requires that science comes to value old age as the final stage in life rather than seeking to eradicate it. On Chapter 20, Chris Phillipson examines the impact of globalization on re-shaping social relationships and social policies in old age. Transnational institutions arising from migration across the globe have transformed the environment in which many older people live. At the same time, international bodies of various kinds now have a major influence on national social policy. A key issue for the future will be the extent to which older people can play a part in shaping those policies which have a direct bearing on the quality of their life. The chapter argues that exploring the lives of older people as active participants in the new global environment will be a major challenge of gerontology in the twenty-first century. In the final chapter, Tony Warnes explores the interplay between globalization and migration. He notes that migration reflects both people's aspirations and their ability to achieve them, and, as a consequence, structures the possibilities for their old age. He sets social change within a large-scale historical and social framework and uses this framework to anticipate the consequences of diverse and continuing migration patterns that impinge on older people. These migration patterns include not only retirement migration but the complex sequences of generation succession which follow the migration flows that globalization opens up. If the ageing of the global workforce is to be considered a problem, the appropriate and efficient use of that population in different parts of the global economy is a vital issue.

Part I

The Future of the Life Course

Old age can be thought of as a stage in the life course, one of a series of transitions that people pass through between birth and death. There are strong normative expectations about appropriate behaviour for different points in the life course, including that of later life. However, life courses vary not only between different social groups – for example, between men and women – they also vary historically.

Models of the life course differ according to the number of life stages identified. There are two-stage models which simply contrast old age with the rest of life (for example, using categories such as adults and children, or working and retired). Three-stage models are also common and are often viewed as typical of modern life. The most common labels used are childhood, adulthood and old age, or pre-work, work and post-work. There are also modifications of three-stage models that bifurcate one of the stages in order to emphasize a particular aspect of that phase of life. Examples here are youth, adulthood, third age (young-old) and fourth age (old-old) constructed in order to emphasize the diversity of old age. In addition, there are models of psychological development across the life course, which tend to be weighted towards the early years (e.g. Erikson's eight stages (Erikson, 1986)). However, questions have been raised about the value of stage-based models, especially in the context of ideas about the 'de-standardization' and greater fluidity of life course transitions.

Distinctions between the pre-modern, modern and postmodern have also been used to characterize some of the changes in the life course experienced in western society. In pre-modern times people were perceived as old at the age at which they ceased to be independent, economically or physically, with, in practice, wide variation between groups and individuals. It is argued that modern society, and in particular the institutions of large-scale industrial capitalism, urban living and the nation state, tend to produce a new series of uniformities in the life course. Retirement is a modern phenomenon and in the twentieth century it has come to dominate our thinking about and understanding of old age (Mann, 2001). However, Featherstone and Hepworth (1989), writing from a postmodernist perspective, suggest that the life course is becoming progressively de-structured. Common social patterns determined by chronological age are becoming less important to people's life experience.

Another set of distinctions cluster around use of the term 'generations' and 'cohorts'. The term 'generation' is as evocative as it is imprecise, having at least three meanings. First and primary is generation as ranked placement within a family lineage. Individuals within a lineage occupy, shape and are influenced by multiple roles that are bound by norms of expectations, obligation and reciprocity. Secondly, at the macrosocial level, the term is used to refer to age groups: cohorts of people born at approximately the same time who experience the same historical changes at about the same stage of life. Issues of primary concern at the macrosocial level of age-cohort relations include public-resource allocation, citizens' expectations of government, and government's expectations of its citizens.

A third meaning is that of 'historical generations'. Karl Mannheim (1952) linked the process of the formation of succeeding generations to social change. He argued that those who live through a period of rapid social change (e.g. the 'Depression Generation') develop a distinct 'historical–social conscience' or collective identity which influences their attitudes and behaviours and distinguishes them from preceding generations. Age cohorts that are so transformed have left, at every life stage, an indelible mark on both its members and on the society through which they passed (Alwin and McCammon, 2003).

Thinking about old age in the future requires anticipation of the impact of specific generations. Those who are now 35 will be 65 in 30 years' time and will bring with them the experiences and culture of their generation. That generational set of knowledge and values means that they experience growing old in new ways. An important question tackled in Part I is: how will the generations of the future change the nature and understanding of old age? The cohort born in the postwar baby-boom in the late 1940s and early 1950s, who experienced the changes in social conventions of the 1960s and 1970s, may not accept the conventional view of old age as conservative and dependent but might seek expression in later life of the sexual liberation, lifestyle experimentation and cultural innovation of their teenage years. One social repercussion of differing cohort experience is sometimes referred to as a 'generation gap'. Although that term originated to describe differences between parents and teenagers, it may well describe the future cultural gulf between those retired and those in work.

How will the third age develop or change? What new divisions in the last part of the life course will emerge? Will older people be increasingly differentiated by wealth and class? What cultural and lifestyle changes can be anticipated? Postmodern approaches emphasize that modern affluence produces a redefinition of old age and creates new cultural agendas based on consumer choice (Gilleard and Higgs, 2000). A significant minority of older people at the end of the twentieth century have financial security unprecedented in the history of the modern west. Set against this, older people in Britain remain among the poorest in the community and may experience exclusion from important areas of social life (Scharf et al., 2002). Power, wealth and economic opportunity vary across time and differentially impact on different generations. Indeed, the increasing differentials between cohorts in terms of their actual and potential access to good opportunities and lifestyles, not least their access to good pensions, has led some to suggest the possibility for increasing conflict between generations. This is sometimes phrased as: 'Will the next, less numerous, generation be willing to pay increased pensions to the retired when the prospects that they themselves will receive a pension are diminishing?'

The questions identified above aim to introduce the reader to a variety of developments affecting the organization of the life course and highlight a range of possible futures for growing old as experienced through different generations and cohorts.[1]

Note

1 The editors wish to acknowledge the contribution of Vern Bengtson and Norella M. Putney to this introduction.

One   Visions of Later Life: Golden Cohort to Generation Z

Andrew Blaikie

Demography does much to produce cultural shifts, albeit inadvertently. Newman's poem 'The Dream of Gerontius' (1866) describes the death of an old man, following his soul into the afterlife. Its popularity was second only to Tennyson's 'In Memoriam' (1850), an elegy for a youngster of great promise taken in his early prime. Today this Victorian fascination with death and religion, promulgated in no small fashion by the Queen's obsessive mourning for Prince Albert, finds little resonance as extended life expectancy pledges greater fulfilment in the here-and-now. Our point of reference has shifted from the brevity of existence and its long aftermath to sustaining ourselves within the good long life. If death was the grand indulgence of our forebears, its status has been usurped by concern for the earthly future, the spiritual dimension eclipsed by matters of physical, psychological and financial well-being. The modern life course, rational, secularized and individualistic, has severed ties with the mystic order of things, and while postmodernity may yet offer possibilities to reconnect with the infinite, these remain limited by social frames of being, the constraints that class, gender, ethnicity, health status, socialization, education and age itself place upon our cultural imagination (Cole, 1992). Different people have different visions, depending on their location within the social system, a fact that directs attention towards generational tensions as much as social inequalities.

What makes the twentieth century and after unprecedented is the remarkable increase in longevity. This 'startling step change' is already evident in the surviving Golden Cohort (born 1918–45), who are living far longer than their predecessors, and the rise will become more rapid. The mushrooming proportion of society in the post-55 age ranges prompts talk no longer of old age, but of two observable categories of mid and later life: the third age of leisure and personal fulfilment, and the fourth age of decline and decrepitude (Laslett, 1987). While sequential, in that decline is an end stage of life, this division is not common to all, for while a majority of baby-boomers (born 1945–65) can look forward to a long span of healthy retirement and a mercifully brief final phase, fulfilment is dependent on rather more than simple longevity (Evandrou, 1997). So long as fourth-agers remain perceived as a 'burden of dependency' on the welfare system and third-agers as 'greedy baby-boomers' enjoying their leisure, tensions of the workers-versus-pensioners type will persist. Normal ageing is only problematic where we assume a particular institutionalization of the life course, namely the reified modernist chronology to which we are accustomed, equating education with childhood, adulthood with work, and old age with retirement. Yet although free-thinking futurologists suggest a collapsing of these 'three boxes of life', with breaks taken from work to enjoy extended leisure, or periods of 'retirement' interspersed with education, retraining and new careers, such liberation will only be for the privileged few so long as the vast majority remain trapped by the constraints of the 'work society' (Best, 1980; Kohli, 1988).

Retirement: pensions crisis or lifestyle opportunity?

Policymakers and theorists have tended to the opinion that there is little point in attempting to deconstruct an elephant when it is fast charging straight at us. In the 1940s, when Britain faced a declining birth rate, the Titmusses warned: 'We are up against something fundamental, something vast and almost terrifying in its grim relentless development. We cannot expect to muddle through.' Arguing that a 'process of the domination of old age and its interests has already been developing for some years', they claimed the country would soon need to produce 'armchairs and bedroom slippers instead of children's foods' while an ageing society would 'lose the mental attitude that is essential for social progress ... The future ... will require greater intelligence, courage, power of initiative, and qualities of creative imagination ... qualities ... not usually to be found in the aged' (Titmuss and Titmuss, 1942: 56, 47, 46). Their fears were unfounded, yet subsequent policy history is replete with generational misgivings. During the late 1980s, the panic took a swipe at third-agers, one journalist claiming: 'All over the developed world, the recently-retired are enjoying a golden age. Though governments everywhere are trimming back on welfare, so far most cuts and extra contributions have fallen on the young

13

and early middle-aged; their pensioner-parents have preserved their benefits largely intact' (Wilshier, 1989). No less alarmist have been the fears expressed over the fourth age. A symposium, 'The Impending Crisis of Old Age', talked of a serious problem 'already casting an unmistakable shadow over the National Health Service (NHS)', namely 'the marked increase in the numbers of the very elderly and frail people which will occur in Britain in the next 20 years' (Shegog, 1981: 11). That happened, but the NHS (and a greatly expanded private care sector) continues to cope despite considerable pressures. More recently, the Pensions Commission (2004b) reported that present arrangements will not provide for those retiring in a decade's time. The 17 million British baby-boomers face a stark choice: increased taxation, working longer, accepting reduced living standards or saving more (The Stationery Office (TSO), 2004). The new century is already witnessing a return to the former gloomy portrayal, entailing a shift 'from living in a fool's paradise to living in a sensible purgatory' (Marr, 2004).

Through its century or so of existence the idea of retirement has been reinvented several times. The common parameter has been that of work-ending: retirement has been defined more by what it is not – work – than by what it is. Yet elders become trapped in a moral and motivational bind, where although leisure practices increasingly become the location for self-identification, these practices are themselves analogous to forms of work. The continuing hegemony of the work ethic, identified in the characterization of 'emotional labour' (Hochschild, 1983) and 'body work' (Gimlin, 2002), is also evident in the earnest pursuit of retirement activities whereby a 'busy ethic' legitimates leisure as worthy rather than simply indulgent, and staying healthy or youthful demands that people 'work at' maintaining their bodies (Ekerdt, 1986). Thus leisure consumption in retirement is driven by similar imperatives to production during work time, provoking two questions: should employers reconsider how people might carry on working as they age; and, if older people do not continue to work, what meaningful role can capitalist societies conceive for this increasingly dominant age group? Both issues concern social integration: the first shifts attention from the rhetoric of pensions crisis to a problematization of work; the second raises the big question of the meaning of the life course in the contemporary world.

Since Generation X (born 1965–80) is less than two-thirds their size, forthcoming labour shortages could mean that many baby-boomers will be unable to retire. Or it may become increasingly practical to treat retirement as a gradual and flexible process rather than a ritualized event. With the 'babybust' already contributing to a skills shortage, it is logical that firms continue to tap the knowledge and experience of older employees by reducing incentives to early retirement. For employers, this could ease the financial burden of maintaining pension schemes while responding to anti-ageism legislation. Meanwhile, owing to the reduced value of occupational pensions, many employees will need to stay in work longer. Phased retirement schemes thus appeal on grounds of both demand and supply. If these become widespread, it will mean the rethinking of career trajectories, away from working up the ladder and reaching the top before retiring to gradual withdrawal from senior positions and, perhaps, re-entry into work after retirement.

It would be misleading, however, to concentrate on work as entirely deterministic in a consumer culture where identities depend less on what one does than how one lives. Modernity did much to devalue the status of the old. Because people are retired it is often assumed that they are no longer making a productive contribution. However, in a consumerist, late-modern environment they are increasingly important as purchasers of goods signifying particular lifestyles. Driven by the urge to remain forever youthful, the third-age habitus embraces 'positive ageing' through the pursuit of health, while enhanced cultural capital demands attention to body maintenance and the consumption of symbolic goods (Featherstone and Hepworth, 1986). 'Midlifestylism' accentuates choice and innovation – in clothing, cosmetics, exercise regimes, residence, pastimes – which are designed to combat ageing itself (Harkin and Huber, 2004). Although the requirements to work at staying sexually active, fit and self-reliant may be construed as imperative rather than liberating, refusal to engage the resources now available, for the sake of ageing 'naturally', could be seen as equally perverse.

The forms of later life once institutionalized through retirement are becoming deinstitutionalized, with individual elders increasingly negotiating paths through a multiplicity of choices. Such opportunities – or risks – come at the price of reduced welfare benefits as citizenship becomes more reliant on possessing sufficient financial and corporeal capital. Those lacking income or transferable skills are restricted to state or charity provision, while in the fourth age the bioethical position becomes fraught. While the sanctity of human life is a moral priority supported by law, questions of public versus private care and the possible rationing of expenditure according to principles of age-based triage point to difficult matters of potential generation disharmony (Binstock and Post, 1991). In Germany, where state pensions have risen by 30 per cent since 1970, the youth section of the Christian Democrats recently demanded, 'it's about time you 65-year-olds started paying for your own hip replacements' (Cohen, 2004). Such activism and invective could be just the beginning. Yet ironically population ageing has swayed voting power away from Generation X to their parents, whose numbers and electoral turnout have both been considerably higher. However, the grey vote remains highly fragmented and far from being simply self-interested, many, unsurprisingly, have their children's and grandchildren's interests at heart. This would question the conflict thesis.

The academics' dilemma

Turner defines a generation as 'a cohort of persons passing through time who come to share a common habitus and lifestyle'. Speculation about the future of class consciousness, racial awareness or sexual understandings would reasonably begin by considering the ways of seeing class, ethnic or gendered groups. By the same token, collective world views can be interpreted as belonging to generations. Moreover, because each generation bears 'a strategic temporal location [sic] to a set of resources as a consequence of historical accident and exclusionary practices of social closure', intergenerational differences are not merely ideological, but can have significant material effects, as with changing welfare polices (Turner, 1998: 302). Nevertheless, in the absence of systematic longitudinal data, comparing the effects of generational histories upon retirement experiences is necessarily speculative (Wadsworth, 1991).

The problem is compounded by the limited vision of sociological inquiry, which has yet to delineate a space for cultures of ageing equivalent to that enjoyed by youth culture, a fact that binds academic discourse itself firmly within the constraints of baby-boom thinking. The very genesis of cultural studies in the youth revolt of the 1960s ensured ageing was constituted as the distant but conservative 'other'. Academic discourse unquestioningly imbibed an essentialism that equated ageing with the languishing of that rebellious attitude seen as fundamental to social evolution. While echoing the views of the 1930s, yet failing to recognize their somewhat illiberal implications, a generation of social researchers disregarded the significance of a major societal phenomenon that paradoxically reflected the decline of youth itself, namely the expansion of the third age (Blaikie, 2004). Consequently, while sociologists have been late in analysing later life, they have often looked in the wrong places, claiming absence of innovation because subcultural equivalents of teenagers are hard to find. Although parallels exist between the emergence of youth culture in the 1950s and the rise of the third age in the 1980s (in some senses driven by the same people, only older), the culture of retirement does not lie with sexagenarians being at the forefront of fashion, underground art, or drug-fuelled happenings; nor is it located in stereotypically defined bingo sessions, Darby and Joan clubs or incarceration in 'homes'.

At the same time, the advocacy shared by many gerontologists and exponents of cultural studies, who decry racism, sexism or disablism, like ageism, lacks the detachment necessary to frame the bigger picture (Rojek and Turner, 2000). Rather, understanding retirement requires the engagement of key sociological concerns – including the body, self and citizenship – with the socioeconomic issues facing particular generations (Gilleard and Higgs, 2000). It is here, in the possibilities for rethinking roles and ways of presenting the self, but also in the erosion of workplace seniority and its potentially constraining effects on status and income in midlife, that cultural changes are being forged (Gullette, 2004). These shifts pertain to a generationally specific experience of values and attitudes, codified through world views that reflect changes in norms and lifestyles. For example, while a strong work ethic has been observed in attitudes to illness and death amongst working-class pensioners in the 1980s, the popularity of holiday cruises reflects both a desire for discovery and the embrace of hedonism by middle-class retirees in the 2000s (Blaikie, 1999; Williams, 1990). This said, observing is not enough: sociologists must examine the motives underlying apparent shifts, for, again, the possibility that leisure is pursued in ways that suggest 'keeping busy' can be read as evidence of continuity rather than change in the work ethic.

After the baby-boomers

The putative motives of separate cohorts clearly inform journalism and popular writing, if not gerontological research (Kotlikoff and Burns, 2004; Mullan, 2002; Wallace, 2001). By the early 1990s *Time, Newsweek* and *Fortune* were referring to the baby-boomers' successors as 'Generation X' (Tulgan, 1996). The 'X' moniker, first used by Fussell (1983) to describe a social group disparaging class, status and money, was reworked as a symbol of youth disaffection via the grunge music of Nirvana, Douglas Coupland's novel *Generation X* (1991) and the cult movie *Slacker* (Jochim, 1997). Characterized by 'short attention span and no work ethic, dropping out of the rat-race to live off parents or barely surviving in low-pay, low-status, short-term "McJobs"', the Xers' absence of motivation by the capitalist creed was starkly contrasted with the entrepreneurialism of their predecessors (Slattery, 1999). Instead, Coupland invoked a guiding philosophy of 'lessness', the reconciliation of self to 'diminishing expectations of material wealth', underlain by 'option paralysis – the tendency, when given unlimited choices, to make none' (cited in Slattery, 1999). While their nihilism found expression both in the suicide of Kurt Cobain, Nirvana's lead singer, and their designation as a depressed 'Prozac Nation', the marketers, though worried over Xers' 'skepticism to advertising claims, and attraction to personal style rather than designer price tags', recognize their relatively small size and have been busy inventing Generation Y (the Echo Boomers or Millennium Generation), the cohort born 1981–95, which at 57 million is 'the largest consumer group in the history of the US' (Onpoint, 2004; Wurtzel, 1994). In contrast to Xers, market researchers claim that Yers hold 'a distinctly practical world view'. Mostly raised in dual-income households with working mothers, although a quarter live with single parents, they have 'already been given considerable financial responsibility'. They expect careers and make five-year plans while still teenagers (Neuborne and Kerwin, 1999). Like their forerunners, they dwell a good deal on the Internet, only unlike today's older people who develop product loyalties and switch brands infrequently, or the Xers who disdain commodification, they see in its diversity the potential to transfer allegiances freely and rapidly as suits their mode.

These trends are less evident in Europe, partly because of cultural differences, but also because both Generations X and Y are to a degree figments of the marketers' sales-driven imaginations rather than established collective entities (Slattery, 1999). The future complexities of such elements as changing family obligations, in a world where 60-year-olds have parents still alive and may have grandchildren to care for as divorce, non-marriage and living alone increase, are simply not evaluated. Nevertheless, the underlying variations identified imply differences in motivation that plead further longitudinal research. If, say, it transpires that Generation X carries its apparently sceptical convictions with it into mid and later life, what are the implications for their attitude towards ageing, and how will those cohorts trailing behind them react? Their anti-consumerism might provide a brake on the materialism of their predecessors, but they would appear unlikely to offer any spiritual salvation in return. Equally, given that compulsory private saving is being mooted as company pension schemes wither, will Generation Y be a more consumer-wise echo of the baby-boomers, and, if so, what consequences await them in later life as the spread of choice and speed of change engulf them?

Conclusion

A recent consideration of inequality and well-being in later life contends that 'it is the prospect of circumventing old age that is now throwing up unexpected challenges' both for older people and for gerontologists (Higgs and Gilleard, 2004: 220). Certainly, research suggests that in wishing to conserve its youthfulness the baby-boom generation is intent upon denying its own destiny by distancing itself from confrontation with the challenges of deep old age, the enactment of this desire being evident in the supersession of 'old age' as a ubiquitous life stage by the sequential, but massively divergent, categories of third and fourth ages (Blaikie, 1999). Indeed, any 'liberation of the elders' relies upon emancipation both from the work and family responsibilities of adult life and from the wretched illness and poverty of deep old age. While this contributes to deepening inequalities between elders in the developed world and those in underdeveloped regions such as sub-Saharan Africa, the global expansion of the third age has attenuated rather than strengthened connections between generations as wisdom becomes devalued and the fourth age suffers from social taboos. Extended well-being, meanwhile, gains currency as 'a form of secular salvation' (Cole, 1992: 239).

Whatever cultural shifts occur henceforth, changes in the socioeconomic structure cannot be gainsaid. A dystopian discourse, framed by a social problems approach that accentuates the structured dependency of older people while condemning most to victim status, is a long way from the optimistic suggestion that third agers can become a cultural vanguard, 'the symbolic conscience of society' (Gilleard and Higgs, 2002; Kohli, 1988: 384). The mismatch between the reality and the dream is a measure of contemporary predilections as much as it is an index of disadvantage. That the numerical rise of those in retirement and the sociological space that this opened up has not been construed as culturally threatening is testimony to the continuing hegemony of youthful attitudes amongst baby-boomers themselves. Because they were the youth generation, so long as they preserve their attitudes and behaviours intact, age cannot wither them. In the generational scheme of things, youth signifies initiative, progress, health and, above all, distance from decline and death; it follows that sustaining youthfulness should defer ageing. Their trick has been to have it both ways, to transpose a synchronic understanding of themselves with a diachronic revision of the life course. But when the cohort that ought to become 'old' does not, we have a society where not just the young are youthful, but the entire society holds youthful values. What happens then to the dichotomy on which the stages of life are founded? Will youth subcultures no longer count as rebellious because they are simply elements of the mainstream? Or, since identities are based upon difference, will we see counter-resistance on the part of Generation X as they accentuate their self-awareness in ways fundamentally opposed to youthfulness as we know it? And if each generation has its own ideas about how to confront (or not) the inevitability of its mortality, where will the X, Y and Zers go? Perhaps we shall see a renewed acceptance of death and dying, not as the pathological celebration of the Victorians, but in their exposing the manifest denial of ageing as a cultural myth.

Two Future 'Conflicts' Across Generations and Cohorts?

Vern L. Bengtson and Norella M. Putney

The problem of generations and ageing, and the resulting problems of generational succession, support, stability and change, represents one of our most enduring puzzles about social organization and behaviour. The question posed by the 'problem of generations' is threefold: First, how will families or societies maintain sufficient continuity of social order over time in the face of continual changes in their membership as a result of birth, ageing and generational succession? Second, how will they adapt to changing circumstances involving economic, social and environmental development? Third, how will they deal with the differences or conflicts that arise between generations and negotiate their resolution to the benefit of individuals, families and the social order (Bengtson, 1993)? These issues underline the significance of both power and affective relationships between the generations and the continuing process of negotiation which characterizes them over time.

But new problems between generations seem to have arisen lately. Macrosocial trends of population ageing and globalization appear to be exacerbating existing socioeconomic and political inequalities between age groups. While the 'generation gap' of the 1960s centred on differences between youth and their parents over social and political values, structures of power, and gender and generational hierarchies, the new debate is over 'generational equity' between elders and everyone else. The current concern is primarily economic and the focus is on the sharing of – or competition for – scarce resources between older and younger generations, or between working and non-working cohorts. Accompanying this debate is a perceived weakening of intergenerational bonds of obligations and exchanges, and indeed concern about the structure and vitality of kinship units themselves. Is the family eroding as a social institution? Will families be able to cope with eldercare demands, for example, in the future?

These debates reflect shifts in the demographic, economic and political conditions of the past two decades, and perhaps a neoconservative cultural backlash against the liberalizing social and normative trends of the 1960s and 1970s. Yet how valid are these concerns? When we examine the empirical research on contemporary families, we find that despite the fears of pundits and politicians – conventional wisdom, so to speak – family functioning has not declined in the past several decades and family intergenerational obligations and exchanges have remained relatively stable over time (Bengtson et al., 2002). The story of intergenerational relations in the first decade of the twenty-first century is that while there may be disagreements or 'distance' between family generations, the predominant pattern is one of emotional closeness and mutual support and exchange.

In the present context of rapid sociohistorical and economic change and the perception of an impending conflict between generations, are there unique characteristics or processes of intergenerational cohesion and support at the microsocial level of families that can influence relationships between age groups at the societal level? While researchers usually consider the direction of such influences as running from macro to micro, are there aspects of intergenerational family relations that can moderate potential conflicts between age groups and buffer the negative effects on individuals of rapidly changing societies?

The line of argument in this chapter is the following – to the extent that relations between societal generations or age groups have become more problematic in the new era of population ageing, globalization and rapid social and economic change, intergenerational family relations may hold the key to resolving these issues. This is because the essential characteristics of multigenerational families – relatedness, interdependence and solidarity, and age integration – can influence and transform societal practices and policies and mitigate potential for conflicts between age groups. In matters of relations between generations and age, there are strong common characteristics between multigenerational families, age groups and society. A viable social contract between generations will remain a characteristic of human society in the future – at both the micro and macro levels of age-group interactions.

The conceptual distinctions in the ways the term 'generation' is used, as set out in the introduction to Part I, are important. They frame analyses of the new issues associated with ageing in industrialized countries as well as their effects on families. While Mannheim's conceptualization of generations as self-conscious historical forces seems intuitively attractive and may have contributed to new insights over the years, we fear such use is too imprecise or historically dependent; moreover, there is no empirical evidence to support it. We feel it is better to use the term 'cohort' or age group at the macrosocial level, restricting the term 'generation' to placement in family lineage. We will use these macro- and micro-level conceptualizations to examine some present dilemmas we face concerning population ageing, how they are reflected in emerging questions about pensions and social welfare for both age groups and families, and the potential for cohort and generational conflict in the future. The issue, simply stated, is this: how can we afford an ageing society of tomorrow? Will conflicts between cohorts become characteristic of twenty-first century life? If so how can such conflicts be mitigated?

Will new cohorts bring new conflicts?

Much has been written about the implications of longer lives, falling fertility and ageing populations. In most industrialized nations, the change in the relative size of cohorts brought about by generational succession, coupled with globalization and economic constraints, is now posing a threat to government provisions for income and health security for the aged. In the US, this threat is generating heated political debate over how to pay for the retirement benefits soon to be drawn upon by ageing baby-boomers and the budgetary crisis this may produce. Interestingly, almost lost in the rhetoric over 'saving Social Security' is the even bigger, nearer-term crisis posed by the Medicare programme and runaway healthcare costs (disregarding for the moment that US healthcare costs per capita are twice those of other industrialized countries (OECD, 2004a)). One implication is that current political arguments about the crisis of the Social Security system (said by many to be sufficiently funded into the foreseeable future with minor programme revisions (Diamond and Orszag, 2004)) are based on ideological more than fiscal considerations. What is less often mentioned in US political discourse is how these government fiscal and policy challenges also threaten families and how the younger generations will be able to care for their elders.

What do the data show about conflict between cohorts or age groups? In 1990, the American Association of Retired Persons (AARP) surveyed a nationally representative sample of 1,500 adults aged 18 to 90 concerning perceptions of inter-age inequities and potential conflicts (Bengtson and Harootyan, 1994). Results showed little evidence of perceived conflicts between age groups in contemporary American society. In fact,

22

younger people seemed to be *more* supportive of ageing programmes than were older people themselves, who in turn did not wish to burden younger generations. Further, compared to younger people, older people were found to hold stronger feelings of parental obligations and lower expectations of their children's obligations toward them. A ten-year follow-up study by AARP found that overall there was continued support for age-based public programmes. Age-group conflict is not a major problem in America today. Interestingly, Americans typically feel that people over age 65 get too little respect from younger people, with younger people more likely to feel this way than older people (Abramson and Silverstein, 2004).

However, support by *younger* respondents of age-based programmes appears to have weakened somewhat over the ten-year period. In related research, Silverstein and colleagues (2001) suggest this is more a reflection of intercohort change than generational replacement. Younger people became less concerned about costs as they got older. They conclude that the interpretation of equity between age groups does seem to have been affected by shifting ideological beliefs about the proper role of government in the lives of individuals and families. In the US, challenges to the existing Social Security system's viability are more frequently framed in terms of the potential harm to 'future generations'. Adherence to the cultural values of individualism and self-reliance probably contributes in no small way to the public's receptivity to claims that older generations are taking more than their fair share of public government resources at the expense of younger generations. The question is: what do these changes portend for relations between age groups, or for relations between generations in families?

How multigenerational families still matter

At the micro level, we now know a great deal about multigenerational families and how members of different generations function over time. Intergenerational bonds of affection, frequency of association, and norms of filial obligation to provide emotional, financial and functional support remain strong across generations at the start of the twenty-first century, despite the dramatic social and economic changes of the past four decades (Bengtson et al., 2002; Silverstein et al., 2002). Research demonstrates that intergenerational status and value transmission have not weakened, and that parents continue to exert positive influence on their offspring's socioeconomic and psychological well-being (except in the case of divorced fathers, who are less likely to positively influence their children's achievement aspirations and self-esteem).

To be sure, larger demographic, historical, economic and cultural changes have affected families, how they are structured and how their members relate to one another. There have been significant changes in family structures as a consequence of longer lives, reduced fertility, and changing family formation and childbearing patterns. Today there are many more three-, four- and even five-generation families, but many fewer members in each generation, giving rise to the metaphor of a beanpole or flagpole family structure in industrialized societies (Bengtson et al., 1996). Beyond changes in family structures, under conditions of late modernity the nature of family relations and their quality have changed. Relationships appear to have become more egalitarian (Cherlin, 1999; Galland, 1997; Giddens, 1991), both between men and women and between parents and children. In the US today, compared to 50 years ago, there is greater emphasis placed on affective bonds and choice, and less emphasis on normative prescriptions and obligations.

Longer lives as well as delays in the timing of expected life-course transitions, such as finishing education, departure from the family home, and family formation have meant there is more time and opportunity for intergenerational exchanges and support, which can strengthen intergenerational bonds and understandings (Putney and Bengtson, 2001). One consequence of these changes is the growing importance of multigenerational family relationships, especially the role of grandparents. In general, longer, healthier lives and reduced fertility mean that there are many more grandparents, and stepgrandparents, who will be sharing many fewer grandchildren. Having fewer grandchildren changes the quality of the cross-generational relationship, altering the investment that grandparents are able, or willing, to make (Uhlenberg, 2004). Also, grandparents are more needed now, particularly when parents have difficulty fulfilling their responsibilities for their own children, as may occur when both parents work, when parents divorce, or when a parent is unable to provide effective parenting because of illness, drug abuse or other incapacity. The incidence of grandparents raising grandchildren has increased substantially in recent years (AARP, 2002).

Will there be more conflict across generations and cohorts?

When scholars consider the linkages between family generations and age-group relations and the potential for age conflicts, their tendency is to focus on the macro to micro direction of influence. However, the converse – starting from the micro level of family intergenerational relations and tracing out their influence to the macro level of potential conflicts between age groups – is important. At the family level, the effects of longer years of shared lives plus the greater interdependence and solidarity between generations that emanates from extended periods of mutual support and exchange can have consequences for macro-level age group solidarity and the reduction of 'generational equity' conflicts. Family affective solidarity and intergenerational exchanges tend to reduce inequality between generations because private family resources are more likely to be allocated based on need (Attias-Donfut, 2003; Kohli, 2004). This egalitarian tendency in turn can extend outward to mediate relations between age groups at the macro level, with implications for policy. We summarize below how other researchers have explored these ideas.

In her study of three-generation families in France, Attias-Donfut (2000) discusses several factors that can decrease differences between generations, including private transfers and shared living arrangements, the intergenerational transmission of values and behaviours, the socialization of elders by younger generations, and processes of intergenerational confrontation and the working through of divergent perspectives and practices. She identifies the degree of social mobility across generations as especially influential. Where social mobility has been more marked, as between many baby-boomers (the pivot generation) and their parents' generation, this has tended to create more intergenerational dissimilarity (in education, values, resources). In recent decades, overall social mobility between generations has slowed (because of growing economic travails and other uncertainties) possibly reducing perceived age differences in experiences and enhancing felt obligations toward one another. The potential diffusion of social change – values and lifestyles – to older persons through their interactions with younger family members may have the further effect of increasing multigenerational solidarity (Attias-Donfut, 2000).

Silverstein and Parrott (1997) documented the positive role of private experiences with older family members, particularly contact with grandparents when growing up, in shaping more general attitudes toward older people as a group. This includes positive attitudes to their entitlement to public support. Contact with grandparents during childhood reduced the generally greater opposition of young adults to current contributory policy, thereby moderating age-group tensions around this issue (Schlesinger and Kroncbrusch, 1994). This framework explicitly takes into account intergenerational exchanges within families and considers intergenerational interactions and transfers at the microsocial level of the family as crucial for explaining views toward public and private fairness across age groups.

Foner (2000) proposes that while it is possible that age-group conflicts may negate trends toward age integration, it is more likely that the opposite will occur: age integration will offset tendencies toward age-group conflicts. Despite predictions of such conflicts in recent years, these have not occurred; young and middle-aged adults have not challenged policies and benefits for elders. Further, there are signs that age barriers are loosening. There are mechanisms within the family related to bonds of affection and exchanges that promote age integration in the larger society, and these micro-level processes are the reason why 'age wars' have not erupted over the growing economic burden on young people, who pay taxes to support the social-welfare programmes benefiting the older cohorts. Foner argues that in the same way that family members pull together when there are family crises, having to cope with such family problems carries over to supportive attitudes about societal-level policies benefiting the old.

The implication of these arguments is that the potential for 'conflict between generations' or age groups cannot be considered separate from relations between generations within families. Furthermore, changing socioeconomic contexts must be considered. The natural age integration of families as well as generational altruism, norms of obligation, and self-interest within the family – the recognition that cutting back public programmes for the elderly means shifting even more burden to families – will tend to dampen receptivity to generational equity arguments about the 'unjust allocation' of public resources to elders at the expense of children. The intergenerational solidarity of families reflects as well as enhances the interdependence and age integration of the multigenerational family with long-term consequences for attitudes toward societal provision for elders and others who are vulnerable.

Is the contract across generations changing?

Central to the concern over generational equity is how the family and society will deal with differences or conflicts that arise between age groups over the economic, moral and social obligations of the middle-aged and young to an ever-growing group of elderly, and in turn, deal with elders' obligations to those younger than themselves in our increasingly ageing societies. Such concerns speak to 'the contract between generations' – shared expectations and obligations regarding the ageing of individuals and the succession of generations through time and within social structures. For industrialized societies, does the second demographic transition mean that government budgetary crises will break the contract between generations? Will the fear of government insolvency translate into an unravelling of the social safety net for those traditionally seen as vulnerable and deserving of collective support?

There have been increased policy concerns about welfare costs and public expenditures targeted for various age groups, especially for the elderly as contrasted with the young. In the US, this concern has become increasingly noisy in recent years as politicians and pundits have drawn attention to the 'crisis' of Social Security and the competition between age groups (Williamson et al., 2003). These concerns reflect much deeper debates over basic social and cultural values: issues of individualism versus collectivism, which emphasizes the interdependence of generations; equity versus entitlement; filial piety versus the special needs of the younger generation; and the proper role of government, valuing the public good versus the imperatives of the market. In the social welfare and corporatist states of Western Europe and Japan, there is little antagonism between age groups. Instead, their growing concern is with plummeting birth rates and shrinking workforces and what these demographic changes imply for long-term economic growth (Commission of the European Communities, 2005). There are several reasons why these countries are less concerned with the generational equity debate, the most important being the existence of social-welfare programmes that support elders as well as families, which in turn promote extensive public–private reciprocal transfers and support, reducing intergenerational inequalities within families as well as within society.

So while concerns over 'generational justice' are essentially macro-level public policy issues, at the micro level of families there are increasing anxieties over providing care for the elderly. In the context of population ageing and rapidly changing economic and geopolitical conditions, we maintain that issues of micro-level family generational obligations and exchanges have remained relatively similar over time. At the same time, issues of macro-level age-group reciprocities and equities may acquire new urgency as a major concern in domestic social policy and economic discussions in contemporary nation states.

Conclusion

Most western governments recognize that current policies for support of the elderly are unsustainable, and some have already initiated some changes to their social-welfare programmes. Yet industrialized nations vary in their responses to the challenges to state treasuries posed by the growing population of elders relative to the working population and expected increases in pension and healthcare costs. In the US, current proposals for dealing with the federal budgetary 'crisis' are focused on changing entitlement programmes. If implemented, these would essentially break the 60-year-old 'contract between generations' and shift more responsibility to individuals and families for care of their elderly. On the other hand, those who see 'generational inequities' fail to distinguish between family and societal-level issues and thus ignore the vast transfers of private resources and life-course reciprocities between generations in the family domain over time.

In the US, we expect there will be increasing attempts by neoconservatives to blame the elderly for getting more than their 'fair share' of public resources, as justification for converting Social Security from a pay-as-you-go social-insurance programme to an individual-responsibility 'defined contribution' programme. We predict this effort will fail. Currently, Americans seem unlikely to abandon the safety provided by the Social Security programme in favour of the dubious promise of higher market returns but far greater risks offered by private investment accounts. The current debate over fairness between generations is a red herring that will primarily benefit market interests, just as it was two decades ago before being silenced by the economic boom of the latter 1990s (Bengtson et al., 1991).

Intergenerational relations at the microsocial level within multigenerational families have a profound but unrecognized influence on relations between age groups at the societal level. While some rhetoric frames the issues in zero-sum terms – there must be winners and losers in intergenerational transfers – the essence of multigenerational families is interdependence between generations and its members, and this will tend to mitigate schisms between age groups over scarce government resources. Further, understanding the relationship between generations at the micro level sheds light on the prospects for age-group cleavage or solidarity at the societal level, perhaps leading to a more holistic approach to the issue of relationships between family generations, societal age groups and 'the problem of generations'.

To deal with the unprecedented demographic challenges of growing numbers of elders and falling populations, the European Union has recently proposed 'a new solidarity between the generations' (Commission of the European Communities, 2005). Noting that families must be supported by public policies that enable women and men to better balance work and family life, the report also acknowledges that *'the family will continue to play an important role in solidarity between the generations'* (emphasis added) (Commission of the European Communities, 2005: 2), and that in this new environment societies will have to invent new ways of liberating the potential of its older and younger citizens. To compensate for the falling working population, policies should promote greater job participation among older people and women, and better integrate young people into the labour market. Policies should also promote non-linear careers for people, enabling them to move back and forth between education, career, family and leisure. The growing numbers of very old who will need support will require greater solidarity of care from both family and non-family networks within the community. In sum, the EU proposes that policies should ensure a balance between the generations in the sharing of time and in the distribution of benefits stemming from growth, and find new links between the stages of life (Commission of European Communities, 2005). It would be very useful for US policymakers to consider these ideas for addressing the dilemmas posed by ageing populations.

Almost two decades ago, Matilda Riley and her colleagues (Riley et al., 1994) foresaw the necessity for greater age integration in the spheres that constitute life's careers: education, employment, family life, leisure and retirement. In the last few years, the macro-level forces of population ageing, globalization and government resource constraints have combined to change the predictable life-course sequence of education, employment and leisure. This leads us to consider again the advantages of eliminating divisions between age groups and an understanding that macro-level relations between cohorts are influenced by relations within multigenerational families. In such a context, we predict that complaints of generational inequity and threats of generational conflict will have little resonance in twenty-first century society.

Three   Developments in the Life Course

Dale Dannefer and Casey Miklowski

The beginnings of life-course studies are generally traced to several independent lines of sociological work in the 1960s in the United States. In 1964, Leonard Cain's foundational paper 'Social Structure and the Life Course' was published, and the following year cohort analysis was introduced to the social and behavioural sciences by the classic articles of Ryder (1965) and Schaie (1965). In the early 1970s, Glen Elder published his classic study *Children of the Great Depression* (1974), following up the Berkeley and Oakland samples originally studied in the 1930s. This monograph still stands as an exemplar of a style of life-course research seeking to understand how events and social-structural conditions of the early life course interact to produce effects that can be traced in later life. This work represents what is still the predominant mode of life-course analysis, focusing on *individual* change and continuity across the life course, and seeking to understand the impact of earlier circumstances on later outcomes. But other kinds of questions also began to be asked about the life course. Demographers began to look at the life course from a *collective* or *population* perspective (e.g. Hogan, 1981), and other analysts identified the life course as a feature of *social organization and culture* (e.g. Kohli, 1986). Each of these three levels – individual, collective and sociocultural – comprises an analytically distinct perspective for life-course analysis (Dannefer and Uhlenberg, 1999). After elaborating these three levels, this chapter discusses some problem areas for life-course studies as they enter the new century.

Three levels of life-course analysis

The three levels of life-course analysis can be defined as follows
(Dannefer and Uhlenberg, 1999): *Individual*-level analyses generally trace
individual lives, explaining outcomes in terms of prior experiences of
individuals. *Collective* analyses consider outcomes for birth cohorts or
other subpopulations. These analyses consider the significance of social
structure and social change encountered by populations as they move
through the life course. Finally, *sociocultural/symbolic* analyses consider
the life course itself as a social construction. Such analyses refer to the
life course not as a property of individuals or cohorts, but of societies –
their social practices, normative expectations and ideas. Within each of
these three levels, both individual-level *personological* hypotheses and
sociological hypotheses have been advanced to explain outcomes. For
each level, we consider these alternative modes of explanation.

Life-course outcomes at the level of the individual

In its basic form, this dominant life-course approach uses an individual's
circumstances, experiences and/or characteristics earlier in the life
course to explain and predict subsequent outcomes, thus setting up a
Time 1–Time 2 logic[1] that typically spans decades. This general model,
well represented in *Children of the Great Depression*, has been elaborated
methodologically and has been applied by researchers to samples drawn
from a wide range of contexts.

The value of this work is evident in the interesting and complex pattern of findings it has generated. It indicates that experiencing deprivation results in the development of personal strengths for middle-class
individuals, but not for those from the working class. Interestingly, such
effects have been shown not only for children, but also for midlife adults.
Women who were parents during the Great Depression showed this same
pattern further across the life course. The women, who were in early
midlife during the Depression years of the 1930s, that were, decades
later, subsequently found to have the highest scores on characteristics of
psychological and social functioning in their early 70s, were middle-class
women who had encountered deprivation (Elder and Liker, 1982). The
authors interpreted this finding to show that mastery of early life struggles enhances adaptive capabilities in later life.

This complex interaction demonstrates the importance of paying attention to social context. Nevertheless, some life-course analysts have focused mainly on individual characteristics, such as personality, as the Time 1 predictors of later life outcomes. For example, Clausen traced the same Berkeley and Oakland respondents over an even longer biographical span – from infancy and early childhood into their retirement years (Clausen, 1993). He contended that the effects of 'planful competence' (presumed to be a component of personality) in youth constituted a strong predictor of life success. Thus, Clausen's view of life-course development was largely ahistorical and decontextualized.

Compared to such an approach, the emphasis on social structure and sociohistorical change central to Elder's work can readily be appreciated for producing a recognition that both social structure and unique historical events play a consequential role in shaping lives, apart from psychological characteristics. It has continued to offer a corrective to the traditional organismic (naturalistic) view of human development, which assumes that age-related patterns are part of nature.

Nevertheless, the general logic of seeking to predict later life outcomes from sociohistorical factors located at Time 1 has itself been subjected to critique on several grounds. One such critique is known as the Time 1 problem. This term refers to the problem that only *outcomes*, and nothing about subsequent or present experiences, are measured after Time 1. Context thus exists in the present only as something carried forward through time by the individual, and thus becomes a characteristic of the individual. Independent effects of contextual variables during adulthood and the question of their continuity with the contexts of adolescent experience are ignored (Dannefer and Uhlenberg, 1999; Hagestad and Dannefer, 2001).

In the United States, the Time 1 problem applies to a large segment of life-course research. More recently, however, some analyses have begun to include contemporaneous variables. In their study of life-course patterns of criminality, for example, Sampson and Laub (1993) follow up the youth sample collected by the Gluecks and examine social circumstances encountered in adulthood as well as early life factors. They find that both early and contemporaneous factors contribute independently to understanding life-course patterns of criminality. Similarly, Crosnoe and Elder (2004) include contemporaneous variables in analysing the relation of early family experiences to adjustment and functioning later in life. They find strong effects on current health and well-being of early life antecedents, but they also find that early experience operates largely through current objective circumstances.

A second problem has been called the *social change problem* (Dannefer and Uhlenberg, 1999; Hagestad and Dannefer, 2001). The pervasive emphasis in life-course studies upon social change and unique historical events seems to encourage an equating of the impact of social forces with social change. In reality, lives are socially organized and sustained under conditions of social stability no less than of change. It has even been suggested that the role of the social is greater under conditions of stability (Caspi and Moffit, 1993; Dannefer, 1993).

Life-course outcomes at the population level

Even those researchers focused on individual change have acknowledged the cumulative effects of cycles of advantage and disadvantage described earlier by Smith (1968), Dannefer (1987) and others (Clausen, 1993; Elder, 1999). The power of such interactive, cyclical processes is evident even at the level of the individual, but can be adequately grasped only at the collective level.

A consideration of the extraordinary diversity and inequality that are observed in older age strata of a population results in inevitable questions: how does such old-age inequality come about? What is the nature of *trajectories of inequality* over the life course with respect to material resources, social support and health? While these questions are in principle applicable to many characteristics, most such analyses to date examine income. Macro-level data on income are relatively accessible, and income is regarded as an index of resources that are related to other resources and to health. A remarkably consistent pattern has been found in several American studies and analyses, indicating steadily increasing inequality within each cohort as its members age. The extent to which the same pattern exists in other societies remains to be clarified.

The key thing to notice about such analyses is that the focus is no longer on individual characteristics directly, but on their *distribution within the population*. From the vantage point of the dynamic occurring in an entire population, it is possible to see that within each cohort, the rich do indeed appear to get richer, while the poor get poorer. Crystal and Shea (1990, 2002) and Dannefer (1987, 1988, 2003a) have interpreted such patterns as reflecting a process of *cumulative advantage/disadvantage.* The recognition of robust and predictable patterns of intracohort increases in inequality as the cohort moves through the life course suggests that cumulative advantage/disadvantage is a regular feature of cohort ageing. Thus, analysts are faced with the question of how to account for such a robust pattern of intracohort increase.

Two main types of explanation have been proposed, one largely psychological and one 'sociogenic'. The first of these, accentuation, refers to the extension and amplification of individual characteristics, strengths and weaknesses as one moves through the life course. The second refers not to individual-level processes at all, but to social processes that produce inequality. The regimes of many hierarchical 'people-processing organizations', such as schools, the military and the corporate workplace, are structured by mobility regimes that ensure the production of inequality among age peers. When they do, they create stratification in the distribution of resources among age peers.

While few would dispute that both the accentuation and sociogenic perspectives have some validity, they imply fundamentally different dynamics. The *strong accentuationist* view suggests that increasing inequality over the life course simply reflects the additive consequence of individual differences in talent, struggle and luck, for which social processes are, at best, of marginal importance. The *strong sociogenic* view suggests that the same patterns reflect the active operation of social processes. This view focuses on the stratified structure of social roles and the mechanisms for allocating individuals to roles as guaranteeing the generation and amplification of inequality, even if the actual individuals involved were clones of one another. The socially institutionalized opportunity structures that assign individuals to positions differing in rewards and future opportunities are sufficient, from this view, to generate the individual-level synergies observed in studies that use the individual as the unit of analysis. Such an argument makes sense when one considers the rigidly stratified, pre-existing role structures of school tracking systems (Lucas and Good, 2001) or military or corporate promotion hierarchies (Dowd, 2002; Rosenbaum, 1984).

A second type of collective life-course outcome concerns the temporal distribution of transition behaviour among cohort members. The question here concerns the degree of age-graded conformity or homogeneity with which cohort members complete key life transitions. Conformity in life transitions has been examined using demographic measures such as the *interquartile range*, a measure based on a compilation of the ages at which each cohort member undergoes the transition in question. The interquartile range reports the number of years required for the 'middle half' of the cohort (26th–75th percentiles) to complete the transition. Hogan (1981) found a steady trend toward a reduction in the interquartile range applied to the transition to adulthood for American males born between 1907 and 1952. This implies a reduction in the age variability of transition behaviour and, correspondingly, an increasing level of age-graded conformity in successive cohorts. As time moved forward, the behaviour of young men became increasingly age graded, as successive cohorts completed the transition in fewer years. Over the second half of the twentieth century, the transition to retirement appears to reflect a similar trend toward greater age homogeneity (Parsons, 1996).

These twentieth-century shifts toward greater conformity and age homogeneity in transition behaviour have also been given both individual-level and sociological explanations. Those advocating an 'individual choice' explanation have suggested, paradoxically, that greater conformity in transition behaviour reflects a higher degree of economic independence and hence freedom for young men, allowing them to marry earlier (e.g. Modell, 1989). Such an interpretation implies a broadly consensual, 'natural' age for marrying (see Dannefer, 1984). Others have seen this trend as indicating the expansion of social policies and institutions that regulate the lives of individuals on the basis of age – the increasing 'institutionalization of the life course' through which the life course itself is constituted as a social institution (Kohli and Meyer, 1986). Both interpretations point to the emergence of *age norms* and the increasingly precise expectations for age-graded behaviour that they imply, which point to the third level of life-course analysis, the life course as symbolic construction.

Life-course outcomes as symbolic constructions and as cultural phenomena

This third category of life-course outcomes is anchored neither in individuals nor in populations, but as ideas in the symbolic apparatus of society, as social ideology (Phillipson, 1982). Such ideas are important elements in defining the values and norms of a social order, and in providing its legitimation. They can be discerned in social policy pronouncements and in the interplay of policy and other such developments with popular culture. For example, the idea that *retirement* demarcates a 'normal life stage' is a recent development that has given sharp age-graded definition to the life course over the past century, bringing with it a growth in the scope and specificity of age norms in western bureaucratic states (e.g. Chudacoff, 1989). These ideas have thus made age-organizing impulses into a normative force integral to the social order of these societies.

The public establishment of an age-graded 'life stage' of retirement is yet another manifestation of a general historical process of what Kohli

(1986) and others have termed the 'institutionalization of the life course'. This process followed the Industrial Revolution and the expansion of bureaucratic modes of organization, and it reflects an increasing reliance on age as a criterion of social organization. Universal public education, an early force for institutionalization, was soon followed by the implementation of age-grading as a general educational practice, and by the institutionalization of retirement. More recently, focus by psychologists and other 'professionals' on 'normal developmental issues' in adulthood – e.g. 'turning 30', the 'midlife crisis' or the 'empty nest' stage has encouraged the continuing development of what historian Howard Chudacoff has called 'age consciousness' and have thus furthered age norms.

Ironically, the institutionalization of the life course refers to the organization of individual lives by social institutions such as school and retirement. It also has produced a bureaucratically organized, age-graded normative organization of society. This age-stratified social organization entails 'age segregation' – the separation of individuals into age-homogeneous groups that are relatively insulated from each other. It is experienced as a taken-for-granted aspect of social life, supported by the notions of normal life-course development supplied by the institutionalization of the life course.

The future of the life course and life-course studies

Currently, the life course as a social institution and as a field of study confront the same broad currents of change that generally confront social life: economic globalization, weakening and destabilization of nation states relative to the private sector, and postmodern cultural trends. These powerful forces have implications for the structuring of the life course, and also for human action and agency. We conclude by briefly considering four such issues, which cut across the levels of life-course phenomena discussed above: 1) institutionalization vs deinstitutionalization, 2) agency vs structure, 3) family vs work, and 4) the meaning of 'linked lives' in a global economy.

Institutionalization vs deinstitutionalization of the life course

As noted earlier, the expansion of the institutionalized life course was a powerful trend across the twentieth century (Kohli and Meyer, 1986; Settersten, 1999: 39–41). Over recent decades, scholars have debated whether the institutionalization of the life course is continuing, or whether the destabilizing effects of economic globalization and postmodern cultural trends are creating a counter-tendency of deinstitutionalization within the same late modern societies where the impulses toward institutionalization have been most powerful and most advanced (Brückner and Mayer, 2005; Dannefer, 2000). This unresolved question may be answered differently in different societal contexts. For example, it has been suggested that the impulses to deinstitutionalization are considerably more developed in the United States than in Germany or Scandinavia (Dannefer, 2003b).

Agency, structure and risk

The accomplishment of social life on a daily basis depends upon the exercise of intentional social action and human agency. This fundamental principle seems sometimes to be overlooked by the life-course scholars and other social and behavioural scientists who seem to fear that acknowledging the power of structure means a negation of agency. In reality, agency cannot be expressed outside of the structure of institutions, since it relies upon the institution of language to formulate and articulate its projects. A good example of how to think about the articulation of agency and structure is by looking at the current discussion of risk. O'Rand (1999; O'Rand and Shuey, 2004) argues that the nature of risk in late modern societies has shifted from the 'old risks' based on a lack of information, to 'new risks' based on information provided to individuals in the form of probabilities, probabilities which are modifiable depending on the efforts one exerts to extend one's information base and to make discerning judgements. The new risks thus place more responsibility upon the individual. An example of this general shift is the shift in the US and the UK from defined-benefit to defined-contribution pension plans, since the former provide a predetermined pension to the earner upon retirement, whereas the latter require the earner also to become a manager of his or her own investment portfolio. Although less structurally imposed, similar trends have also developed in other areas such as lifestyle, healthcare and education.

It is unclear that such changes necessarily imply more 'agency' for individuals. More knowledge and more control can also mean more risk and more stress. Some individuals may prefer not to spend their time becoming amateur investment counsellors, but they may perceive little choice in that matter. The lack of such choice is an indication of the ways that structure constrains and organizes agency (Dannefer, 1999). An emphasis on such a structuring of opportunity and hence of the parameters of agency suggests an alternative formulation of some of the themes of life-course studies.

Family, work and the life course

From the beginning, life-course studies has made family-related issues more central and problematic than those that derive from the workplace. Given the importance of family relations, the close connection to family is understandable, yet the omission is consequential. Work has implications not only for household economy but also for a range of personal consequences of job and career, such as place of residence and geographic mobility, physical and mental health and the quality of family life. As globalization imposes new kinds of economic challenges and struggles upon the working- and middle-class earners of North America and Western Europe, what has always been true may become more apparent: that family well-being is linked to economic well-being, and for most individuals and most families, economic well-being is linked to one's occupational position.

Globalization, inequality and 'linked lives'

Recently, it has been claimed that inequality *between* societies has decreased in recent decades (Firebaugh and Goesling, 2004). At the same time, others suggest that in many cases inequality *within* societies is increasing (Kawachi et al., 1997). Both trends are manifestations of globalization (e.g. Stiglitz, 2002).

In traditional life-course discourse, 'linked lives' refers to familial and other personal attachments that create contingencies and interdependencies between individuals in their life-course circumstances and transitions. As the global economy reshapes the relations of production and consumption globally, an expanding supply of consumer goods is provided to the globe's minority of late modern consumers by the younger, poorer workforces of 'underdeveloped' countries (Bales, 2000; Dannefer, 2003b). The producer-consumer relation is consequential for the life course of all parties to the transaction, yet it is hidden from view in everyday social life, and has been largely ignored by life-course research that has been too content with those obvious modes of social intercourse that are premised on conventionally superficial definitions of reality and relationships. Grasping the life-course implications of such intricate global economic interdependencies remains a challenge for life-course studies as we look to the future.

Conclusion

The life course as an area of study has made an enormous contribution in identifying the importance of historical contingency and specifying the significance of structure and social change in shaping lives, in explicating the problems of graded societal patterns of resource allocation and role transitions, and in suggesting connections between patterns of social change and changes in normative and cultural definitions of age, ageing and the life course. It has thus contributed important correctives to commonsense ideas and scholarly misunderstandings of age and life-course patterns across several disciplines and subfields in the social and behavioural sciences.

Intertwined as the field has been with issues of social change, it is perhaps not surprising that the changes of the late twentieth century and of the new millennium are confronting life-course studies with a new set of difficult challenges. Addressing these challenges seriously can move life-course studies further to the centre of scholarship within the sociology of age and can raise issues and provide a window on social processes beyond the discipline of sociology.

Note

1 Experimental designs in empirical life-course research typically measure change in a set of variables for a sample of individuals between two points in the life-course, one earlier called 'Time 1' and the other later called 'Time 2'. This design raises issues which are discussed later in the paper.

Part II

The Future of Social Differentiation

Understanding the intersection of age and generation with different kinds of social inequality is vital to an understanding of old age and its futures. In gerontology, a largely classless view of old age was prevalent until the emergence of the political-economy perspective, which pointed out that stratification, such as social class, gender and ethnicity, played crucial roles in the ageing experience. Even though older people may have left full-time employment or previously had little part in the labour market, the effects of their work situation endure even into late old age (Estes and Minkler, 1984; Phillipson, 1982, 1998; Townsend, 1981; Walker, 1980, 1981). Early political economy analyses focused chiefly on occupation, but more recent research within this paradigm has emphasized gender and ethnicity (Arber and Ginn, 1991a; Blakemore and Boneham, 1994), as well as the interconnections between them (Estes, 1991, 2004; Walker, 2005).

In retirement, the influence of social class is a function of accumulated advantage or disadvantage built up over the life course (Dannefer, 2003a; Walker, 1981). Economic resources such as savings, pensions and property are owned through inheritance or as a result of employment and, in older age, help to determine the material quality of life. Thus a political economy of old age draws on a life-course perspective which acknowledges the influence of resources and experiences acquired earlier in life (Arber and Evandrou, 1993; Hockey and James, 2003). Because 'the life course is experienced not in a vacuum, but in societies that are continually changing' (Riley, 1983: 1) there is a dynamic interaction between the individual life course, the social structure, economic relations and social policy that determines the material conditions of later life.

Understanding the history of gender is key to understanding the current and future situation of older women. The formative years of the current generation were spent before, during or shortly after the Second World War, periods of austerity and the maintenance of traditional gender roles. Although young women were called on to work during the war, they were then encouraged to return to the domestic sphere to free up jobs for returning servicemen (Brown, 1992). This generation of women was largely engaged in childcare and domestic support for their husbands, and, if in employment, tended to work part-time with few occupying higher non-manual positions. Alongside married women, who were primarily identified as 'housewives', was a group of unmarried 'career women'.

The next generation of older women will be very different. Those retiring from 2010 onwards grew up during or after the 1960s. The 1960s represents a landmark in numerous ways, from the growth of educational opportunities, availability of birth control and the sexual revolution, to the rise in divorce following the Divorce Reform Act 1969. The Women's Liberation Movement challenged and changed the assumptive worlds of young women and men and had long-lasting consequences. The 1970s saw legislation in terms of equal pay and sex discrimination, which particularly enhanced women's employment opportunities. Thus, the generation of women born in the 1950s and 1960s have had a radically different life experience to the current generation of older people. This experience, however, still includes discrimination in employment and pensions and disadvantages in terms of domestic responsibilities and other areas of gendered social expectations (Arber and Ginn, 1991a, 2004). Old age will continue to be a gendered experience.

Stratification on the basis of race, culture or religion is frequently labelled 'ethnicity', but these terms are much debated and US and UK usages are different. Unlike most of the US 'black' population, most British ethnic elders have direct experience of migration. They are consequently influenced by the economic and social climate into which they arrived, and which shaped their lives as they grew older. How these experiences impacted on economic fortunes, health and, perhaps most important, their sense of identity, is essential to understanding the future of ethnicity in old age in Britain. Data from the 2001 Census on the ethnic makeup of the UK population show that the non-white minority groups made up a relatively small 7.9 per cent of the UK population and include a considerable range of ethnic backgrounds, with the main groups reflecting close connections with former British colonies. (See Table 6.1, page 67)

Any ethnic description is inevitably theory-based, even if this is not explicitly recognized (Nazroo, 1998; Modood et al., 2002). Gender, age or country of birth as demographic 'facts' are complicated by social and historical context, but there is a good case that 'ethnicity' is even less straightforward. The 2001 Census measure of ethnicity contains an acknowledgement that it is a subjective characteristic covering a variety of domains of experience and the pertinence of particular domains will vary across contexts and individual biographies (White, 2002). Nevertheless, it is also a characteristic that is routinely observed in population studies, perhaps because as well as being subjective, contextually experienced and theoretical, its relevance to everyday life is obvious and acknowledged in commonsense ways. This is reflected in the typical measures of ethnicity that are utilized in social research, with the 2001 UK Census questions being typical, covering notions of skin colour, nationality, country of origin and ethnic 'mixing'. In the US the use of the term 'ethnic' is equally problematic. The US census terminology uses both 'race' (Black, Native American, etc.) and 'ethnic' (Hispanic). There are great differences in the material conditions of US elders on the basis of such 'racial' and 'ethnic' divisions which seem unlikely to diminish in the near future.[1]

Note

1 The editors wish to acknowledge the significant contribution that Alan Walker, Liam Foster, Sara Arber and James Nazroo made to this introduction.

Four   Ageing and Social Class: An Enduring Relationship

Alan Walker and Liam Foster

Social class is a critical factor influencing how people experience old age and, in particular, the quality of the lives they lead. In general, social class is an important indicator of a person's position in the social stratification system in any society and his or her access to material resources (Gjonca and Calderwood, 2003). It is a potent indicator of inequalities in income, wealth, status and power, with equally strong influences on morbidity and mortality (Townsend, 1979; Townsend and Davidson, 1992; Westergaard, 1995; Wilkinson, 1996). However, the role of social class in everyday life is contested. The main reason for this is the origin of class analysis in Marx's theory of social reproduction. Thus the essential place of production in the construction of identity has long been regarded as problematic (Giddens, 1991; Miller, 1991). It is observed that the class relations that used to underlie political consciousness and voting patterns have shifted substantially as a result of changes in production and employment, such as the decline in the blue-collar working class, the increased participation of women in the workforce, the restructuring of working life and the destandardization of employment (Bauman, 1998; Giddens, 1998). Hence it is argued that social class derived from occupation is less relevant to social behaviour and identity formation than it was previously.

This chapter asks how far these trends will influence the future of old age. Has the centrality of occupation been replaced, or will it be, in the determination of pensions and the other material circumstances in which people experience older age? We focus primarily on what is known – the current class divisions and those among the coming generations of older people – although, towards the end, we speculate on future trends. First of all it is necessary to explain why a political economy perspective is essential to understanding the relationship between social class and old age. In capitalist society older age is characterized by detachment from paid employment so that older people are no longer in a socially defined 'productive' sector of the economy (Phillipson, 1982; Walker, 1981). However, the dynamics of class continue to exist in the older person's everyday life independent of the workplace. Occupation, regardless of whether it is Fordist or post-Fordist, modern or late modern in form, remains one of the most important ways of acquiring material resources across the adult life course (Dale, 2004).

Furthermore, occupational status, underpinned by educational attainments (Dale, 2004; Estes, 1991), can still have a direct impact after retirement in the form of non-wage benefits such as access to private healthcare. Nevertheless, this detachment from the productive process, in the traditional Marxist sense, means that workplace relations do not constitute the primary dynamic of class relations for older people (Estes, 1991). (There is not space here to dwell on the inherent weaknesses of social class defined in terms of occupational classification, but the common exclusion of 'pensioners' (Saunders, 1990) and equally common classification of married women according to their husband's current or last occupation (Arber and Ginn, 1991b) are serious problems for gerontology.)

Older age does not always simply reproduce the class-based pattern present in earlier years (Moody, 2002). Living conditions may be degraded as older people outlive their economic resources, such as when widowhood, serious illness or entry into an older people's home, causes a drastic depletion of assets. Indeed it is usual for income to decline relatively over the course of retirement as a result of inflation and the gradual rundown of assets.

Pensions

Pensions are the main source of income in retirement and the subject of the whole of the following part of this book. In the opening decades of the twentieth century, two parallel systems of pensions were developing: one organized by the state, which tended to cover the poorest two-thirds of the population, and another covering a smaller group of employees of major firms with internal labour markets and bureaucratic employment features. In the early history of occupational pension schemes certain employees, most notably women, were excluded from these schemes, whereas for some others it became a problem that they were obliged to join an employer's scheme as a condition of employment. At times this represented an unhealthy balance between exclusion and conscription (Hales and Gough, 2003). It was this dichotomy which led Titmuss (1958) to warn of the emergence of 'two nations in old age': the majority of whose pensions were supplemented by National Assistance and the relatively few more affluent whose supplementation came from an occupational pension, with the gap between them growing wider over time.

Subsequent research has borne out the accuracy of Titmuss's (1958) predictions. He correctly identified the inequalities developed through the greater rewards, privileges and benefits gained by managerial, professional and administrative staff, whereas, particularly among the unskilled and semiskilled, opportunities do not increase in the same way as a result of wage and non-wage disparities and their job insecurity. Figure 4.1 shows the class bias in private pensions. It is evident that 90 per cent of males aged 65-plus whose last occupations were professionals or managers in large organizations have a private pension, compared with less than 60 per cent of males employed in unskilled manual work (Ginn and Arber, 2001a: 55). Table 4.1 also indicates that socioeconomic classification has an impact not only on the number of people receiving private pensions, but also on the amount they receive. Furthermore, those aged 65 and over who were last employed in higher socioeconomic groups are also less likely to require income support than those in routine and manual occupations (Summerfield and Babb, 2004: 9–11). Occupational pension coverage is skewed towards the higher socioeconomic groups, generally those with a higher earning capacity, and voluntary early retirement is also most common among these groups. To them that hath shall be given: the highest pensions are paid to the highest earners, and this inequality is rooted primarily in the hierarchical occupational structure. Unemployment, part-time work and early retirement affect the building-up of non-state pension contributions for certain groups (Johnson and Falkingham, 1992).

Over the past 50 years the economic situation of a large number of older people has improved. The development of private pension schemes and the acquisition of private-sector assets has created a situation in which many pensioners are well off compared with their predecessors (Craig, 2004). On the other hand, changes in the level of state pension caused by the 1980 de-indexation of the basic state pension from earnings has left many of those without access to these other income streams in a financially precarious situation in older age. By 2005 the basic state pension had fallen to 15 per cent of average earnings (£543 per week in April 2005 for full-time adult workers).

In April 2006 the flat-rate basic state pension stood at £84.25 per week for single people and £134.75 for couples and is still the main source of income for a majority of pensioners.

The after-tax incomes for occupational pensioners increased rapidly in the 1980s in real terms compared with the incomes of non-occupational pensioners. For single pensioners in the bottom income quintile, on average 91 per cent of their income is made up from benefits with only 4 per cent coming from occupational pensions. By contrast those in the top fifth have an average income made up of 38 per cent from benefits, 32 per cent from occupational pensions and 22 per cent from investment income (Balchin and Shah, 2004). The average real incomes from occupational pensions rose by an estimated 152 per cent between 1979 and 1996–97, whereas state-benefit incomes increased only by 39 per cent during this time (House of Commons, 2003). The doubling of occupational pensions contributions between the 1960s and 1980s benefited only those fortunate enough to belong to a pension scheme (Ginn and Arber, 1993).

The class implications of access to occupational and personal pensions are significant. While occupational pensions have provided an excellent source of income in old age for middle and high earners, especially those with stable long-term service with the same employer (Field, 2002), they are a key source of inequality among pensioners (Mann, 2001; Walker, 1980). Moreover, this engine of inequality is fuelled by state fiscal subsidies (Cutler and Waine, 2001; Mann, 2001; Sinfield, 1981, 2000), which reinforce class-based occupational privileges. There has been a recent decline in the receipt of occupational pensions – from 51 per cent in 1994–95 to 44 per cent in 2000–01 among single pensioners – and this is expected to continue as employers replace these mainly defined benefit schemes with personal defined contribution ones (Pensions Policy Institute, 2003a). This is a policy encouraged by both government (Department of Social Security, 1998; Department for Work and Pensions, 2002, 2003a) and international governmental organizations (World Bank, 1994).

Personal pensions are likely to provide lower incomes than occupational ones because of their lower levels of employer contributions and lack of inflation-proofing, as well as the absence of a guaranteed pension level (Ginn and Arber, 1999). The mis-selling of such pensions in the 1980s and 1990s and the recent poor performance of the stock market are further sources of uncertainty (Hales and Gough, 2003). Does this mean that the class-based inequality between pensioners will disappear in time? Certainly not, because those in secure, well-paid occupations will continue to enjoy defined benefit pension schemes or have sufficient income to fund personal ones, whereas those in part-time or insecure employment (mainly women) will find it hard

Figure 4.1 Percentage with a private pension, women and men aged 65+, by socioeconomic category

Key socioeconomic categories

1. Professional managers in large organizations
2. Intermediate non-manual/managers in small organizations
3. Routine non-manual
4. Skilled manual/supervisory
5. Semiskilled manual/personal service
6. Unskilled manual
7. Employers/self-employed
8. Never employed

Excluded: Armed forces/PT students/inadequate description

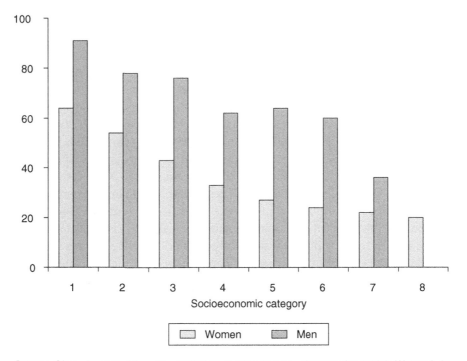

Source: Ginn, J. and Arber, S. (2001) 'A Colder Pension Climate for British Women', in J. Ginn, D. Street and S. Arber (eds) *Women Work and Pensions*. Buckingham: Open University Press. p. 55. Reproduced with the kind permission of the Open University Press/McGraw-Hill Publishing Company.

to contribute enough to provide for a decent pension. However, while personal pensions are portable, without subsidies from the public purse they cannot cover the whole workforce and guarantee it a retirement free from economic insecurity (these issues are discussed in depth in Part V).

Table 4.1 Private pensions[1] provision of those aged 65 and over, by marital status and socioeconomic group[2], 2001/02

Great Britain					Percentages
	Percentage receiving		Median amount for those with private pension (£ per week)		Ratio of females' to males' median income
	Males	Females	Males	Females	(percentages)
Marital status					
Married/cohabiting	74	28	92	34	37
Single	52	61	65	70	108
Widowed	70	56	61	46	75
Divorced/separated	57	36	78	48	62
Socioeconomic group					
Professional/managerial	90	64	172	95	55
Intermediate non-manual	60	51	84	43	51
Routine and manual	62	34	50	28	56
All	71	43	83	44	53

1 Occupational or personal pension, including survivor pensions.
2 Based on own occupation and classified according to the National Statistics Socioeconomic Classification (NS-SeC). The data are unweighted.

Source: http://www.statistics.gov.uk/downloads/theme_social/Social_Trends34/Social_Trends 34.pdf

In the absence of a basic state pension that is universal in coverage and provides for an adequate standard of living, a significant proportion of pensioners must rely on means-tested benefits or live below the poverty line (some 600,000 in the UK do so). Again, this situation is likely to persist in view of the inadequacies of personal pensions and the fact that means-testing is an explicit aim of government policy (Department of Social Security, 1998) – unless, that is, a rumoured citizens' pension is introduced to address the social exclusion and high marginal withdrawal rates associated with means tests. In other words, without a significant change in policy both poverty and social exclusion are likely to persist (Phillipson and Scharf, 2004).

Other inequalities in old age

Income inequalities derived from the interaction of vertical social divisions, such as class and gender, are mirrored in other areas. For example, older owner-occupiers are more likely to have an occupational pension than those in some form of social housing (Evandrou and Victor, 1989). Indeed there is a strong negative association among pensioners between income and other key determinants of quality of life and living in social housing (Breeze et al., 2002; Taylor et al., 2004). The continuing rise in owner-occupation is likely to diminish these inequalities but by how much we cannot predict, nor whether this will increase the proportion of asset rich but income poor pensioners.

Education

There is a strong correlation between a pensioner's success in the education system and his or her position in the income distribution (Taylor et al., 2004). In 2001, 64 per cent of pensioners in the poorest fifth of the income distribution had no qualifications, compared with just over a third of those in the top 60 per cent of the distribution. Table 4.2 shows how educational attainment is strongly linked to a person's socioeconomic classification, both for those still in employment and those in retirement (Gjonca and Calderwood, 2003). Education affects health and mortality through a number of pathways, such as lifestyle, social relations, health behaviour and problem-solving abilities, as well as through income and occupation. It is expected that educational inequalities will diminish with the rapid rise in higher education participation rates, but that is a long-term prospect. Meanwhile, although the coming (boomer) generations are more highly educated than their parents, there are still 14 per cent of men and 21 per cent of women among them with no qualifications at all (Huber and Skidmore, 2003).

Health

There is an enduringly strong relationship between health status and occupational class. Older people previously in unskilled occupations are twice as likely to have a moderate or greater level of disability as those previously in higher middle-class occupations (Evandrou and Victor, 1989; Ginn and Arber, 1993). Life expectancy also varies significantly by socioeconomic class. For instance, Table 4.3 shows that among women in social class I, life expectancy at 65 is nearly four years higher than for those in social class V, and the gap has grown wider over time (Pensions Commission, 2004b: 48). Increases in life expectancy have occurred at

Table 4.2 Educational attainment by occupational class, gender and age group

	Age			
	50–59 %	60–74 %	75+ %	Total %
Men				
Managerial and professional				
Degree/higher	40.4	33.8	24.0	35.0
Intermediate	53.8	52.1	47.5	52.0
No qualifications	5.8	14.1	28.5	13.0
Intermediate				
Degree/higher	10.3	8.7	3.6	8.6
Intermediate	62.0	39.4	30.8	43.3
No qualifications	27.7	37.9	61.1	37.2
Routine and manual				
Degree/higher	3.7	1.2	0.7	2.0
Intermediate	55.5	39.4	30.8	43.3
No qualifications	40.8	59.3	68.6	54.7
Women				
Managerial and professional				
Degree/higher	33.7	20.5	15.1	25.4
Intermediate	58.5	63.9	58.9	60.6
No qualifications	7.8	15.7	26.0	13.9
Intermediate				
Degree/higher	6.4	4.4	2.2	4.6
Intermediate	72.5	58.3	42.7	59.5
No qualifications	21.1	37.3	55.0	35.9
Routine and manual				
Degree/higher	1.8	0.7	0.3	1.0
Intermediate	44.1	25.5	14.6	28.9
No qualifications	54.1	73.8	85.1	70.2
Bases (weighted):				
Men	2078	2167	948	5192
Women	2130	2404	1475	6009
Bases (unweighted):				
Men	1892	2247	961	5100
Women	2237	2558	1320	6115

Source: Gjonca and Calderwood (2003:43), data from the English Longitudinal Study of Ageing: Wave 1.

different rates across the social classes since the 1950s, resulting in a widening of differences between the least and most advantaged groups (Acheson, 1998; Arber and Ginn, 1991b; Grundy and Sloggett, 2003). For example, among civil servants after retirement, an 86 per cent increase in mortality has been observed among men in the lowest grade compared to the highest (Marmot and Shipley, 1996).

Table 4.3 Trends in female life expectancy at age 65 by social class, England and Wales

Social Class	1972–76	1977–81	1982–86	1987–91	1992–96	1997–2001
I	19.3	20.0	18.6	18.7	20.9	20.6
II	17.1	17.8	18.0	18.8	19.5	20.1
IIIN	17.8	17.6	18.0	18.4	19.0	19.7
IIIM	16.3	16.9	16.8	16.9	18.0	18.2
IV	16.8	16.8	17.4	17.0	17.2	17.8
V	16.4	16.3	16.1	16.0	16.5	16.9
All women	16.2	16.7	16.9	17.3	18.0	18.8

Source: ONS Longitudinal Study, 1972–2001
(http://www.statistics.gov.uk/StatBase/Product.asp?vlnk=8460&Pos=&ColRank=1&Rank=272)

The association between morbidity and social class has an impact on the need for care and also on the living arrangements of older people. Class is directly associated with the material, financial and cultural resources which are necessary to enable an older person to remain autonomous within his or her own home. Those who lack resources, including access to care, are most likely to have to enter residential care. This is usually associated with a marked reduction in the older person's autonomy and independence (Arber and Ginn, 1993; Townsend, 1981; Walker, 1982). Financial resources may be used to adapt or purchase appropriate housing or aids to promote independent living and pay for substitute care. It is also thought that education and cultural resources may increase the older person's knowledge about available services, which may reduce the need to rely on informal carers.

Social-class differences in health can be seen as the biological correlate of socially structured and differential exposure to health hazards. (The issue of the future of health in old age is discussed in Part V of this volume.) An optimistic case could be made that the main occupational causes of health inequalities are now largely in the past, with the decline in mining and other heavy industries and improvement in health and safety in the workplace. However, this must be qualified by the increasing divergence of some lifestyle factors between socioeconomic groups, especially the prevalence of smoking and obesity, along with continuing differences in working conditions and the increasing prevalence of factors such as stress (Pensions Commission, 2004b).

Conclusion

It has been shown that there is an enduring relationship between old age and social class. Although the parameters of class will continue to change as the occupational structure and nature of work itself change, their power is likely to diminish, but it will take a very long time for the effects to be felt in old age. Retirement is not a homogenizing experience. Social class position early in life casts a long shadow over future attainment and health outcomes (Donkin et al., 2002). We have used a political economy perspective to demonstrate how an older person's prior labour-market status has a determining influence on his or her current material resources and the relationship between occupation, health, income and assets (Arber and Ginn, 1991a; Bowl, 1986; Dale, 2004; Walker, 1986). It must be remembered that cultural processes are also embedded within specific kinds of socioeconomic relations. Therefore, class should be seen not only in terms of employment relations but also in terms of collectivities of people who, in essence, share identities and practices (Bottero, 2004). This emphasizes the need to examine cultural aspects of ageing (Gilleard and Higgs, 2000), although the relative importance of such factors in shaping living standards, as opposed to identities, must be borne in mind (Baars et al., 2006). Not all inequalities can be reduced to social class. As the other chapters in this section show, older age, ethnicity, gender and other sources of structural inequality need to be taken into account and their interactions with class demonstrated.

Although this important task has slipped down the scientific research agenda in recent years, partly as a result of the late (post)modernists' celebration of variation, it is necessary now more than ever, and it will remain so in the foreseeable future. Class will remain salient as a result of continuing occupational segregation between the core and peripheral labour forces, increasing labour-market insecurity mirrored by pensions insecurity, and as the prospects for decent public pensions, based on solidarity, are undermined by neoliberal-style economic globalization. Thus, although it will be intertwined increasingly with other social divisions, the relationship between ageing and social class looks set to endure.

Five   Gender and Later Life: Change, Choice and Constraints

Sara Arber

This chapter will examine how both demography and the nature of gender differences among the older population will change by the 2030s. Will the next generation of older women be more likely to 'grow old disgracefully'? The Hen Co-op (1995) used the term 'growing old disgracefully' to emphasize that older women in future should focus on what *they* want. 'We stressed the idea of letting go of the "shoulds" and "oughts" that many of us have lived with during our lifetimes of service to everyone except ourselves', arguing that women should have greater agency in determining the way they live their lives. They contrasted this with the traditional expectation that women 'grow old gracefully', a situation in which you 'live out your life passively and unnoticed' (Hen Co-op, 1995: 180, 181). The baby-boomers and subsequent generations of older women will be more educated, and have grown up and spent their working lives expecting greater equality in employment and other spheres of life. They are less likely to be content to spend their later years in a stereotypical passive old age.

To what extent older women are likely to be able to do this will depend on their balance of choices and constraints. Constraints in old age relate primarily to three areas: the availability of money and adequate material resources; caring, i.e., both the expectations that older women will care for others (grandchildren, partners and older parents) and their access to adequate caring resources should they become disabled; and their own health and functional ability (Arber and Ginn, 1991a). Following a discussion of the changing demography of ageing and new partnership forms in later life, the chapter will examine the first two of these potential constraints on autonomy and independence. Older women have greater levels of disability than men (Arber and Cooper, 1999; Arber and Ginn, 1998), but this will not be addressed here (however, see Chapter 13).

The diminishing feminization of later life

The feminization of later life – or numerical predominance of women – is diminishing, and projected to fall further in the time span considered by this book. Later life was disproportionately female throughout the latter half of the twentieth century. This situation is changing, because of faster recent declines in men's mortality over women's. Between 1971 and 2001, the sex ratio fell from 161 women to 138 women for every 100 men over age 65 in England and Wales. Above age 85, women outnumbered men by over 3:1 in 1981; this fell to 2.6:1 by 2001 (Arber and Ginn, 2004).

While expectation of life at birth has increased for both men and women in England, the improvement has been more rapid for men, increasing from 71 years in 1981 to 76 years in 2001, and for women from 77 years in 1981 to 80.6 years in 2001 (Office for National Statistics, 2004a). Thus, the faster reduction in male mortality has diminished women's advantage in life expectancy, from 6.0 years in 1981 to 4.6 years in 2001 (Office for National Statistics, 2004a). Sex differences in mortality reflect differences in health-promotion practices (associated with diet, smoking, drinking and exercise), the hazards of occupations, lifestyles and engagement in risky behaviours (Arber and Thomas, 2001).

Government assumptions are that mortality will continue to fall for both men and women, with projections of expectation of life of 81.3 years for men and 85.2 years for women by 2031 (Shaw, 2004). This seems highly unrealistic, given the recent growth in obesity, work stress, and engagement in risky health behaviours. Since women and men increasingly lead comparable lives and lifestyles – for example, there is no longer any gender difference in smoking – it might be predicted the sex difference in life expectancy will continue to diminish. Such demographic changes would mean that later life will increasingly become *less* feminized than in the past. This will decrease rates of widowhood among women, and result in more older people experiencing longer marriage into very old age. These changes will have implications for living arrangements and social relationships of older people.

Changes in marital status

Marital status and living arrangements are pivotal to an older person's financial well-being, social relationships and access to carers should they become frail or disabled (Arber et al., 2003). Most older men are married and therefore have a partner for companionship, domestic-service support and for care if they become physically disabled, whereas currently this is not the case for the majority of older women.

As outlined by Kate Davidson in Chapter 17, the marital-status contours of late life are projected to change between 2001 and 2021 (see Table 17.1, page 183). Fewer older men will be married, due to increasing divorce, although even by 2021 two-thirds are projected to be married. This contrasts with older women, where the proportion married is projected to increase from 40 per cent in 2001 to 45 per cent by 2021. As discussed above, this change is due to improvements in mortality at older ages, especially among men. A sharp decline in widows is projected between 2001 and 2021, from almost half to 35 per cent of older women.

More older people will have experienced divorce at some stage in their lives. The proportion of older people who are divorced is projected to rise to 13 per cent by 2021 (Table 17.1). There are important policy implications of a growing proportion of divorced older people, as Davidson discusses. Research shows that older divorced men are more likely to be socially isolated from family and friends, and engage in more risky health behaviours, such as smoking and high alcohol consumption, than are other groups of older men (Arber et al., 2003; Davidson et al., 2003), while older divorced women *and* men have particularly poor material and financial circumstances.

Gender and new forms of partnership

Legal marital status is becoming a poorer indicator of living arrangements and partnership status among older people, in the same way as for younger age groups. Some of these issues are discussed in Part VI on the family. Older people are increasingly establishing lasting intimate relationships in which each partner continues to live in their own home. This alternative to marriage is usually referred to as 'living apart together' (LAT) (Borell and Ghazanfareeon Karlsson, 2003; and see Chapter 17 of this volume). Research suggests that it is older women who prefer to continue in a LAT relationship rather than enter cohabitation or remarriage, because a LAT relationship enables women to maintain greater autonomy and personal control by staying in their own home and not having full-time domestic responsibilities for their partner. LAT relationships can offer solo older people a fulfilling intimate relationship while maintaining a significant degree of autonomy (Davidson and Fennell, 2004).

Couple relationships are the locus of practical and emotional support, as well as 'disclosing intimacy' (Jamieson, 1998). Among the next generation of older people, who have experienced greater gender equality during their working lives and in childrearing, there is likely to be more equality among older partners in terms of domestic labour, emotional closeness and caring support. Sexuality in later life has often been considered a taboo subject, with a tendency to desexualize ageing (Gott, 2005). The next generation of older people, who experienced the sexual revolution of the 1960s, are likely to have very different views about sexuality (Davidson and Fennell, 2004). In the future there is likely to be greater recognition and acceptance that close emotional and sexual relationships are important for both older women and men.

A barely recognized and under-researched area is same-sex relationships in later life (Cronin, 2004; Heaphy et al., 2004). The Gay Liberation Movement had a major impact in reducing the stigma associated with gay and lesbian relationships in the late twentieth century. Rosenfeld (2003) argues that the experience of lesbians and gay men in later life is profoundly influenced by the historical period when they first identified as lesbian or gay. Given societal changes, and the larger proportions of young and midlife people living in same-sex relationships, more individuals will enter later life as part of a same-sex couple, while more older people are likely to begin same-sex relationships following divorce or widowhood. In the future, lesbian and gay older people will be more vociferous about their rights and expect their chosen living arrangements and sexuality to be accepted by health- and social-care providers, to a much greater extent than they are today.

Among the gay community, there is a greater emphasis on 'families of choice', representing flexible and supportive networks of friends, as well as lovers (Weeks et al., 2001). However, these gay communities are often youth-focused, resulting in older gay men feeling excluded from these groups and communities, and ageing being seen as a crisis of midlife among gay men (Kimmel and Sang, 1995). In contrast, lesbians in later life are more likely to live in partnerships and have more extensive friendship networks than do gay men (Heaphy, forthcoming). Thus there may be gender differentiation, with lesbians having greater access, and gay men more fractured access, to support and informal care in later life.

Caring: gender differences in constraints and needs

The expansion of paid employment for women, and lack of available and affordable childcare in the UK, means that grandparents often provide childcare for grandchildren on a regular basis. Whether an older person is constrained by grandparenting roles is likely to become increasingly socially divided. It is those daughters (in law) who have to work full-time for financial necessity yet earn insufficient money to pay very high child-care costs, whose mothers are most likely to be constrained by routine grandchildcare. Thus, working-class women in mid and later life are more likely to have their lives constrained by grandparenting than are middle-class women.

In contrast, parent and spouse care hits midlife and older people irrespective of their socioeconomic standing. Care for a disabled partner is often particularly intensive, with older people providing round-the-clock care. However, whether the burdens of informal caring for partners or parents can be relieved by paying for care depends principally on the financial resources of both the person in need of care *and* the carer. To the extent that England continues to operate a system whereby 'social' care is not free for older, frail or disabled people, there will be increasing inequities in later life due to the constraints of having to provide care for loved ones.

The married or partnered in later life, who become frail or disabled, largely rely on their partner for care. The widowed depend heavily on children, if they have any, to provide care 'at a distance'. Divorce fractures relationships with children to a greater extent for men than women, with divorced older men having little contact with their children (de Jong Gierveld, 2003). The proportion of women who remain childless has increased over recent years, with 26 per cent of women born in 1965 remaining childless by age 38 (Berrington, 2004). An important future issue will be the availability of informal carers for the greater proportion of older people who are childless. It remains unclear how the increase in remarriage, and step-parenting, will influence the availability of carers for older people in the future, and to what extent these effects are likely to be gendered.

There is little research on the nature and extent of informal care support for older lesbian and gay people, either from relatives or friends. However, this is likely to become a more significant issue over the next 30 years. The literature on caring is only just beginning to examine informal care by non-heterosexuals for their own parents, and to what extent their sexuality, which may have led to more ambivalent family relationships earlier in the life course (Connidis, 2003), impacts on their provision of care for parents and other relatives.

Entering a care home is usually considered a major threat to autonomy which older people resist until there is no alternative. Older women are twice as likely as men to live in such a 'communal' setting: 2.6 per cent of men and 5.9 per cent of women over 65, and 23 per cent of women and

12 per cent of men over 85 in England in 2001 (Arber and Ginn, 2004). The main reason for the higher communal residence of older women than men relates to gender differences in marital status, since the widowed and never married are more likely to live in care homes than those who are married, and these groups are disproportionately women (Arber and Ginn, 1991a, 1998, 2004). Thus, marital status provides a proxy for the availability of family carers. The widowed have half the level of communal residence of the never married, illustrating the role of adult children in providing care. The low proportion of married people who live in care homes demonstrates the major role of marital partners in providing intensive care and delaying residential admissions. Thus, the changing contours of gender and marital status in later life over the next 30 years will influence the chances of a person spending his or her final years in a residential setting, and result in a relative growth in the proportion of male care-home residents.

Income, poverty and well-being in later life

Material resources, especially income, are crucial for well-being and quality of later life. Income inequality is growing among older people with increasing polarization between well-off pensioners and those on means-tested Pensions Credit, who live at poverty or near-poverty levels. In 2001, 24 per cent of older non-married women received income support, compared with 15 per cent of non-married men and only 6 per cent of older couples (Arber and Ginn, 2004). Among older men, the married have the highest income, but among older women the never married and widowed have the highest personal income (Ginn, 2003; Arber and Ginn, 2004). The precarious financial position of older divorced women is evident.

How gender interacts with marital status in influencing an older person's income mainly reflects inequalities in ability to build private (occupational or personal) pension entitlements during working life (Arber and Ginn, 1991a; Ginn, 2003). The gender division of labour associated with childrearing reduces women's lifetime earnings, as does the gender pay gap. Earnings and access to an occupational pension also depend on occupational class, with manual workers less able to build good private pensions. To the extent that the state pension in Britain remains below means-tested benefit level, an adequate retirement income will depend on having a substantial private pension.

A key issue is whether the next generation of older women will be financially better off than the current generation. Full-time work is essential in order to accumulate an adequate private pension. However, Table 5.1 shows

Table 5.1 Percentage of women (a) in full-time employment and (b) contributing to an occupational or personal* pension, by whether they have had children and age group

	20–29	30–39	40–49	50–59	All 20–59
(a) % in full-time work					
Never had a child	70	73	64	43	66
Had a child	15	23	39	33	30
All women	50	38	43	34	41
(b) % with pensions					
Never had a child	39	60	58	42	48
Had a child	15	32	42	33	33
All women	29	39	45	34	37

*Personal pensions are other than rebate-only pensions.

Source: *General Household Survey*, 2001 and 2002 (analysis by Debora Price). The sample of women aged 20–59 was over 10,000.

that under 40 per cent of women in their 30s work full-time, with a similar proportion contributing to a private pension. The proportions are only barely higher for women in their 40s. The figures are lower for women who have ever had a child. Thus having children will continue to differentiate the financial well-being of older women in Britain over the next 30 years.

Another gender-differentiated constraint and aspect of quality of material life is having a car. Among older cohorts of women the norm was to depend on their husband for transport, as it was less usual to obtain a driving licence themselves. Thus, widowhood or divorce for women often represented more than the loss of a breadwinner and partner – it included loss of geographical mobility. In 2001, only 42 per cent of women aged 75–84 and 25 per cent over 85 had a car in the household, compared with 66 per cent and 45 per cent of men of these ages (Arber and Ginn, 2004). Although future generations of older women will be more likely to have learned to drive, to the extent that they are living on poverty level incomes, they will lack the financial resources to run a car.

Conclusion

Diversity in later life is set to increase further. Greater longevity gains for men than women are likely to continue, reducing the numerical predominance of women. The higher proportion of older people who are married, and thus advantaged by greater material well-being, living in a couple relationship, and having their partner as a potential carer, contrasts with the growing proportion of divorced older people. Being divorced in later life equates with material disadvantage for women and men, and for men equates with weaker social support networks and fractured access to potential carers. Meanwhile, new forms of partnership, such as LAT relationships and same-sex relationships are likely to become more common among older people in the next 30 years.

Older married men will continue to be the most advantaged group, both in terms of pensions and access to carers should they become sick or disabled. Older women in the future are likely to expect greater independence and autonomy. However, many are likely to continue to be constrained in their aspirations and expectations by low financial and material resources, as well as the constraints of caregiving. There is little evidence that the next generation of older women will be better off financially, since in Britain bearing children still represents a major constraint on women's full-time employment and ability to accumulate a private pension sufficient to keep them out of poverty in later life.

Six   Ethnicity and Old Age

James Nazroo

As described elsewhere in this volume, dramatic changes are affecting life at older ages in the UK, but the extent to which their impact might vary across different ethnic groups is uncertain and has rarely been studied. Indeed, there is a general paucity of research on the experiences of older ethnic minority people in the UK, together with a real concern that they may face considerable inequality as a result of the disadvantage associated with both older age and ethnic minority status, so called double jeopardy or multiple hazard (Blakemore and Boneham, 1994; Ebrahim, 1996; Mays, 1983; Norman, 1985). Such a concern, though, needs to be placed in the context of changes in the situation of older people across cohorts and variation in the experiences of ethnic minority people across specific groups and, possibly, over time (Modood et al., 1997). This chapter will address the future of ethnicity and old age in three ways: first, by outlining, briefly, the current situation of older ethnic minority people; second, by exploring how far we can identify elements of their situation as a consequence of generation-specific experiences; and, third, by examining how far the trends for younger ethnic minority people suggest that they will have similar or different outcomes at older ages.

There are two essential starting points to understanding the ageing of ethnic minority people in the UK: first, to consider the meaning of ethnicity and the problems with using the concept as a research variable (touched on (see my contribution to the introduction on pages 44–5)), and second, to describe the complexity of the ethnic composition of the UK population and how it has developed historically. Much has been written on ethnicity in the UK and the experiences of ethnic minorities (see, for example, Barot, 1996; Mason, 2003; Modood et al., 1997). In the context of the future of ageing, it is worth noting that older non-white ethnic minority people are almost exclusively migrants, many arriving in the period of reconstruction after the Second World War. Indeed, most of the migration of non-white people was driven by the postwar economic boom and consequent need for labour, a need that could be filled from Commonwealth countries. Postwar migration varied across countries of origin, with migrants in the 1950s predominantly coming from the Caribbean. Migration from India and Pakistan was concentrated in the 1960s and was followed in the 1970s by the arrival of South Asian refugees from East Africa, in the 1980s by migration from Bangladesh and China, and in the 1980s and 1990s by migration from Africa.

Generally, the initial period of migration involved young adults seeking work, with spouses, children and, sometimes, older relatives joining later. The young adults who migrated in the 1950s, 1960s and 1970s are only now reaching older ages. Analysis of the Labour Force Survey suggests that ethnic minority groups have a much younger age structure than the white population (White, 2002), with 16 per cent of the white group aged 65 and older, compared with around 6 per cent for non-white ethnic minority groups. Age profiles also vary across ethnic minority groups, reflecting migration history. For example, 9 per cent of the Black Caribbean group, 6 per cent of the Indian group and 4 per cent of the Pakistani group are aged 65 or above. The current generation of older ethnic minority people will have had a range of experiences that migrants before them did not face and that will be markedly different for their children.

We can describe the ethnic makeup of the UK population from the 2001 Census. The questions on ethnicity varied between the different countries of the UK but was most detailed for England and Wales. These data on the makeup of the population of England and Wales are shown in Table 6.1.

The circumstances of older ethnic minority people in the UK

In some dimensions there is evidence of clear and marked inequalities across ethnic groups at older ages. Figure 6.1, using data from the Health Survey for England (HSE)[1] (Erens et al., 2001), shows the proportion of men aged 55 or older who report that their health is bad or very bad (rather than fair, good or very good) and who report a diagnosis of diabetes. The figure shows very clear inequalities, with Bangladeshi and Pakistani men reporting particularly high levels of bad health and diabetes, followed by Caribbean and Indian men, then Chinese men, with the men in the general population sample having the lowest rates (despite their younger age profile even within this restricted age group).

Table 6.1 Ethnic composition of the population of
England and Wales, 2001

	Number	Per cent
White	**47,520,866**	**91.3**
British	45,533,741	87.5
Irish	641,804	1.2
Other White	1,345,321	2.6
Mixed	**661,034**	**1.3**
White and Black Caribbean	237,420	0.5
White and Black African	78,911	0.2
White and Asian	189,015	0.4
Other Mixed	155,688	0.3
Asian or Asian British	**2,273,737**	**4.4**
Indian	1,036,807	2.0
Pakistani	714,826	1.4
Bangladeshi	280,830	0.5
Other Asian	241,274	0.5
Black or Black British	**1,139,577**	**2.2**
Black Caribbean	563,843	1.1
Black African	479,665	0.9
Black Other	96,069	0.2
Chinese or other ethnic group	**446,702**	**0.9**
Chinese	226,948	0.4
Other	219,754	0.4
Total	**52,041,916**	**100**

There is a substantial body of evidence suggesting that ethnic inequalities
in health are largely driven by economic inequalities (Davey Smith et al.,
1996; Nazroo, 1998, 2001, 2003). Not surprisingly, the pattern of inequalities
in health shown in Figure 6.1 is also present for economic inequalities. Again
using data from the HSE, Figure 6.2 shows tertiles of household income for
households with one or more members aged 50 or older (Nazroo, 2004). The
figures are equivalized to account for variations in household size and show
that the Bangladeshi and Pakistani groups are particularly poorly off (with
93 per cent and 77 per cent, respectively, in the lowest-income third), followed by the Indian and Caribbean group (both with just over 50 per cent in
the bottom-income third) and the two white groups best off. In terms of the
top-income third, the Chinese group is equivalent to the two white groups,
but there are also substantially more Chinese households in the bottom-
income third – 59 per cent. Although income is a crude marker of economic
well-being at older ages, these figures are dramatic and reflect estimates of
pension income provided by the Pensions Policy Institute (2003b) and
broader estimates of economic well-being (Bajekal et al., 2004).

Figure 6.1   Ethnic difference in health, men aged 55 or older in England

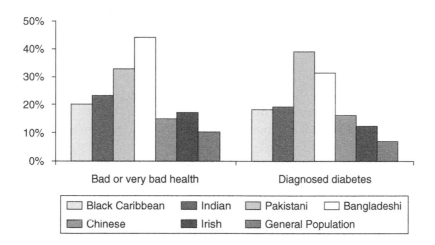

Figure 6.2   Equivalized household income by ethnic group for households with one or more persons aged 50 or older in England

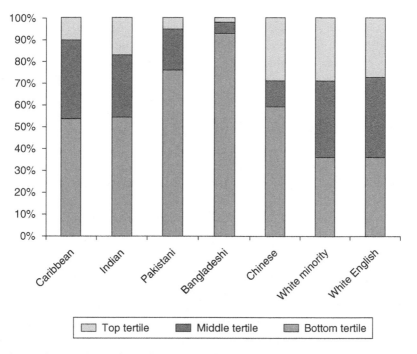

For other dimensions the pattern of ethnic inequality is much less clear. One striking feature of the circumstances of ethnic minority people in the UK is their concentration in quite specific locations. Analysis of the 2001 Census shows that ethnic minority people are more likely to live in England, in large urban areas, and that 45 per cent of the ethnic minority population live in the London region (White, 2002). However, regional location varies by ethnic group with, for example, more than half of Black African (78 per cent), Black Caribbean (61 per cent) and Bangladeshi (54 per cent) people living in London compared with about a fifth of Pakistani people. And, considering small areas, analysis of the 1991 Census suggested that more than half of ethnic minority people lived in areas where the total ethnic minority population exceeds 44 per cent, compared with the national average of less than 6 per cent at the time (Owen, 1994). As might be expected, this concentration of ethnic minority people is primarily in areas that are rated very deprived according to statistics such as the Index of Deprivation 2000 (Department of the Environment, Transport and the Regions, 2000). In direct contrast to such formal estimates of deprivation, however, older ethnic minority people rate the areas in which they live more highly than do white people in terms of the availability of amenities and no worse in terms of crime and the physical environment (Bajekal et al., 2004). Interestingly, in-depth interviews with older people suggest that this 'mismatch' between respondents' reported experiences and formal assessments may be a consequence of ethnic minority people settling in areas together and investing in developing the local infrastructure (appropriate places of worship, shops, clubs, etc.) to meet their needs – so-called community building. Such communities have then offered opportunities for older ethnic minority people to engage in social and civic activities and to take up roles that they find rewarding (Grewal et al., 2004), despite being more deprived according to objective assessments of factors such as housing stock and amenities.

As well as rating the areas in which they live highly, older ethnic minority people, as a growing body of literature suggests, have more contact with family and social networks than do white people (Evandrou, 2000). Focusing on respondents aged 45 to 74 in four ethnic groups – Caribbean, Indian, Pakistani and white – and using questions covering the frequency of seeing, writing to and speaking on the phone to relatives, Bajekal et al. (2004) show that contact with family was, on average, significantly higher in Indian and Pakistani groups compared with the white group and, if anything, higher as well for the Caribbean group. Of course, within ethnic groups there will be significant variation in contact with social and family networks.

This brief description of the position of older ethnic minority people in comparison with their white peers indicates that the situation is a little more complex than suggested by simple claims that older ethnic minority people face multiple sources of disadvantage. On the one hand, while measures of economic position, local-area deprivation scores and health suggest significant disadvantage, other, perhaps more subjective, assessments of community and social networks are less clear. On the other hand, economic and health disadvantage are not experienced uniformly among older ethnic minority people – the disadvantage is greater for some groups compared with others and even within particularly disadvantaged groups there are gender (Bajekal et al., 2004) and class (Nazroo, 2004) differences.

Generation, period or ethnic inequality?

As indicated earlier, older ethnic minority people in the UK are a generation who have had unique experiences. Their current situation might relate directly to their pre-migration and migration experiences and how these influenced economic opportunities, social networks and health. It might also relate to the period-specific context within which the migration occurred, for example, postwar UK economic structures or racist ideology (see Winder, 2004, for a historical account of migration to Britain). However, it might be a consequence of more general and more persistent post-colonial ethnic relations, or, more likely, some combination of these processes and structures. An examination of how these processes and structures operate helps us understand not only the position of the current generation of older ethnic minority people, but also how the experience of growing older might be the same and different for younger generations.

Given the more or less complete overlap between age, generation and period for ethnic minority people in the UK, it is difficult to separate their effects empirically and, thereby, to estimate how we might see shifts in experience between generations. Two approaches are, first, to examine individual biographies and to attempt to identify factors that have led to particular circumstances at older ages and how unique these are to particular periods or generations, and, second, to examine how far current circumstances are different for older and younger ethnic minority people and the extent to which this might be a consequence of period effects or of ageing.

The difficulty of these tasks is illustrated by Figure 6.3, which shows the cross-sectional relationship between age, ethnicity and self-reported fair or bad health, using data from the HSE (Nazroo, 2004). The figure is

Figure 6.3 Fair or bad self-reported health by ethnic group and age, England 1999

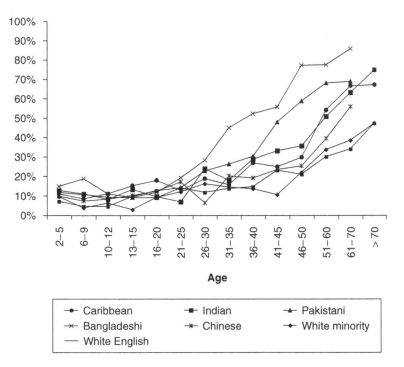

striking. Alongside the increase in fair or bad health with age for all ethnic groups, ethnic inequalities in health increase markedly with age (although there is some diversity in experience – compare the Bangladeshi, Indian and Chinese groups, for example). The small differences in early childhood disappear in late childhood and early adulthood, but then reappear in early middle age and grow dramatically throughout the rest of adulthood. There are many potential explanations for this observed pattern. It could be a consequence of: a differential experience of the ageing process (perhaps as a result of differences across ethnic groups in the accumulation of exposures to social and economic risk over time); the generation-specific impact of migration (for example, the impact of pre-migration circumstances, or the process of migration and post-migration circumstances, on health); or contextual/period effects that vary across age cohorts and first and subsequent generations of migrants (such as economic opportunities, transformations in identities, and acceptance into and participation in social and civic life).

There are other dimensions of experience where we can observe or anticipate generation or period effects. Evidence indicates significant downward social mobility for most postwar migrant groups (Heath and Ridge, 1983; Smith, 1977), but there is also evidence of a correction of some of this downward mobility for second-generation and younger ethnic minority people, which is illustrated using two markers of economic position in Table 6.2 (Nazroo, 2004). The first part of the table shows the proportion of men who are in a manual rather than non-manual occupation, focusing on those of working age (16 to 65) and split between migrants and non-migrants. It shows that there is no difference within the Indian group, while for all of the other groups second-generation men are less likely to be in a manual job than are first-generation men. The second part of the table shows the relationship between ethnicity and economic activity for men in two age groups. For the white English group just over a third of men aged 50 to 65 were not in paid employment. Figures are higher for all of the ethnic minority groups, except for the Chinese group, with particularly high rates in the Pakistani and Bangladeshi groups. Similar, though smaller, ethnic differences in participation in paid employment can be seen for men aged 30 to 49. Comparing rates for those aged 30 to 49 with those aged 50 to 65 shows that the fall in activity rates is greater for all but one of the ethnic minority groups (Chinese men being the exception) compared with the white English group, and is particularly large for Pakistani and Bangladeshi men, for whom rates drop by around two-thirds. As for health, the ethnic inequality in economic position increases for older age cohorts, but the same questions as to the drivers of this increase in inequality remain.

Other evidence also suggests changes in context and differences in experience. For example, although more than 40 per cent of Bangladeshi people of working age have no qualifications, compared with less than 20 per cent of white British people, 40 per cent of Bangladeshi boys and around 50 per cent of Bangladeshi girls aged 16 achieved five or more GCSEs in 2002, compared with only slightly more white boys and girls (45 per cent and 55 per cent, respectively) (White, 2002). This suggests a significant decrease in ethnic inequalities in education for younger generations. Also, data from the British Crime Survey series suggest that the number of racially motivated offences fell by more than a quarter in the four years between 1995 and 1999 (White, 2002), implying a shift in the extent and nature of racist ideology, although how far this trend is likely to have continued into the twenty-first century, in a period of likely increases in Islamaphobia, is uncertain.

Finally, the form and strength of ethnic identity is another dimension where we might expect to see change across different generations of

Table 6.2 Employment and class by age, ethnicity and place of birth: England 2001

	Caribbean	Indian	Pakistani	Bangladeshi	Chinese	White English
Per cent in manual classes						
Not born in England	73	53	64	77	50	N/a
Born in England	56	52	43	35	32	N/a
Per cent in paid employment						
Men aged 50–65	42	57	31	16	62	63
Men aged 30–49	74	86	78	55	88	88

ethnic minority people. Analysis of the Fourth National Survey showed that a measure of a traditional identity (covering behaviours such as wearing traditional clothes, speaking traditional languages, thinking of oneself as a member of an ethnic minority group, not thinking of oneself as British, and believing that close relatives should marry a member of the same ethnic group) correlated strongly with a number of demographic factors, including age and generation, though not in entirely consistent ways, reflecting the complexity of transformations in ethnic identities (Nazroo and Karlsen, 2003). Relevant to this context, is the earlier discussion of the significance of investment in building local communities by migrant generations, where it seems clear that a range of rewards for this investment have accrued. However, it is not certain whether younger generations will, as they grow older, also live in ethnically concentrated areas, have the same degree of engagement in local ethnically specific communities and reap the same rewards.

Conclusion

There are marked ethnic inequalities in the areas of economic position and health, inequalities that have been documented elsewhere (Mason, 2003; Modood et al., 1997). Evidence summarized here suggests that ethnic inequalities in health and economic position are at their greatest for older people. The extent of the economic and health disadvantage faced by some ethnic minority groups at older ages is extreme and the significance of this cannot be overestimated. However, it is important to recognize that older ethnic minority people do not uniquely face these circumstances and that they are not uniformly experienced in ethnic minority populations, but they are far more common.

The origins of the economic disadvantage of older ethnic minority people undoubtedly lie in their post-migration experiences, with employment opportunities on the whole restricted to jobs with poorer pay, poorer security and often with more limited pension rights (Brodie, 1996; Pensions Policy Institute, 2003b). Even those who were recruited into professional occupations, such as medicine, faced considerable disadvantage in employment (Kyriakides and Virdee, 2003). It is also worth recognizing that the impact of economic decline in the UK in the 1980s was particularly significant for this generation of ethnic minority people, many of whom spent the period before state retirement age unemployed, or unable to work because of poor health. There is considerable evidence suggesting that ethnic inequalities in health are driven by economic inequalities, evidence that shows how closely related experiences of poverty, unemployment and poor health are; and evidence that, it is suggested, shows the significance of racism and discrimination to the life chances of those ethnic minority people who migrated to the UK in the 1950s and 1960s (Nazroo, 2003).

This portrayal of disadvantage does not, however, fully capture the experiences of older ethnic minority people. Most notably, older ethnic minority people appear to do relatively well in terms of community, social and family networks. Again this can perhaps best be understood in relation to the experiences of a migrant generation. In one study, respondents described the rebuilding of ethnic communities post-migration, a rebuilding that was aided by close settlement patterns and employment in local industries (Grewal et al., 2004). The investment of this migrant generation in the building of a local ethnic community is something that many seemed able to draw on in their older ages. Of course the development of such communities occurred in the face of considerable local and national hostility (Winder, 2004). It is here that it becomes apparent that we need to consider the situation of older ethnic minority people not just in terms of the ways their lives have been structured by economic and social forces, but also in terms of how this structuring has been resisted by individuals and groups. The building, in response to post-migration hostility and exclusion, of communities in the context of ongoing significant economic hardship and poor health, has evidently done much to enhance the lives of at least some older ethnic minority people.

A remaining task is to consider how these experiences will change for future generations of ethnic minority people, who will grow older in what will be very different and possibly more positive contexts. There is some suggestion of improvements in the economic fortunes of younger generations (Nazroo, 2004) and it is likely that there will also be important demographic shifts. It is, of course, impossible to determine the impact of such changes in a complex open social system; however, it might be worth posing some questions:

- Will lower relative rates of unemployment in ethnic minority groups lead to reductions in inequalities in incomes and pension wealth at older ages?

- Will relative improvements in economic well-being lead to reductions in ethnic inequalities in health?

- What impacts will increases in female participation rates in the labour force and decreases in family size, for some ethnic minority groups, have on the provision of informal care?

- How will possible increases in geographic mobility impact on family and community networks?

- What implications does a possible shift in government policy towards 'integration' and the dispersal of new migrants have for the formation and maintenance of supportive ethnic communities?

The last point is a reminder that policy interventions are important and that their full significance needs very careful consideration.

Note

1. The HSE is an annual survey covering a nationally representative sample identified using a stratified sampling design. The HSE covers a wide range of health outcomes, together with conventional risk factors and demographics. Its focus shifts from year to year and in 1999 it contained a boosted sample of ethnic minority people.

Part III

The Future of Retirement and Pensions

In the modern world the single most important transition that is seen to mark entry into old age is retirement. It is a historically recent phenomenon, and is characteristic of the urban, industrial societies of Western Europe and North America. Thane (1978, 2000) argues that before the early nineteenth century individuals retired from their occupations at whatever age they felt unable to carry them out. The conventional definition of old age as starting at 60 or 65 stems from bureaucratic organization of the life course around the administration of retirement pensions. In more recent years, the practice of standardized retirement ages has become less rigid. A number of factors have been influential in these changes. Two in particular stand out: first, there is the use of early retirement to manage fluctuations in the labour market, and the use of pension funds to attract older workers to withdraw from paid employment. Second, there is the cultural re-evaluation of the post-work phase of life in which the positive attractions and opportunities for personal growth in retirement have been highlighted. Finally, there are pressures, from a variety of public agencies, not least governments, to raise the retirement age and extend working life.

The discussion of the future of pensions has been dominated by what are presented as mainly demographic issues. Ageing of the populations across the world are seen by some to be placing an unsustainable burden on current pension schemes (World Bank, 1994). It is difficult to open a newspaper without an article describing chaos in the UK pension system or an impending crisis in social security. In the future there will be more older people and fewer people of working age, because in recent decades life expectancy has been increasing and birth rates have been falling. These alterations mean that there is widespread concern as to whether productivity can be sustained among the reduced cohort of those of working age, sufficient to support the incomes and purchasing power of the retired. The ageing of the 'baby-boomers' (Evandrou, 1997) has been a focus of concern, with larger cohorts entering retirement and the consequent increased costs of pensions and healthcare. Particularly alarmist versions of this argument have been called 'apocalyptic demography' (Robertson, 1999). However, there is a need to retain a healthy scepticism about the ways that demographic projections are used uncritically to forecast additional pensions and healthcare costs. The arguments raging around the policy implications of these effects are complex, subtle and highly politicized.

Three sets of questions stand out in this area: first, should pension systems be financed on a pay-as-you-go basis, or should they be funded? This means, should current workers pay taxes out of which current pensions are paid, or should they volunteer to or be forced to save in a fund which will ultimately provide for their own old age? Second, what is the correct balance between state-run schemes and those which are privately organized? And, third, what form should private schemes take? Predominantly this debate takes place among economists and policymakers concerned with fiscal sustainability, and the effects of pension systems on labour and capital markets (see for example OECD, 2004b; Rein and Schmähl, 2004). Within these debates insufficient attention is given to the social costs and social implications in terms of inequalities and of stratification of differing systems. Indeed, debate about pension reform is often so technical that it obscures the choices to be made and how these relate to societal values and questions relating to adequacy and equity (Whiteford, 2004: 14).

Globalization has had a profound influence on national pension schemes and some have argued that there is a particular modern form of international finance called Pension Fund Capitalism. In the 1990s public-pensions crises contrasted with the enormous expansion of privately controlled pension funds. The subsequent downturn in world stock markets and crises in private pension funds have exposed pensioners to new risks. Despite pension funds having supplied significant numbers of older people in the US and UK with a good retirement, it has been argued that global financial markets and the international elites who operate them undermine many of the conditions necessary for a secure, prosperous old age across the world (Blackburn, 2002; Clark, 2000; Minns, 2001). The institutions through which the pension schemes operate must have a stable multigenerational continuity to be capable of reliably supporting people in old age. A secure old age including income maintenance and health and social care can be achieved only within a framework of social solidarity. A key issue is to identify what in the future will be the basis of achieving social solidarity and support across generations?[1]

Note

1 The editors acknowledge the assistance of Debora Price, Jay Ginn and Sara Arber in writing this introduction.

Seven The Future of Inequalities in Retirement Income

Debora Price and Jay Ginn

The possible impact of population ageing on fiscal, economic and social policies has led to an explosion of interest in pension systems and the stresses that they are predicted to encounter (Bonoli and Gay-des-Combes, 2003; OECD, 2005). These same factors have also led to a widespread perception that the welfare state, provider of insurance and income in old age, is under threat (Castles, 2004; Pierson, 2001; Taylor-Gooby, 2004). The extent to which this is an accurate perception is contested (Castles, 2004), but even if expenditure on 'welfare' is not reducing, massive restructuring of the provision of welfare is under way. All Western European countries have been examining and reforming their pension systems – one of their greatest welfare expenditure items (Bonoli and Gay-des-Combes, 2003). In the UK, this reform has taken the form of increased reliance on private and occupational pensions for the provision of adequate income in old age, in the face of dwindling state provision (OECD, 2005; Pensions Commission, 2004b).

This political construction of pension systems is especially evident in the light of economic theory that the macro-economic differences between state-run pay-as-you-go pensions and funded pensions accumulated in the private sector are often overstated and misunderstood (Atkinson, 2004; Barr, 1998; Pensions Commission, 2004a). The ageing of the population affects both systems adversely. The extent to which an individual can expect a pension through the state and to which he or she must accumulate private pensions to ensure adequate income in old age depends largely on political choices made over time, rather than on other factors.

In the UK, these political choices have led to our current position of reliance on the private sector. Beveridge's welfare state of the post-Second World War era was predicated on the assumption that men would be the breadwinners and women would perform unpaid work as housewives and mothers, with pensions accruing to men through paid work on behalf of the family (Beveridge, 1942; Harris, 2005). Since this distinctly male but ideologically egalitarian vision of the 1940s, we have moved from a universal pension system that promised (although never fulfilled) alleviation from poverty for all older people, through attempts by the Labour government in the 1970s to provide a secure pension future for most citizens, to a neoliberal highly individualized pension system that depends on private investment for adequate income in retirement. Without a reasonable amount of such private investment providing household income, dependency on the means-tested 'pension credit' system[1] at some point in old age is almost inevitable. Earnings from paid work in the formal economy have thus become a crucial element of the ability to make sufficient and adequate pension provision.

This growing reliance on the private sector for income in old age also explains something of the crisis that we have more recently endured in the UK in the governance of pension schemes, as a series of scandals and funding deficits have rocked the private pensions industry. These have included fraud, misselling, incompetence and the emergence of pension 'black holes' where once there were assets. We have witnessed the large-scale closing down of salary-related occupational pension schemes, and increasing reliance in the UK on schemes based on contributions, which build up a fund from which an annuity (pension) will be purchased at retirement. This has led to many employers massively reducing the pension contributions that they pay, and the transfer of much of the risk of investments and interest rates in the future to individuals. In addition, and related to these structures and events, as a society we are facing increasing challenges as evidence grows that there is insufficient investment in these private schemes to provide adequate incomes in retirement (Pensions Commission, 2004b). The public now trust neither the government nor private providers to fulfil their pension promises (Taylor-Gooby, 2005).

Inequality in later life

There are other implications of the focus in the UK on private sector pensions, and these relate to the way that inequalities emerge in society. The debate about pension reform generally focuses on sustainability, and rarely ventures into the social costs and social implications of different pension systems, of inequalities and of stratification. Yet inequality is both created and perpetuated by the structure of the pension system, and the policy choices made can either contribute to its growth or ameliorate its effects. Whiteford (2004: 14) comments that pension reforms have given little attention to the economic well-being of older people, and the House of Lords Select Committee on Economic Affairs (2003: 45–7) describes the notion of 'fiscal sustainability' as 'vacuous' in the absence of a clear understanding of the social purpose of a pension system.

Inequalities in old age are finally surfacing into the policy arena, as it becomes increasingly clear that in a system so reliant on private means of financing retirement, histories of paid work and earnings become crucial in determining inequality in later life. Thus groups disadvantaged in participation in and rewards from paid labour are at particular risk of poverty in later life. Women still provide the bulk of unpaid family caring, impacting heavily on their participation in paid work. Widespread discrimination in the ability to accumulate human capital through the life course, and in the operation of the labour market, still exists against women, some ethnic minority groups, some religious groups, older workers, and people with disabilities. Resulting inequalities in participation in paid labour, in levels of pay, and in terms and conditions of employment all translate into wide inequalities in income in later life (Bardasi and Jenkins, 2002; Falkingham and Rake, 2001; Ginn, 2003; Ginn and Arber, 2001b). The cost of such inequality is millions of older people living below or on the margins of poverty, that is, the reliance of some 2.7 million claimants[2] on means testing in old age, and the abject poverty of a further 20 to 33 per cent who are entitled to claim but do not do so (Department for Work and Pensions, 2003b; House of Commons, 2005; Office of National Statistics, 2003).

The continuing problems for women particularly in accumulating pensions in a society which assumes that they will be available to provide care for children, grandchildren and frail, ill and disabled adults, as well as care of home and hearth, are well documented and indicate the ongoing assumption by governments and individuals of financial dependence by women on men (Ginn, 2003). But in modern UK society almost half of children are now born outside marriage (Kiernan and Smith, 2003) and the risk of relationship breakdown is high (Ermisch and Francesconi, 2000; Shaw, 1999). In depending so heavily on private pension accumulation over a full-time working lifetime, the pension structure does not take into account lifetime working patterns interrupted and/or affected by caring and domestic responsibilities, nor the low earnings of women, nor the low wage economy and large inequalities of earnings that characterize the neoliberal political economy of the UK today (Brewer et al., 2005; Palmer et al., 2004).

Of course, not all those belonging to generally disadvantaged groups are equally disadvantaged. Among women, there are rising inequalities, for example, according to education and social class, and especially according to whether women have children. Childless women with good education and a reasonable position in the occupational structure will accumulate similar pensions to men, although still substantially disadvantaged by gender pay gaps. For women with children, however, class and educational advantages are much less striking (Ginn and Arber, 2002; Warren, 2003), with all mothers severely disadvantaged in paid work and in pension accumulation.

Policy options for pensions

If pensions were not so closely connected to histories of paid work, then unequal chances in life, unequal gender relations during the working life and workforce discrimination would matter less for income in later life. In countries where there is more support, institutionally, for women's paid work, and where business and labour depend on a full-time regulated workforce, rather than a part-time flexible workforce, there is less disadvantage at the bottom of the wages distribution. In countries where pension accumulation does not depend to such a great extent on paid work, inequalities in later life are not so profound.

To what extent should those who fare less well in the labour force be penalized in pension provision in later life? Women's identity is often structured around an ethic of care, of considerable benefit to the nation's economy in the provision of unpaid household labour. Disadvantages because women undertake housework and care should not reflect in poverty in later life. Similarly, discrimination suffered along other dimensions – ethnicity, race, religion, age, disability, social class – should not be compounded by lack of pension accumulation in later life. These are structural and societal constraints and disadvantages, and the social cost should be shared by society. A pension system should prioritize the needs of the less well-off, compensating for structural inequalities arising out of the norms and values prevalent in society, which have often been institutionalized within social policy, within industry, and within family structures. There is widespread public support for all older people to receive adequate pensions from the state, and also for state pensions to keep pace with living standards.

A pension system that achieved social aims of ensuring the well-being of all older people and reducing inequalities arising in these ways would need to be fair,[3] adequate, simple, stable and secure, and allow older people to live in a dignified manner. Our current system does not achieve these aims, and will serve to exacerbate rather than reduce inequalities in the future.

Primarily, pension accumulation in the British state schemes – which are redistributive – is too low to ensure adequate, secure, dignified income. Most women do not have a full state pension, but even for those who do, this is now only 16 per cent of national average earnings, and well below the poverty line (Disney and Emmerson, 2005). The very low rates at which our state pension system replaces income[4] lead to the prevalence of means testing as a form of poverty prevention in later life. Under current policies, this is set to get worse, as over time the state pensions will fall further and further below the poverty line. About half of pensioners are currently entitled to means-tested benefits, projected to increase to four-fifths of pensioners by 2040 (Clark and Emmerson, 2002). Means testing not only penalizes those on low wages who did save towards pensions (by providing high withdrawal rates on additional income), but it forces people to display their poverty: it is complex, stigmatizing, bureaucratic, invasive and burdensome. It also consigns claimants to a lifetime on the margins of poverty, with no hope of acquiring an adequate income for the enjoyment of a 'modern retirement' (Howse, 2004).

The combination of National Insurance entitlements (with various credits and boosted accrual for the low paid), means testing and several types of private sector pensions with different risks creates complexities well beyond the grasp of most people – indeed justifies description as the most complex in the world (Pensions Commission, 2004b). A simple, secure, stable system would allow people to understand what their pension income would be at all stages of the life course, without tricky calculations dependent on assumptions on which even experts cannot agree. If everyone had a guaranteed income above poverty levels, and knew that any additional income would be theirs to keep and would enhance their retirement, they could make sensible plans for their old age. For this to happen, state systems would have to pay above-poverty pensions to all, and remain stable and predictable over very long time spans. This implies that political cycling must be removed from pension decisions.

Can a private system deliver fairness, adequacy, stability and simplicity? In the UK our private pensions are driven by tax concessions, which predominantly benefit those already best off (mostly privileged men) and do little to encourage or aid saving to those struggling with low wages (Agulnik and Le Grand, 1998; Pensions Commission, 2004b). This is not a fair system. Structures of defined benefits schemes are themselves unfair – providing disproportionate rewards to those who end their working lives on high salaries after many years of unbroken employment with the same employer (again, mostly privileged men), at the expense of other members of the scheme and non-members. The transition that we are witnessing, away from defined benefit schemes and towards defined contribution schemes or other forms of personal pension, leads to individuals bearing risks previously borne by employers or collectively by scheme members – of interest rates, stock market volatility, inflation and longevity. These are risks which those on low wages have little means of hedging or managing. The last decade, with bankrupt schemes, failing schemes, falling equity values, variable investment performance, high charges and low interest rates, has shown that it is extremely difficult for the private pension sector to ensure predictable pensions and stability across cohorts. Moreover, the interaction between the state scheme and the private sector is making it impossible to know how to advise those on low and moderate incomes about pension savings.

The future of pensions

For many men and most women, material and substantive improvements in their income in later life will result only from the detachment of pension income from labour-force participation and wage level. In other words, the rapid decline in the level of pensions provided by the state and the increasing reliance on private pensions for pension adequacy in old age must be reversed. Simultaneously we must emphasize unpaid care as a qualifying criterion for state pension entitlement, to supplement that of paid work. It is only in state systems that redistributive policies towards the low paid or those with low lifetime accumulation can be effected, and it is only within state pensions that care work can be adequately credited. If we do not ensure that caring is adequately recognized, unjustifiable inequalities will persist.

Inequalities arising from private systems imply that, for a socially just system, the state, with its economies of scale, ability to ensure progressive benefits and ability to underwrite risk[5] should have a role in the acquisition of pension provision above the minimum poverty line. This was the role initially envisaged by Barbara Castle[6] for the State Earnings Related Pension Scheme (SERPS), but subsequently eroded by successive government policies, both Conservative and Labour. Yet if low-paid workers, and those who provide care, are to have sufficient incomes to enjoy their old age and participate fully in society after retirement, state pensions need to ensure income adequacy for all citizens in later life. However, whether this should be done at all and, if so, how, are heavily contested questions. The current Labour government seems wedded to the ideology of means testing to relieve poverty, despite disincentive effects and persistent low take-up.[7]

81

While support of non-governmental bodies for improvements to the state sector is growing, motivations and reasons vary. The insurance and pension sector, such as the Association of British Insurers, or the National Association of Pension Funds, believe that a higher baseline income for the population is necessary to enable them to sell top-up pensions to higher-paid workers, i.e. mostly to men. Their principal concern is poverty traps created by the gap between the basic state pension and the means-tested limits.

Liberally minded commentators, such as the Pensions Policy Institute (PPI), believe that the basic state pension should be improved because the current combination of state pension and means testing is a highly inefficient and often anomalous way of preventing poverty; but liberals (and the PPI) have no belief in the role of the state as anything more than a stringent provider of residual welfare. The Trades Union Congress wants improvements for reasons, ironically, similar to that of industry – a better base upon which their members can build occupational pensions associated with their provision of paid labour – though in this instance, through increased compulsion of employer contributions. But such reforms would not improve pensions for those who are excluded from or severely disadvantaged in the workforce. This loose coalition of business, liberals and the trade unions is acting as a self-interested but powerful lobby for setting state pensions at or just above the poverty line.

Organizations concerned with the interests of pensioners now and in the future – including women's lobby groups such as the Fawcett Society, pensioners organizations and charities concerned with older people – value the ability of state pensions to redistribute towards the disadvantaged and reward care, and believe that the political risks are less severe than the financial risks in the open pensions market. They want to see the state providing pensions that not only eliminate poverty but also provide adequate replacement rates, with higher returns for those with lifetime low wages. A compulsory state supplementary pension that provided much higher levels of income replacement, and that compensates for periods of caring and low wages ensures inclusion of most women in second tier saving, eliminating the elements of choice that have so bedevilled women's participation in voluntary pension schemes.[8] Systems along these lines would benefit not only women, but all those who suffer systematic disadvantage in the workforce.

For state pensions to resist politically expedient erosion over time, it is important that people trust that they will last into the long term; otherwise there will be little political support for them and constant pressure to scale back payments (Atkinson, 2004; Taylor-Gooby, 2005).

Ironically, the rhetoric of the unsustainability of state provision of pensions is in danger of becoming a self-fulfilling prophecy.

Conclusion

The UK policy regime of heavy reliance on the market for the provision of financial welfare in old age means that citizens can only achieve an adequate retirement income if they are able to participate in private pension savings. In turn, this means their working lives must follow a pattern of relatively stable, full-time employment at high wages, for it is this pattern upon which good private pension accumulation is predicated. These are the structures that lead to inequality in later life, with advantages compounded for the rich, and the poor left with multiple disadvantages, reliance on means testing, and inadequate incomes for a fully integrated and meaningful retirement.

There are two possible ways to reduce differentials in the accumulation of provision for old age. Either the reliance on the market must be substituted with a system which redistributes financial benefits from paid workers to those providing support in the home through care and other forms of domestic work, and to those on low pay and who have more chequered histories of paid work, or all cultural, structural and social inequalities in the provision of paid labour must be eradicated. It is difficult to envisage rapid progress towards the eradication of all such inequalities, particularly in a society where many jobs are low-waged, where women are expected to provide unpaid care and where the 'flexible' labour economy is highly prized. This leaves as the only solution the strengthening of the state pension schemes so that they provide adequate, safe, secure, simple and fair incomes for older people. The retention of a second tier National Insurance pension scheme on top of much-improved basic provision would seem to offer the best chance of ensuring an adequate income for all in old age.

The more general challenge for politicians is to restore faith that government can and will provide for the well-being of its citizens. As pressures on state and private pension schemes increase in the coming decades, and as the government and opposition parties contemplate the long-term future of our pension systems, political choices will be made affecting the well-being of both current and future generations of pensioners. It will be more important than ever to ensure that the least advantaged members of society are able to enjoy their old age, with self-respect and security.

Notes

1 Formerly Income Support and then Minimum Income Guarantee.

2 A claimant may be living alone, or have a dependent spouse.

3 In this chapter, we consider fairness in the sense of reducing inequalities within cohorts, and do not consider the issues raised by debates on intergenerational equity, which ask whether overlapping generations should share the burden of changing longevity and fertility equally, or in some other proportion. See Howse (2004).

4 Contrasting with the state pensions in many European states and in other English-speaking countries, where replacement rates are much higher.

5 By ensuring that risks are shared among the population, and, if necessary between current and future populations.

6 Barbara Castle was a leading Labour politician and the Minister responsible for pensions in Harold Wilson's 1974-6 administration.

7 The reasons for low take-up are complex, but include people's fear of appearing in need, and losing their independence (Department for Work and Pensions, 2003b).

8 Compulsory membership of private pensions for all workers would also eliminate choice, but would be forcing low and moderate earners to invest in high-risk, high-cost schemes, possibly for no financial benefit because of poverty traps, and where their income may be better spent elsewhere, for example on debt reduction or the care of children.

Eight   Will the Baby-boomers be Better off than their Parents in Retirement?

Maria Evandrou and Jane Falkingham

It is often assumed that children will be better off in retirement than their parents. Certainly the evidence over the last century bears this out, with successive generations of people in the twentieth century retiring with better pensions and higher incomes (Department of Social Security, 2000). However, recent changes in the family and the workforce, as well as in the benefit system, mean that in future this may not be the case.

The value of the basic state pension relative to average earnings is decreasing, and by 2040 the basic state pension is predicted to be worth 9 per cent of average earnings (Curry and O'Connell, 2003). Many people do not expect there to be an adequate state pension in their own retirement and instead expect to rely on pension income from non-state sources (Mayhew, 2003). This shift towards greater private pension provision means that there will be a greater reliance in later life on earlier labour-market experiences. At the same time, postwar industrial change has resulted in the emergence of alternative working practices, and the notion of a *lifelong* career has all but disappeared. Rather, part-time, temporary and transitional jobs have become a permanent feature of the employment experience for many young people today. US research has led some to project that the baby-boomers will be the first American generation to be less well off than their parents on reaching retirement age (Levy and Michel, 1991). However, little research has been carried out on the financial prospects of the British postwar baby-boom generations.

This chapter investigates whether the 1960s baby-boom cohort in Britain will be better off than their parents in retirement.[1] It examines the social and economic experiences of four different birth cohorts over the last 30 years in order to assess how the experiences of the baby-boomer generations to date are likely to shape their future. Key predictors of financial well-being in later life include employment history, income, membership of occupational and personal pension schemes and housing tenure. The research focuses on these factors for each of the four cohorts, looking at how their experiences differ at the same chronological point in their life course. By adopting such an approach, it is hoped to shed light on what the baby-boom cohorts might look like in 30 years' time and how they may differ from older people today.

Data and methodology

There is no single source of longitudinal data in Britain that currently provides information both across an extended time period and for a range of different birth cohorts. The British Household Panel Study at Essex University is producing exciting and useful data but its usefulness for this research is limited in that data collection commenced only in 1991. This research therefore uses a pseudo-cohort approach to examine the experience of four birth cohorts at the same chronological age and to compare the differences between them.

The analysis uses cross-sectional data from 30 years of the General Household Survey (GHS), 1973–2003, to track the experiences of representatives of each birth cohort. It uses a pseudo-cohort approach since the individuals are not the same from year to year. Instead, those respondents aged, for example, 53–7 years old in the 1973 GHS are taken as being representative of the birth cohort born in 1916–20. The same birth cohort is then represented by those aged 54–8 in 1974, 55–9 in 1975, and finally those aged 83–7 in 2003. Rather than tracking individuals per se, it is the group mean that is taken. Thus the unit of analysis is the cohort and what is measured is the *average* experience for the cohort.

The main advantages of using a pseudo-cohort approach are that it is less expensive in time and money as the data already exist and cover a long time period and avoids the problem of sample attrition, as with panel data. However, there are limitations to employing such a method. First, it is not possible to examine the duration of events for individuals, but only the average duration for the cohort as a whole. Second, as with any analysis of cross-sectional data over time, there may be problems with consistency of data. Third, there is the problem of sampling error in the successive cross-sectional samples. However, the large sample size of the GHS means that the sample errors around the estimates are relatively small. Finally, the results are affected by both age and period effects which are often difficult to disentangle. Despite these limitations, pseudo-cohort analysis can provide useful insights into inter-cohort differences and help to inform policymaking.

The cohorts

The four cohorts selected are people born in the years 1916–20, 1931–5, 1946–50 and 1961–5. There is often discussion as to the arbitrary nature of cohort boundaries. The choice here reflects a group of people born in the same five-year time period, who consequently have many historical experiences in common.

First, those born in 1916–20 represent today's 'older' elderly, being aged 80–84 in 2000. Twenty-five years earlier, in 1975, they were aged 55–9 and approaching retirement. Second, the cohort born in 1931–5 are today's 'younger' elderly, aged 65–9 in 2000. In 1975 there were entering midlife, constituting the group aged 40–44. Third, the cohort born in 1946–50 represents the 'first baby-boom generation'. They were aged 25–9 in 1975 and by 2000 they were aged 50–54 and starting to plan for retirement. Fourth, the cohort born in 1961–5 represents the 'second baby-boom generation'. In 1975, aged 10–14, they were still at school. By 2000 they had reached their mid to late 30s. This reflects a stage where their education and training have largely been completed, and occupational pathways are well established, along with family life.

Given that the mean age at motherhood in 1961 was 28, those born in 1931–5 can be viewed as representing the parents of those born in 1961–5 (Office for National Statistics, 2005a). Similarly those born in 1916–20 may be considered as being the parents of those born in the period 1946–50.

Marked differences are to be expected between the cohorts, as they were born into and grew up in very different economic, technological and social climates (Evandrou and Falkingham, 2000). The differences between the experiences of the postwar and pre-war cohorts is considerable with neither of the latter groups having experienced large-scale war and both growing up under the umbrella of the welfare state. However, the experience of the two postwar cohorts has been far from similar. The first baby-boomers (1946–50) were born in a period of postwar austerity, experiencing rationing and selective education. However, when they entered the labour market in the early 1960s, the economy was entering a period of relative *prosperity*. Not only was the job market buoyant, but the rapid expansion of higher education in this decade also meant that a growing number stayed on at school and entered university. In addition to new opportunities in education and work, the introduction of 'the pill' heralded a new sexual freedom.

In contrast, the second baby-boomers (1961–5) were born in a period of prosperity, grew up during the consumer spending boom of the 1960s, and 'enjoyed' the benefit of comprehensive secondary education. But by the time this generation came to enter the labour market at the end of the 1970s, the economy was entering a recession, resulting in sharp rises in unemployment. Individuals born during the peak birth year of 1964 reached school-leaving age in 1980 at the depth of the recession. Some may have *never* had a permanent full-time job. Furthermore, the spirit of radicalism and freedom, enjoyed by the preceding baby-boom cohort, was missing, not only in terms of employment and income, but also in other spheres of life. The first diagnosis of a person with AIDS was in 1984 – marking the end of the sexual revolution.

These very different economic and social environments will have affected the respective life chances of the different cohorts, as well as cohort members' expectations of employment, the welfare state and life in general. As the findings illustrate, the trend towards greater inequality is a persistent theme throughout the lives of the second baby-boomer cohort. The two baby-booms in the postwar period are clearly illustrated in Figure 8.1, mapping the annual number of births in England and Wales since 1916. It is the ageing of the 1960s baby-boom, constituting around nine million people, which will present a particular challenge for social policy both in terms of their numbers and the diversity of experience.

Work and pensions

Financial well-being in retirement is critically dependent on past work histories and pension-scheme membership. Membership of occupational and private pensions has increased significantly over the last 30 years (Table 8.1). Men and women from the 1960s generation are generally more likely to have private pensions (occupational and personal pensions) than were older generations at the same age. This is particularly true for women in full-time employment. At age 40, over three-quarters of full-time employed women from the 1960s cohort are members of a pension scheme compared to just two-fifths of their mother's generation at the same age (Table 8.1). Pension membership is lower amongst women in part-time work, but nevertheless 43 per cent of the 1960s women had such coverage at age 40 compared to just 11 per cent amongst the

Figure 8.1 Annual Number of births, England and Wales, 1916–2003

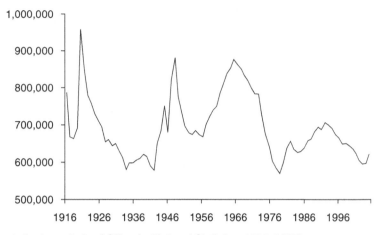

Source: Author's analysis of Office for National Statistics, 1984, 2005b.

Table 8.1 Membership of occupational or private pension scheme at selected ages, by gender and birth cohort (%)

	1916–20 cohort	1931–35 cohort	1946–50 cohort	1961–65 cohort
Employed men				
Age 25			53	65
Age 40		62	88	71
Age 55	68	85	75	
Full-time employed women				
Age 25			42	56
Age 40		39	66	77
Age 55	42	75	73	
Part-time employed women				
Age 25			25	20
Age 40		11	20	43
Age 55	9	25	45	

Source: Authors' analysis of the GHS, 1973–2003/4.

1930s cohort at the same age. Interestingly, although pension-scheme membership is higher amongst men from the 1960s cohort than amongst those from the 1930s cohort at age 40, it is lower than that for the 1940s cohort, suggesting that the growth in private pension scheme membership has fallen off.

In addition to better pension coverage, a higher proportion of the baby-boom cohorts will have access to housing wealth, both through their own tenure and through inheritance, than previous generations had.

Figure 8.2 Proportion of men in employment, by birth cohort

Source: Authors' analysis of the GHS, 1974–2003/4, using three-year moving average.

At age 55, over four-fifths of the 1940s cohort owned their own homes, compared to 70 per cent of the 1930s cohort and around half of the 1920s cohort. It is likely that a similar proportion of the 1960s baby-boomers will also enter retirement owning their own homes. Thus, rising membership of pension schemes and greater levels of owner occupation both point to the baby-boomers being *better off* in retirement than today's older people, that is, their parents' generations.

However, the 1960s baby-boomers faced particular problems entering the labour market during the recession of the early to mid-1980s. The poor timing of their entry into the labour market was exacerbated by their size; being a member of a large generation in a context of high unemployment is likely to reduce their level of lifetime earnings. Furthermore, they are likely to be the first generation to experience the full extent of industrial change, with the growth of flexible labour markets, the decline of the manufacturing industry and the expansion of part-time working.

Changes in the labour market have affected men and women differently. The proportion of men in employment at selected ages by birth cohort is shown in Figure 8.2. The combined employment trajectories of

Figure 8.3a   Proportion of women in full-time employment, by birth cohort

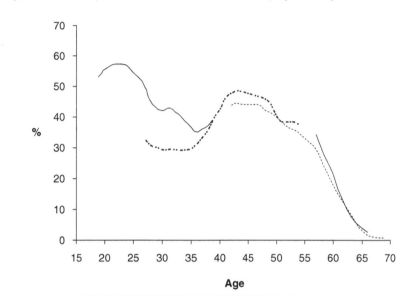

Source: Authors' analysis of the GHS, 1974–2003/4, using three-year moving average.

the different cohorts broadly outline the typical employment profile of men, rising at young ages, then levelling out between the late 20s and 50s, and then declining as people progressively retire. However, it is clear that successive cohorts of men are both entering the labour market *later* and leaving *earlier*, and have lower overall participation rates at any given age.

In contrast, women from the 1960s cohort experience *higher* rates of participation at any given age than the earlier cohorts, although their participation rates are still lower than those of men (see Figures 8.3a and 8.3b). They are much more likely to work full-time than women in earlier cohorts: at age 30, 42 per cent of the 1960s-cohort women were in full-time employment, compared to 30 per cent of women from the 1940s cohort. Although the proportion of the 1960s baby-boom women working full-time drops as they enter their peak childbearing years, levels are not as low as for previous cohorts and start to increase again from age 35. Moreover, the proportion of 1960s women working part-time is higher than the proportion of the previous generation. Thus overall, more women in this cohort are working. The extension of women's retirement

91

Figure 8.3b Proportion of women in part-time employment, by birth cohort

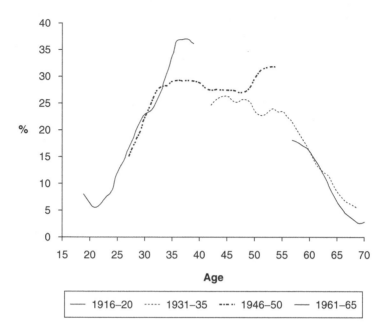

Source: Authors' analysis of the GHS, 1974–2003/4, using three-year moving average.

age to 65 may well lead to longer working lives, which will mean that women will have longer to build up their pension entitlements.

These trends have implications for the level of resources in later life. More women will have *longer* working lives, enhancing their potential for accumulating pension entitlement in their own right. The shorter working lives of men, however, will tend to have the opposite impact, *reducing* overall pension entitlements. This may be exacerbated by the fact that the proportion of 1960s baby-boomer men that had ever experienced unemployment by the age of 35 is very much higher than for previous generations. The two recessions of the early 1980s and 1990s are clearly visible in Figure 8.4 and the unemployment rate during each recession has been greatest amongst the baby-boomers. In 1983, a staggering 19 per cent of the 1960s cohort were unemployed and some had never had a full-time job. Although unemployment rates for the baby-boomer men fell during the 1980s, it is not until the late 1990s that unemployment levels reach those experienced by the older cohorts during the *height* of the 1980s recession. The mixed employment experiences of the 1960s baby-boomers have resulted in a high level of income inequality within the cohort.

Figure 8.4   Proportion of men unemployed, by birth cohort

Source: Authors' analysis of the GHS, 1974–2003/4, using three-year moving average.

Income

Given the growth in real wages over the last fifty years, it is not surprising that, on average, the 1960s baby-boomers are significantly better off
than their parents' cohort (1931–5) at the same age. The average (median)
monthly income of each cohort at age 40 is compared in Table 8.2. In
order to take into account variations in household size as well as
economies of scale in consumption, gross monthly household income is
equivalized using the original OECD equivalence scale (OECD, 1982).
Income values are expressed in 2003 prices, with data from earlier years
deflated using the retail price index for all goods and services. The 1960s
baby-boomers have an average income of £1,159 per month compared to
their parents, who had £529 per month at the same age (Table 8.2). In
other words, the baby-boomers are, on average, 119 per cent better off
than their parents were in early middle age. Interestingly, analysis by
Easterlin and colleagues of the US situation found that the American
baby-boomers were, on average, two-thirds better off than their parents'
generation at the same stage of the life course (Easterlin et al., 1993).

Table 8.2 Absolute and relative income position at age 40 amongst the different baby-boomer cohorts and their parents' generation

	1931–35 cohort	1946–50 cohort	1961–65 cohort	Difference 1960s–1930s
Average monthly income (median)	£529	£1,050	£1,159	+119%
Poorest (10th percentile)	£191	£425	£369	+93%
Richest (90th percentile)	£1,040	£2,917	£2,667	+156%
Relative position				
10th P/50th P	0.36	0.40	0.32	–12%
10th P/90th P	0.18	0.20	0.14	–22%
Gini coefficient at age 40	0.348	0.335	0.396	

Note: Income is household adult equivalent income per month in 2003 prices, equivalized using OECD equivalence scale. The relative position is calculated by 10th percentile/50th percentile.

Source: Authors' analysis of the GHS, 1973–2003/4.

However, this *average* picture masks significant diversity within the baby-boomer cohort. Table 8.2 also shows the level of income for the richest and poorest 10 per cent of each cohort. The richest 10 per cent of the 1960s cohort are significantly better off relative to their counterparts in their parents' generation, with an income of £2,667 per month, compared with £1,040 enjoyed by the most successful amongst the 1931–5 cohort at the same age. This is a wider differential than was found for the cohort as a whole. Although even the poorest 10 per cent of 1960s baby-boomers are better off relative to their counterparts in the parental cohort, the advantage is much smaller – £369 per month compared to £191. Moreover, the top and bottom of 1960s cohort appear to be doing less well than the 1940s cohort at the same age, despite being separated by 15 years of real earning growth.

Furthermore, if economic well-being is taken to be a relative rather than an absolute concept, a different picture emerges. Table 8.2 also shows the position of the poorest 10 per cent relative to the richest 10 per cent within each cohort (the 10th percentile compared to the 90th percentile). Amongst the 1930s cohort, the poorest members had an income 18 per cent of that of the richest members. However, amongst the baby-boomers, the poorest 10 per cent have an income just 14 per cent of the richest. In other words, the poorest amongst the 1960s cohort are less well-off in relative terms than the poorest in their parents' generation at the same age.

Table 8.3 Inequality within birth cohorts at selected ages: Gini coefficient of adult equivalent household income

Midpoint of age group	Birth Cohort			
	1916–20	1931–35	1946–50	1961–65
25			0.322	0.339
40		0.348	0.335	0.396
55	0.346	0.372	0.425	
70	0.313	0.351		

Note: Income is gross household adult equivalent income per month in 2003 prices, equivalized using the OECD equivalence scale. The Gini coefficient is a statistical measure of inequality. The higher the value of the Gini, the greater the degree of inequality.

Source: Authors' analysis of the GHS, 1973–2003/4.

The degree of income inequality between and within the cohorts is summarized by the Gini coefficient (Table 8.3). Two key findings stand out: first, income inequality within cohorts appears to rise with age and then falls in retirement. This is not surprising, as differences in earned income during working life tend to be greater than pension income in later life. Second, income inequality at any given age is higher amongst younger cohorts, reflecting the growing gap between 'rich' and 'poor' during the last 30 years (Goodman and Webb, 1994; Goodman et al., 2005). Thus, although the 1960s baby-boomers are on average 'better off' than their counterparts in their parents' cohort, the 'average' economic position masks significant heterogeneity within the cohort. The higher proportion of full-time workers and dual-earner families within the 1960s cohort has had a positive effect upon income, but the higher proportion of unemployed and economically inactive families has had a negative effect on average income (Evandrou and Falkingham, 2001).

Conclusion

With increasing emphasis on private and occupational pensions and the declining real value of the basic state pension, economic well-being in later life in the future will be more closely tied to work histories than in previous generations. The fact that membership of private (occupational and personal) pension schemes is higher amongst the 1960s baby-boomers than amongst their parents' generation bodes well for those who are in such schemes. On average, younger cohorts are currently considerably

Figure 8.5 1960s baby-boomers at age 40: pension membership, housing tenure and any children

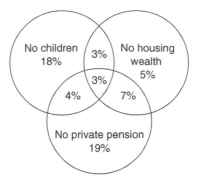

Has private pension, is owner-occupier
and has children – 43%

Source: Authors' analysis of the GHS, 2003/4.

better off in terms of income than their parents were at the same point in the life course, and it is likely that this will continue to be the case into retirement. However, the fact that the baby-boomers are also more polarized than their parents' generation has important implications for policy and society.

Moreover, it appears that being disadvantaged in terms of pension membership often overlaps with being disadvantaged in the housing market, meaning that those baby-boomers without private pensions may not be able to rely on equity release to make good this shortfall. A third of all 1960s baby-boomers who were not contributing to a private pension scheme at age 40 also did not have any housing wealth (i.e., were not owner-occupiers) (see Figure 8.5).

Looking at total welfare, rather than focusing purely on economic welfare, we also need to take into account changes in household and family composition across cohorts. Previous research has shown that a higher proportion of the 1960s cohort will enter retirement without a partner and a fifth will have no children (Evandrou and Falkingham, 2000). Amongst those baby-boomers without a spouse or children, options in later life regarding informal care from family may be limited. Some will be in a position to pay for such care, but for those who will not have the means to do so it is uncertain what levels of support the state will provide in 2030. Of those 1960s baby-boomers without a pension and without housing equity at age 40, a third were also childless. This amounts to 3 per cent of the total cohort born 1961–5, i.e. around 150,000 individuals.

Thus, there is no doubt that many of the 1960s baby-boomers will be better off in retirement than their parents' generation. There has been real economic growth over time, which the baby-boomers as a whole have benefited from. However, there is evidence that the poorest baby-boomers have benefited relatively *less* from this growth than has the cohort on average, reflecting widening inequality within the cohort. New Labour's strategy to ensure that more of tomorrow's pensioners can retire on a decent income has largely focused on extending private pension saving while concentrating state help on poorer pensioners via means testing (Evandrou and Falkingham, 2005). The increasing emphasis on the individualization of risk means that incomes in later life are likely to be more unequal in the future. Restoring the link between the basic state pension and earnings, and widening entitlements through more generous credits to carers and those with discontinuities in their labour market histories, would be two simple but critical steps in ensuring that all future elders benefit from today's economic growth.[2]

Notes

1 This chapter updates and extends work published in Evandrou and Falkingham (2000, 2001).

2 We are grateful to the Office for National Statistics, The Data Archive and the ESDS for access to the GHS data 1973–2003, which has been used by permission. The analysis and interpretation of the data is the responsibility of the authors alone. The research is part of the ESRC SAGE (Simulating Policy for an Ageing Society) Research Group funded under grant number M565-28-1001.

Nine   The Future of Stock Market Pensions

Richard Minns

Five years into the new millennium, we are faced with an almost total collapse in the principle of private provision, aided by a state sector which provides minimal and declining provision. Literature continues to warn of crises and 'demographic timebombs', while scandals in private provision continue. The first of the scandals for the new millennium was the gross underfunding of schemes in the private pension backyard, namely the US and the UK (the accumulated assets were insufficient to meet forecast liabilities). By 2001, 360 out of the 500 top US companies (the Standard and Poor's 500) had seriously underfunded schemes amounting to $350 billion, while in the UK 80 out of the top 100 companies had run up deficits of over £50 billion (later estimated at over £100 billion). Companies could have deficits in their pension plan which were larger than the value of the company itself. Pension liabilities started to become deal breakers in corporate acquisitions,[1] upsetting the *raison d'être* of the stock market – and threatening the lucrative fees to be generated from takeover activity. The British government admitted in July 2004 that, since 1997, 65,000 people had lost more than 20 per cent of their pension when companies were wound up. The government was forced to introduce a Pension Protection Fund and an interim Financial Assistance Scheme of £400 million in order to provide some compensation to contributors to occupational plans which were left underfunded when companies went bust.[2] In addition, for some years private pension schemes had been shifting from 'defined benefit', where there was an assumption that pension was linked to final salary, to defined contribution, where the pension was dependent on contributions and stock market returns. In an era of falling stock markets this proved to be no solution either.

As if nothing had happened, the need for reform of the public sector and increase in the private sector were still promoted by expert bodies. The argument continued that there were insufficient numbers of people in work to pay for the increasing numbers of old people; that the imbalance in generations meant that when current workers retired and their pension assets were sold there would be a massive collapse in share prices and accrued benefits (the 'asset meltdown hypothesis');[3] or, contrarily, that by shifting from the state to the private sector, there would be an increase in demand for the assets as savings were privatized; or that the life-cycle hypothesis (LCH), whereby people saved while working, then dis-saved when retired, could recreate the asset meltdown. On the other hand, there was evidence that contradicted the LCH, as well as statistical uncertainties about asset meltdowns in general. The exhortations to save more continued, despite there being little evidence that this was going to produce anything worthwhile.

Why save more?

The question is, given the claims and counter-claims, the confusing and inconclusive arguments, why are we, and the populations of many countries, encouraged to save more and to support private savings mechanisms over the next decades? The answer is that there are enormous financial interests involved, and, most fundamentally, 'pensions' are rarely just about 'pensions'. The financial interests market the idea of private pensions, but there is always some other reason for implementing the concept. Even the World Bank felt it had to justify its proposed reforms by maintaining that they would promote economic growth by encouraging private saving and subsequent investment.[4] Unfortunately no part of its thesis has been verified. Since 'investment' of people's savings does not actually contribute to economic growth through real investment or increase the 'capital stock' (by which advocates optimistically mean new assets or productive capacity), or add to the real value of people's savings as the World Bank would like, pension contributors are left to rely on the world's stock markets. The aim of expanding stock markets is the real reason for the rhetoric of pension reform. Let us consider this in the context of recent expansions in the system of private pensions and stock markets.

Territorial expansion

Europe

A significant development here has been the marketing of private pensions to former Soviet-bloc countries and the expansion of the European Union into Central and Eastern Europe and the Mediterranean. The extension of private pension provision in many of these states has been well documented (see, for example, OECD, 2004b). The battle in some EU countries has been very intense and has provoked widespread industrial action and political crises. The most significant battle for the beginning of the new millennium was that in Italy. But after the accession of the ten new member states in 2004, there was a majority of countries in the EU where private stock market pensions were either predominant or increasingly significant. Over the ensuing years this will make EU policymaking in the area of pensions more weighted towards the private sector lobby.

The OECD report listed the countries which had undertaken 'radical' reforms to enhance the role of private sector and invested pensions. Of the new EU members these included Hungary (1998), Poland (1999), Latvia (2001) and Estonia (2002). Reforms in other countries included Kazakhstan (1998), Bulgaria (2002), Croatia (2002) and the Russian Federation (2002). There was an interesting and, in some cases, instrumental role played by the international financial institutions, in particular the World Bank, especially where there was leverage over a country's overall 'transition' policies and its need to demonstrate its commitment to market-oriented reforms in general. Where some of these conditions were not present, such as in the Czech Republic and Slovenia, 'policy makers did not opt for the iconoclastic move toward the "new pension orthodoxy"'. 'The World Bank, the main promoter of pension privatisation elsewhere, was absent from the Czech reform arena. The Bank's lack of leverage in the Czech Republic coincided with a low level of external debt' (Mueller, 2004: 24, 31).

Whiteford (2004: 9) summarizes the World Bank position as 'funding accounts can accelerate the development of capital market institutions and efficiency in capital allocation, therefore leading to higher growth' and goes on to say that 'the authors of the World Bank Report also note that these assumptions are more attractive in CEE countries, where the objective is to catch up with the EU'. The promotion of stock markets is key to the World Bank's arguments about economic growth. The growth in stock markets in the new member states is shown in Table 9.1. Private pension arrangements may or may not have contributed to this (putting the major downward blips to one side). The main point is that the World Bank and others think they have.

Latin America

Latin America was a major area of experimentation for the World Bank model. Countries in Central and Eastern Europe, and Russia, were

Table 9.1   Growth in stock markets in new EU member states

(Equity Market Capitalization: US $m)

Country	1993	2000	2002	% GDP*
Czech Republic	–	11,002	15,893	28.2
Hungary	812	12,021	13,110	25.0
Poland	2,706	31,279	28,750	16.4
Slovakia	–	1,217	1,904	9.7
Slovenia	–	2,547	4,606	24.4
Estonia	–	1,846	2,430	46.0
Latvia	–	583	715	9.4
Lithuania	–	1,588	1,483	12.5
Cyprus**	981	11,516	1,489	132.3
Malta	–	2,009	1,382	56.2

*Stock market as % of GDP, 2002 as % of 2001, except for Cyprus, 2000/1999, and Malta, 2000/2000.

**Cyprus is classed as a 'developed' market. The rest are 'emerging'.

Source: Author's analysis of Standard and Poor's (2003) and OECD data.

encouraged to copy the Latin American experience. The results in Latin America are salutary. The developments have been substantially reviewed in professional literature and by the World Bank itself (Claramunt, 2004; Gill et al., 2004; Taylor, 2003). The test case was always Chile, but substantial reforms were introduced in other countries, including Argentina, Peru, Colombia, Bolivia, El Salvador, Venezuela, Mexico, Costa Rica and Nicaragua. The overall conclusion is that the privatization reforms have been disappointing and have not fulfilled the expectations of the proponents. The problems include poor coverage, high management fees charged by the private sector (half the contributions by Chilean workers who retired in 2000 went to management fees) and a questionable impact on economic growth. But assets held by pension funds as a share of income as a percentage of GDP doubled between 1998 and 2002, so the business of asset management and fees expanded, but with no comparable impact on either economic growth or pensions.

In Argentina, for example, it has been forecast by the Argentine Institute for Social Development that only 50 per cent of people over 65 will have pensions in ten years' time (*Buenos Aires Herald*, 2005: 2). The issue is the nature of employment, not the privatization of pensions. The other major concern in Argentina is the extent to which the privatization of pensions contributed to the public debt and the massive default to the IMF and private creditors in 2001. This led to political crisis, street demonstrations and violence. Subsequent economic recovery appears to owe very little to the policies of the international financial institutions

Table 9.2 Stock markets in the Middle East

(Equity Market Capitalization; $US million; figures for 2002 unless stated)

Country	Market Capitalization	% GDP (2001)
Israel	45,371	53.2
West Bank/Gaza	723	1.9
Jordan	7,087	71.5
Egypt	26,044	24.5
Lebanon	1,401	7.3
Saudi Arabia	74,000	39.3

Source: Authors analysis of Standard and Poor's (2003) and OECD data.

(IMF and World Bank) (for example, Burgo, 2004). And so the sad story of privatization continues, with the major beneficiaries not being pensioners.

The Middle East

Where else does this leave for the 'new pension orthodoxy' to apply its theories in the following decades? I believe that the Middle East is under-estimated in this context, despite its prominence in other areas of debate and conflict. The extension of neoliberal financial ideology would seem to be consistent with other claims to export democracy and 'economic freedom' more widely to the region. Already the stock markets of Israel and five surrounding countries are together three times larger than those of all ten of the new EU entrants (see Table 9.2). But what do these stock markets mean? And why would the region want privately funded pensions? The example of Israel and Palestine goes some way to answering these questions.

During the initial years of Israel's development a national and partially funded, defined benefit pension scheme evolved which covered most non-public-sector workers. When it was formalized under the State of Israel, over 90 per cent of assets had to be invested in government bonds issued at preferential rates. Benefit formulae were generous in terms of years of contribution, the aim initially being to offer very generous benefits to the huge numbers of new Jewish immigrants who were part of the state's demographic policies. The most telling aspect of its pension fund philosophy was summed up by the large labour federation, Histadrut, which managed the pension fund arrangements. The pension funds never served solely as a 'savings fund'. The pension funds served as an instrument for applying the national and social policies of state institutions. Throughout the years – and in accordance with dictated government policy – the funds acted to benefit various populaces, such as new immigrants (Histadrut, 2004).

By the 1980s the politics and economics of Jewish demographic policy had begun to change with the increasing emphasis on the territorial occupation of the West Bank and the extension of settler communities. The pension fund had served its purpose and was seen as a labour-oriented legacy of a different era of Israel's history. Prompted by allegations of actuarial deficits, corruption and bankruptcy (similar to arguments heard elsewhere about pension systems which need 'reform'), proposals were made by a special commission to close the funds to new members and to introduce new benefit formulae. It was also proposed to increase the investment substantially on the Tel Aviv stock market in order to help in changing the structure of the economy, to diminish the power of Histadrut, and to promote economic growth.

In the Palestinian Territories the public sector has been the main beneficiary of the retirement provisions inherited from Jordan and Egypt as the previous occupying forces from 1949 to 1967. The end result has been substantial coverage for the government (Palestinian National Authority), security forces, universities, professional associations and latterly for employees of the UN, and not very much for the private. The Palestine Economic Policy Research Institute, after consultation with governmental institutions and trade unions, had already called for a national social security system for the West Bank and Gaza Strip (WBGS), including a funded pension scheme: 'A new type of pension fund geared to WBGS society is required which would be more comprehensive in nature and would be influential in WBGS financial markets, thus encouraging economic growth' (Hilal et al., 1998: 19). Other models were rejected.

Conclusion

'Reforms' have been and are under way in most regions of the world. But the reformers have failed to prove that there is any real economic, as opposed to political or marketing, reason for reducing the role of the state or for introducing or extending the risk of privately financed insecurity in old age. In all the case studies there is always some other reason for the pension reforms. This has led to an increasingly vulnerable global system of private stock market pensions, with little foundation in the

Table 9.3 European Union: Productivity gains necessary to absorb increased social transfers over the next forty years

Sweden	0.06
Greece	0.08
Austria	0.09
Portugal	0.18
Luxembourg	0.19
Finland	0.23
France	0.24
Germany	0.24
Belgium	0.24
European Union	**0.25**
Italy	0.26
Denmark	0.28
Spain	0.28
United Kingdom	0.31
Netherlands	0.35
Ireland	0.40

Note: The figures show the average annual increase in productivity that is necessary to finance increased expenditures for the dependent population (pensioners, unemployed, children) during the period 2000–2040. The ratio of average current transfers per dependent to the average wage is supposed to remain constant over the whole period.

Source: Concialdi (2004).

economics of the productive economy. If the real economy were the basis of reforms, the situation for many countries could be very different. Table 9.3 shows the productivity gains needed to absorb increased social transfers over the next 40 years for all the countries in the pre-2004 European Union. The average annual increase is only one-quarter of 1 per cent (Concialdi, 2004).

Private Anglo-American pensions are the only aspect of public social policy which has territorial expansion as a central plank of its rationale, for ideological, commercial and political reasons. This is because the Anglo-American pension model is a crucial part of the neoliberal economic project. Pensions are sold as a means of promoting economic growth through the promotion of stock markets and private financial infrastructure. But the evidence is hard to find. They may extend financial markets, but that is all. The enormous expansion of financial-market risk exposes pensioners to asset meltdown of a serious kind. World stock market capitalization was around $23 trillion (thousand billion) at the end of 2002. Global private pension assets probably represent over half of that figure. This $23 trillion represents a drop of 35 per cent over no more than three years. This drop is coincidentally almost the same as the total value of global private pension assets. It is an extreme case of the continuing and expanding financial insecurity.

What is being sold to many new EU countries and the remaining accession candidates, and to other countries such as Israel and Palestine and those of Latin America, is the image of a modern, developed, as opposed to an underdeveloped, economy. Private financial institutions are a crucial part of this brand image, and private pensions are presented as a way of getting there, although we all know that the introduction or expansion of private pensions is really about something else entirely.

To sum up, pension reform is rarely about pensions; there are other interests involved which we need to understand. The market is a poor provider of security in old age: the evidence from around the world points to continuing disaster. The growth of stock markets should not be an objective of social policy, but in practice that is how it has turned out. The exhortation to people everywhere to accumulate more private savings shifts the responsibility from collective provision for societal risk to individual provision for personal risk.

The stock market model of social welfare is divisive within and between generations and social groups, wherever you look. This private model simply cannot handle the concept of social solidarity as the basis of social policy. It sticks to the fantasy of being able to create economic growth which will solve the vexing issues of where the money for pensions will come from, and who gets it. If the present global trends in the stock market model continue, the prospects for the coming decades are bleak indeed.

Notes

1 In July 2004, the private equity group Permira dropped its plan to acquire WH Smith after failing to agree the funding of a £250m pension fund deficit. Discussions between the bidder for Marks and Spencer and the Marks and Spencer pension fund with a £585m deficit played a significant part in the failure of the bid.

2 By the end of July 2004, the bankruptcy of T&N (Turner and Newall) in the UK, and its US parent Federal Mogul, put a further 20,000 pensioners in the UK at risk, and placed a large question mark over the adequacy of the government's proposed £400m Financial Assistance Scheme. See also *Financial Times* (2004). In 2003 the Pension Benefit Guarantee Corporation in the US was itself put on the list of high-risk government institutions.

3 The 'asset meltdown hypothesis' is outlined in OECD (2004c).

4 The link between pension reform and economic growth is crucial to the World Bank and reformers' argument. The title of the seminal World Bank report is *Averting the Old Age Crisis: Policies to Protect the Old AND Promote Growth*. The word 'and' is emphasized in the original but is inadvertently 'de-emphasized' in many references.

PART IV

The Future for 'Self' in Old Age

Most of the discourse of self in old age has been concerned with self as defined by cognitive capacity and personality. Are we as clever and cognitively capable with age as we were in youth? Which elements of our intellect improve, which decline? This interest in cognition sits comfortably with the belief that self requires intellect and reason, and that self is in some way measurable, quantifiable. There is a long philosophical tradition of argument that self requires reason and the capacity for internal examination of oneself (e.g. Parfit, 1984). Such notions of self as inherently rational are closely linked with ideas of self as autonomous and a-contextual and a-historical. They argue that self exists independently of, and unaffected by, historical time and sociocultural context. From such a framework those with failing cognitive capacity are considered to be at risk of losing their selves. Such a rational concept of personhood suggests that people with dementia who have lost memory of the past are 'biographically dead' (Post, 2000). A person with dementia who has lost their memory of their past is assumed to have lost connection with his or her former self. Because they cannot communicate coherently, it is assumed they have stopped being a person. Such a hyper-cognitive view of personhood and self has been criticized by Jennings (2004), Kitwood (1997), and Post (2000) who argue for an understanding of self in more relational and aesthetic terms.

The idea of self is tied up with the distinction between mind and body and associated with concepts such as 'individuality', 'personality', 'consciousness' and 'the mind'. The idea of an interior self, the real or inner person different from the external appearance, is the dominant 'commonsense' one. However, these 'commonsense' notions are, at the start of the twenty-first century, increasingly viewed as problematic. In the mid-1900s the notion of the self as being largely social and a function of relationship to, and with, others was postulated, most famously by Mead (1934). Critical feminists, among others, argue that self will be constructed differently depending on one's race, ethnicity, class, gender, power, sexuality and location within particular communities at particular points in historical time (Qin, 2004). This leads to the idea of situated selves, selves determined by different socioeconomic, political and racial contexts. Others, as illustrated by Gubrium and Holstein in this section, argue for a 'narrative self', reflexively constructed with others in specific interactional circumstances.

Jenkins (1996) argues that individual and collective identities are both essentially social and are, for most practical purposes, inextricably entangled. Identities are neither chosen at will by individuals nor rigidly determined by the social order; they are the consequence of a process by which internal and external events generate identities in particular contexts. So both the 'interior' and the 'exterior' processes of identity formation are social. Some approaches to the study of identity emphasize the sources of individuality – these approaches will tend to look at issues of mind and body and how each of these may come to be considered to have unique or individual characteristics. The question of social process then becomes: how are the uniqueness of each person's various identities accomplished in social settings? How are these accomplishments problematic for older individuals? Other approaches emphasize how social similarity is produced. These emphasize, on the one hand, historical and cultural features which impinge on the possible range and variety of meaningful social identities. On the other hand, they draw attention to the production of institutionalized and administered identities associated with powerful groups such as the state, commercial and administrative bodies. The problematic nature of self for older people can be viewed from both these perspectives. One of the most problematic situations for establishing personal identity in old age is in the area of mental and physical infirmity. If identity is a social accomplishment based in interaction, what impairments inhibit its achievement? One may ask, is there a time when interaction is so impaired that people cease to be able to negotiate a satisfactory identity?

Psychologists, philosophers, psychoanalysts and sociologists have all been interested in what happens to our sense of self as we age. Across these disciplines there is a tendency to see selves as constructed in interaction with social and cultural contexts. As these contexts change in the future, what will happen to this sense of self? In the contemporary world, on a day-to-day basis we have never seemed to be so much in control of creating our selves. We are told we can be all that we can be (if only we have the will) or can (re)create our selves with makeup or makeovers. Yet the sense that the self exists as an entity with integrity and meaning persists. It is timely to ask in what ways self in old age will change in coming years?

Ten   Ageing Selves and Others: Distinctiveness and Uniformity in the Struggle for Intergenerational Solidarity

Simon Biggs

A key factor influencing how relations between self and others might change lies in the probability that there are going to be as many more older, fitter adults around than there are younger adults. This can be expected to influence citizenship and social rights (Phillipson, 2002) and is increasingly likely to be the case within the 'developing' as well as the western world (Sidorenko and Walker, 2004). Up until recently it has been assumed that older people are a small and dependent part of the total population, and this view influences attitudes in everyday interaction and within gerontology itself. Robert Butler's famous characterization of gerontology as an amalgam of advocacy and science (Moody, 2001), for example, contains within it the assumption that an older minority require the support of more powerful groups in society and that it is right that such forces should give it. As older adults live longer and healthier lives, these expectations appear to be dissolving, producing more neutral age environments, based on continuing productive roles more deeply into later life than previously expected. An upside of this might be that age differences begin to disappear, a downside that different generational groups are forced to compete for the same ground, with little recognition of different age-based priorities and capabilities. The possibility of old age becoming an 'unthought-known' of contemporary society (something that tacitly influences social action but with powerful thoughts and feelings remaining unacknowledged) may move ambiguity in age identity towards ambivalence and even antagonism, with unpredictable implications for intergenerational relations.

Contemporary ageing

At the end of the twentieth century there appeared to be two trends influencing relations between self and others based on age. The first of these was the possibility that previously fixed life stages were giving way to a more blurred and indistinct set of categories (Featherstone and Hepworth, 1989). In other words the features that had previously been taken to characterize particular parts of the life course were ceasing to identify qualities specifically attributable to later life. Second was the continuing presence of ageism, as a prejudice specifically pertaining to age difference (Bytheway, 1995, 2003). To a certain extent these trends pulled in different directions. The first indicated that older and younger adults were becoming closer to each other in what they feel, think and do. The second, however, suggested that there were enduring differences of interest that shaped the quality of intergenerational behaviour and the distribution of resources. Whilst older adults were encouraged, in Andrew Blaikie's words 'not just to dress "young" and look youthful, but to exercise, have sex, take holidays, socialise in ways indistinguishable from those of their children's generation' (1999: 104), the contradictions and power implications of such a new alignment were only loosely sketched out. And it is possible to divine a hope that changes in lifestyle would lead to the elimination of differences and age-based antagonisms. Identity, so often at the crossroads of the inner world of self and the external world of social expectations, was now moving in directions that promised greater age neutrality yet nevertheless allowed personal integration and self expression.

Taken together, these factors present interesting times ahead for age, identity and intergenerational relations. Traditional assumptions appear to be fragmenting, opening possibilities for new, more flexible identities to take shape. However, novel attempts to fix expectations of what it is to 'age well' are close on their heels and it is an open question whether we will end up with a more tolerant or intolerant relationship between generations as a result. Age-based relations are poised between simple ambiguity and more complex forms of ambivalence, and it is this combination that is explored in more detail below.

Uniformity through diversity

In everyday adult relations, age is rarely referred to directly. In this respect explicit awareness of age difference is little greater today than it was almost 40 years ago when Simone de Beauvoir (1970) observed that 'when we are grown up, we hardly think about our age anymore'. In consequence we continue our progress through life, especially in midlife working environments, as if ageing is irrelevant.

Where adult ageing is perceived as personally inescapable and a threat to self-identity, its significance is largely denied in everyday life. A number of writers (Gilleard and Higgs, 2000; Smith and Gerstorf, 2004) have observed that the roles and lifestyles available to older people have become more diverse and there is more variation within generations than between them. Therefore whilst older people may be becoming more varied in the lives they lead, this variation itself increases the overall similarities between older and younger age groups, making it more difficult to identify patterns that distinguish one generation from another. Increasing diversity of lifestyle and life chances in later life paradoxically contributes to an erosion of visible differences based on age.

Similarities between age groups are also emphasized by contemporary trends in social policy. Here, an original emphasis on social inclusion has evolved into attempts to define what it is to 'age well' (Biggs, 2004). The most powerful of these trends has been to associate legitimate forms of ageing with continuing productivity. Encouraging the productivity of older people (Hinterlong et al., 2001) through engagement in work, and worklike activities such as volunteering, has the fiscal advantage of turning the 'burden' of an unproductive social group into one that is not only not drawing pensions, but also generating taxes directly through paid activity, or indirectly by facilitating the productive labour of others. Moody (2001) has observed that this trend not only makes older people more acceptable to other generations, it makes older adults more similar to them in terms of their daily activities.

So, whilst the ageing population may be becoming more diverse through the proliferation of many different 'cultures of ageing' (Gilleard and Higgs, 2000), an outcome of this process has been to reinforce the life course blurring first identified by Featherstone and Hepworth (1989). The adult life course appears to be more uniform because there is, at least on the surface, less that is distinctive about later life itself.

Distinctiveness through common experience

This dominant view of age uniformity, outlined above, significantly underplays differences between adults based on age. Satisfying identities in later life may not simply require 'more of the same' in terms of lifestyle and work or worklike activities. There are a number of factors that suggest later life contains a unique set of qualities when compared to other parts of the adult life course. First is the possibility that our priorities change in later life and that this has deep-seated roots in the process of ageing itself. Historically Jung (1967 [1934]) and Erikson (1986), have both emphasized the differences that can occur as the life course progresses. The developmental life tasks of an adult at 20, for example, will, according to these writers, differ significantly from those of some-one at 40 and at 70. Both concur that to hold on to priorities of a younger part of life and extend them into the next is a recipe for social and psychological dysfunction. More recent writing by Cole (1992), Tornstam (1996) and Biggs (1999) point to important existential differences in priority between the first and second halves of life. Increased integration of personal potential that could not be expressed in earlier phases now allows the growth of an identifiably mature imagination that may ultimately be a consequence of a natural patterning of the adult life course.

Secondly, it is by no means clear that living longer and healthier lives is an indefinite process. Baltes and Smith (2002) have argued that bodily ageing is a continuing factor that places limits on possibility of continued participation in society and that an over-preoccupation with a 'third age' of active retirement in our 60s and 70s should not obscure a 'fourth age' in which the hazards of a failing body do indeed lead to disengagement and a decline in social participation. Economists such as Schultz (2001) suggest that unless there is a radical reform of both the nature and structure of work, it is unlikely that older adults will in reality be able or willing to compete with younger adults.

Mature adulthood may, then, allow greater personal integration, and therefore individuality, based upon a common experience of ageing. It also confronts us with undesirable aspects of the human condition that do not fit easily with contemporary ideas about the adult life course. Commonality and distinctiveness are rooted in the long game through which the life course plays itself out in each of us. This source of collectivity is, however, obscured by a growing cultural desire to avoid the consequences of growing old.

The unthought-known of contemporary ageing

What emerges from these different trends is a situation in which the features that define different generational groups are becoming more than simply ambiguous. Becoming more 'oneself' also means becoming increasingly distinct from others, while increasing diversity in cultures of ageing contributes to a feeling that there is nothing particularly distinctive about being old. There are growing numbers of older people, thus making them more visible as a social group, yet the particular tasks and challenges of growing older are becoming increasingly hidden. The future of intergenerational relations and age identity depends upon how these various currents play themselves out.

We are faced, then, with a confusing, ambivalent cultural situation. As Margaret Gullette (2004) puts it, contemporary ageing is used as a basis for social behaviour, yet is barely recognized as such: 'Although it operates in plain sight, it is almost invisible.' Everyone knows they are likely to grow old, and much older than has historically been the case, yet few show a desire to acknowledge this situation. It has become, to use the term of Christopher Bollas (1987), the 'unthought-known' of our everyday social and personal experience.

Bollas' ideas have arisen in the context of psychodynamic psychotherapy and concern the fact that in order to suppress or deny the existence of something, we have already at some level to have knowledge of it in order to defend ourselves against it. The unthought exists on the boundaries of conscious awareness, a tantalizing, yet potentially disruptive, force influencing an existing state of affairs. We 'know' something, but have as yet been unable to think it and must rely on others in order to recognize what this might be. Until the issue is openly faced, experiences and intuitions can cast their shadow over thoughts and feelings towards others, leaving a residue of discomfort and a tendency toward avoidance.

The unthought-known of twentieth-century ageing was maintained by creating physical distance between generations. Older people were seen as different and, when that difference became unbearable, were placed outside everyday encounter in age ghettos masquerading as forms of care (see for example Townsend, 1962). Riding on a shift toward blurred characteristics and identities based on continuing productivity, contemporary trends appear to subsist by actually placing distinctiveness itself out of bounds. The logic of arguments that turn on personal productivity and expecting others to behave in the same way fails to take social, psychological and bodily barriers seriously into account because of the threats these pose, both at a personal level and to the structure of the discourse itself. We know that at one level there is a problem but are avoiding complex thought about it. This can result in some curious combinations. As a society we find it quite possible simultaneously to celebrate scientific progress increasing longevity and to express resentment about the growing numbers of older people drawing pensions, to take an obvious example. Such debates can appear to be pragmatic, but subsist on an absence. Unpleasant or inconvenient facts of life tend to be ejected, and, interpersonally speaking, projected into a conveniently positioned 'other'. Jung's (1967 [1934]) appreciation of this shadow side of the personality 'the thing a person has no wish to be' leads to the suspicion that a moral problem is being avoided. A problem 'that challenges the whole ego personality, for no one can become conscious of the shadow without considerable moral effort. To become conscious of it involves recognising the dark aspects of the personality as present and real' (Jung, 1967 [1934] (9): 13).

Accordingly a cultural denial of ageing runs the risk of not addressing an unthought shadow of resentment, disgust and envy that can so easily occupy the gap left by intergenerational distinctiveness. Old age holds an image of self in future time, that is, eliminated from thought, while nevertheless shaping formal policies and interaction. If ageing well is narrowly defined as a relationship to work activity, either sharing the same ground as other parts of the adult life course, or as a time of hedonism and leisure while 'the rest of us' work hard and have no time, the possibilities of competition, or rage and envious attack, become multiplied. The point here is that this antagonism can easily become the unthought-known of intergenerational relations. It shapes debate and behaviour and is justifiable because older adults are, where it counts, no different anymore to anybody else. Age simultaneously becomes a site of projective identification and of a denial of distinctiveness. It becomes ok to engage in generation wars because, paradoxically, there's no difference anymore.

Is this line of thinking about the future of old age playing, as Gullette (2004) usefully describes her own age criticism, 'Cassandra amongst the joggers'? There would appear to be evidence to suggest not, and that rivalry, in one form or another, has a longstanding intergenerational pedigree. De Beauvoir's seminal work (1970) refers to a covert antagonism towards older adults, verging on 'biological repugnance'. Intergenerational exchanges are marked, it is claimed, by duplicity, with formal deference travelling hand in hand with resentment, depreciation and manipulation of the older person. More recent reviews by Coupland et al. (1991) and Williams and Nussbaum (2001) point to a recurring finding that younger adults base their talk to older people on stereotypic assumptions, centring on failing physical and cognitive capabilities, a trend that increased linearly with the age of their conversational partner.

This ambivalence, verging on antagonism, is nowhere more evident than in the experience of the US baby-boomer population, who are emerging as the 'new' old of the twenty-first century and for whom the dogma of productivity in later life has been especially crafted. Moody (2001) argues that in encouraging older adults to build identities on productive ageing, a fundamental change is occurring in the way that value is attributed to old age. Rather than being based on past contribution, resulting in a 'well earned rest', old age is now valued in terms of current input to economic processes. Gullette (2004) herself argues that rivalry and resentment towards the 'boomer' generation, by the succeeding cohorts of 'Generation X', has been deliberately encouraged by the same political interests that attempted to generate age/race wars over taxes and benefits (Minkler and Robertson, 1991) between younger and older adults in the 1980s. The ground on which this antagonism is being expressed is that of work productivity, with a study by the American Association of Retired Persons (AARP, 2004) showing that the current midlife population (aged between 39 and 57) have views, anxieties and aspirations that are significantly closer to those of younger adults (18–38) than to those of older adults (58–plus).

Thus a consequence of trying to build a new identity for later life on productive ageing is that adult generations are increasingly sharing the same ground, where competition over resources is at its most acute. Psychologically speaking, it is less easy to use either denial or avoidance in such close proximity. One is required to encounter intergenerational difference and rivalry directly without the cultural supports of intergenerational solidarity historically based on a small and dependent older population. If, as has been argued by Gilleard and Higgs (2005), we are moving towards cultural distinctions based on generational consciousness, rather than on social structure and position, then the possibilities of moving beyond ambiguity and ambivalence towards active antagonism are considerably enhanced.

Conclusion: building bridges between self and other

What hope, then, of building bridges between self and other based on age? In order to do this, it is important to engage with the unthought-known of adult ageing, a process that overcomes the difficulties of stepping beyond one's own age-based perspective and recognizes age distinctiveness as a basis for social solidarity.

First, the ability of each age group to place themselves in the position of the other is key to recognizing the complementary priorities and perspectives of different generations. Unfortunately, blurring of age distinctions makes it easier, rather than more difficult, to mistake the priorities of one's own generation in the behaviour of another. Where there is an absence of empathy and a cultural premium on similarity, the possibility of a more powerful generation 'recognizing' itself mirrored in the age-other mistakenly, when what it is actually observing is a masquerade of sameness, conforming to social expectations. We need to be more comfortable and familiar with the distinctiveness of different ages as a basis for recognizing complementary qualities.

Second, there is a pressing need to rediscover a more critical and complex way of thinking about work-based productivity. Work appears in the public policy of the early twenty-first century as a universal panacea that confers social meaning and personal satisfaction. It is presented as a unifying discourse that squares the circle of increasing numbers of older adults, the continued blurring of age differences and fixing legitimate social roles in the context of an ageing population. However, there is scant reference to the cumulative inequalities that it generates, its negative effect on physical and psychological health, and the suppression of dissent through work discipline. In particular, social inclusion based on work stokes competition between generations. This competition is based on, yet denies, age differences. It allows working conditions, such as life-course-based improvements in pay and conditions, to be eroded and alternative sources of public support to be dismantled. Work can also supply social solidarity between generations and a source of resistance to age-unfriendly policies. It can generate forms of power through control of productive processes that the traditional roles given older people have historically denied. But the discourse is not being set up like that.

Third, bridges between self and other have to be based on recognizing the distinctiveness of late-life experience as a valued part of the human condition. Later life should not simply mean 'more of the same' and solidarity should not be based on age similarity alone. If there are distinctive features associated with old age, a genuine and more natural contribution by older adults should be based upon the facilities that are most available at that part of the life course and not by mimicking the characteristics of other life phases. It may then give birth to a deeper understanding of life's priorities. Good teams are not based on everyone being the same, but on a recognition and deployment of complementary qualities. In this respect, life-course solidarity is no different to any other of life's projects.

Psychologically speaking, a key characteristic of current constructions of adult ageing is their reliance on an unthought-known. It allows contradictory directions to be held simultaneously, avoids the consideration of uncomfortable consequences and entrenches whatever discourse is currently most favoured by dominant interests. It is, however, difficult to think creatively about these social challenges without making the unthought conscionable. As older people become greater in number and thus more visible, it will be increasingly difficult to avoid an encounter with the other based on age. Solutions that base themselves on a denial of age distinctiveness, in whatever combination of economic and intergenerational reasoning, run the danger of exacerbating the very problems they claim to solve.

116

Eleven Biographical Work and the Future of the Ageing Self

Jaber F. Gubrium and James A. Holstein

How shall the future of the ageing self be conceptualized? Is it to be an entity that begins with childhood, develops through experience, unfolds with maturity, and comes to resolution in later life? This is the familiar self whose essential contours remain constant through time, but whose features may be transformed – sometimes gradually and at times precipitously – as life goes on (see Langer, 1969). It is the self of both depth and developmental psychology, a self whose characteristic elements persist through the life course, even as they may change in detail or nuance. This self is categorically in place despite significant social, cultural and historical influences. Whether we dwell on its hidden meanings or are satisfied to discover behavioural patterning in relation to environmental contingencies, it is a self whose basic formulation permits one to wonder how it comes to be what it is in its final decades, after a lifetime of experience.

Or is the self in old age to be the residual product of the many social forces that define and shape it through time? This is the well-known self of the social and cultural sciences and of history. It is the self whose organization and disorganization are read from the parallel details of larger social schemas. It is the venerable self whose human nature is drawn directly from social order (Cooley, 1964 [1902]). It is the self of this community, that nation, this culture, and that particular historical era. It is a self that befits, or is oddly out of step with, its time and place. Its variations do not so much develop through time, as they are artifacts of the broader social influences that produce and reproduce it. The essential parameters of this self are transformed by its social influences.

This chapter reflects upon these time-honoured conceptions and how they will continue to figure the self in old age. As an alternative, we suggest that viewing the self as a product of practical, situated 'biographical work' frees it from such totalized schemas. The self in old age is open to myriad interpretive possibilities, limited only by the social, cultural and historical circumstances that mediate, but do not determine, biographical work.

Two reductions

Of course we have exaggerated the two conceptions of the self in our introduction. The many social psychologies, on the one hand, and psychological sociologies, on the other, belie a more complicated conceptual landscape. We exaggerate in order to highlight and contrast two reductions we wish to avoid in presenting a different view of the future of the self in old age. Reduction is the habit of representing a phenomenon such as the self as if it were, in principle, an appendage of something else. That something else is not itself viewed as an empirical option but, instead, is treated as a fixed source of explanation.

Let us explain in relation to the alternative conceptualizations. To view the self and its future in old age along the lines of the first alternative reduces the self as entity to the generalized experiential patterning identified through time. Patterning may be described in terms of distinctive life challenges, in which case we might explain, for example, that individuals become who and what they are as a result of the strength and sequence of the challenges. Having mastered the challenges (or the developmental tasks, as some say) of childhood, individuals become the selves that result from dealing with or resolving the challenges in particular ways. The patterning is general to experience, the resulting selves represent its particulars. Whether patterning through time comes in the form of essentialized depths, resolution processes readily open to observation, or even in the form of behaviouralized contingencies of experience, the self derives from, rather than being played out in relation to, the patterning.

This reduction portends a specific future for the self in old age – a future that is essentially predetermined or fixed in its broad design. The future of such a self is reduced to the patterning identified as more or less developmentally universal. One of the most familiar reductions of this kind is Erik Erikson's (1963, 1976) eight-stage view of human development. While dated, its logic remains a significant and widely applied way of thinking about the self through time. Informed by clinical impressions and Freudian concepts, Erikson views the experiential values and tensions of later life as centred in concerns with personal generativity as opposed to stagnation in middle adulthood, and with ego integrity as opposed to biographical despair in old age. The final stage, whose onset is a growing awareness of finitude and closeness to death, features the developmental task of evaluating the path of one's life, resolving tensions, tying loose ends, and affirming the meaningfulness of the whole. In this framework, the future of old age is reduced to either the felicitous resolution of personal and interpersonal difficulties, or despair, if not disgust, with one's life (see Black, 2003, for a contrasting view). Absorbed as old age is with developmental resolution in the face of death, the self is removed from the broad spectrum of social, cultural and ethical issues of every-day life. This is a self that is, well, self-absorbed. The future of such a self has exceptionally thin moral fibres, virtually immune to transformative influences such as civil war, colonialism, national independence, urban relocation, economic depressions, changing social sensibilities, extreme poverty or wealth, and diverse institutional practices (Gubrium and Holstein, 2003).

In contrast, to conceptualize the self and its future in old age along the lines of the other reduction consigns the self to social and historical patterning. For example, when patterning is conceptualized historically, the familiar contours of selves that form in particular eras emerge, such as the self of the Enlightenment or of the post-Second World War years. To describe the self-conceptions of Americans, say, in the decade of the 1950s as opposed to earlier and later periods, as David Riesman (1950) did in his classic book *The Lonely Crowd*, reduces the self to the moral principles of particular times in American history. The longer term also may be an ostensible source of difference – such as comparing the self of the ancient Greeks with the self of contemporary times – even while deconstructive critique casts significant doubt on such comparison (Gubrium, 2000).

Patterning also may be conceptualized culturally, in which case one obtains, for example, the distinctive cultural contours of the self. Margaret Mead's (1973) controversial book *Coming of Age in Samoa* is an exemplar of this sort of reduction. Mead shows how dramatically different the self can be by virtue of its cultural influences. Here again, the self derives from generalized patterning; culture's influence is determinant.

This reduction portends a different kind of future for the self in old age. It is a future whose identity is as categorically varied as its location in historical time and social space. In this view, the future of the self in old age flows with individual experiences in relation to the development of larger sociohistorical processes. Glen Elder (1974, 1994), for example,

119

has argued that cohorts, or 'children', of the Great Depression had formative experiences that generated particular views of the world, leading them to orient to life in distinctive ways. Historical differences in the period of birth confront individuals with specific challenges and opportunities, which set the stage for particular patterns of growth and development. As John Clausen (1993) looks back and describes American life in the 1920s and 1930s, he simultaneously portrays a generation whose indelible experiences of lost opportunity imprinted them for life. Theirs is a grim, silent, resilient or hopeful future, depending on their earlier relationships to the distinct features of their times. Such reductions present selves in later life that are not immersed in the resolution of universalized developmental tasks, but, rather, selves fuelled by the lingering particulars of historical challenges. Whether they are generations of the Great Depression, the so-called 'greatest generation' of the Second World War (Brokaw, 1998), or some other generalized cohort, the future of the self in old age takes form in relation to the sociohistorical and cultural particulars of socialization.

Biographical work

Our view of the future of the ageing self avoids assigning the self a contrasting agency of its own, separate from individual and social patterning. Rather, our aim is to offer an approach that works against reduction. In the two reductions described, developmental and social patterning are treated as if they had lives of their own, as if they were agents that determined who and what we are, were and would become in old age. But we must ask, in what ordinary sense are we products of early life? How is it that, in practice, we become the characters of the crucial decades in which we lead our lives? In what way will the futures of old age derive separately from either of these? How does the self, again in practice, get shaped through experiential time? Alternatively, as a matter of everyday life, how does the self take the contours of its social, historical or cultural environment? Something surely must be done to secure the linkages. What is the process of 'doing' these forms of self?

We ask these questions in relation to lived experience, which directs us to the give-and-take of a mundane world with its own categories, reasoning and sense of credibility. In turn, this points us toward the ways theorists of the self themselves conceptualize the way the self and its future are shaped. In the practice of everyday life, patterns are not just there, variously imposing their wiles on the likes of the self and other forms of life. They must in some way be articulated, represented practically in their determining functions if that is the way patterning is to be conceived and put into place.

If we figure that members of the world of everyday life name, categorize and theorize it on their own terms, we then begin to rein in the reductions. If we ask who theorizes ageing (Gubrium and Wallace, 1990), are we to exclude mundane folk theorists of developmental tasks, challenges, the formative years, historical eras, and social and cultural contexts? Is the task of naming, categorizing and theorizing the life course completely owned by academic theorists? We would argue to the contrary: all persons, in the course of everyday life, theorize the very experiences academics and professionals contemplate. Such theorizing is an integral part of everyday life as individuals narratively construct and experience themselves and each other as subjects living through time.

We refer to the ordinary activity of assigning meaning to experience through time as *biographical work* (Holstein and Gubrium, 2000a). Biographical work is no respecter of professional or academic credentials. It is the province of an 80-year-old veteran's discovering new pride and experiential integrity as a member of the 'greatest generation'. It extends to mundane 'death talk' and the distinct transformations of the dying experience reported by Elizabeth Kübler-Ross (1961). Indeed, it even leads the 80-year-old veteran to incorporate Kübler-Ross' stage model into a biographical scheme for understanding the meaning of life's end for both him and his dying wife. Drawing the line between the credentialed and non-credentialed obscures the ways in which scholarly and folk theorizing reflexively intermingle in everyday life, especially as formal theoretical frameworks become popularized and theoretical frameworks, in turn, parallel social and cultural developments.

Thinking in terms of biographical work as a matter of practice encourages us to ask 'where' and 'when' meaning is assigned to experience through time. How common is the reduction of the ageing self to the central experiential dilemmas of developmental stage models? Is the issue of resolving Eriksonian-type tensions a matter of consideration 24 hours a day, seven days a week? Or is it engaged on occasions when adherents to Eriksonian and similar kinds of developmental thinking ask us to address later life in such terms? In our own ethnographic work on the narrative organization of identity in people-processing institutions such as courts, nursing homes and counselling centres, it was not at all uncommon for staff members, clients and their families to frame 'what it means' to grow old in professionalized, Eriksonian terms (see Holstein and Gubrium, 2000a). In various guises, such reductions have become the discursive stock-in-trade of the diverse institutions whose business it is to construct

who and what we are for various ameliorative purposes (Rose, 1998).
Institutionally sponsored biographical work mediated by local discourses
produces 'institutional selves', which are lodged in time and place,
reflecting when and where the identities under consideration are discur-
sively constructed in particular ways (see Gubrium and Holstein, 2001).
Questions of when and where, in turn, point us to the everyday practices
of reduction, transforming reduction from abstract theory to practical
usage. In the process, the ageing self is freed from conceptual totality and
its behavioural diversity relocated in particular times and places (see
Holstein and Gubrium, 2004).

The same would apply to reductions to social and cultural order. Here,
too, we might ask whether cohorts such as the generations of the Great
Depression or the 'greatest generation' are identified by others or identify themselves in those terms, around the clock, on all occasions. Do
members of these cohorts continuously construct themselves in those
global terms? Or do individuals frame themselves and others in such
terms to which they are accountable on specific occasions?

Gubrium's (1992) work on narrative identity is telling in this regard.
It was not uncommon, for example, for counsellors and other therapeutic staff members in two family therapy agencies to instruct clients about,
and hold them accountable for, dealing with their troubles in terms relating to sociohistorical pasts. Recalcitrant grandparents would be viewed as
products of the wariness drawn from the disadvantages experienced
growing up in the 1930s. Ethnic and cultural differences also were used
to explain differences in caring, caregiving and intergenerational support.
Ironically, on rare occasion, individual staff members would literally
remind others not to 'reduce' otherwise complex matters to such universalized explanations, noting that such-and-such individuals weren't just
puppets of their circumstances or backgrounds, for example. If this was
infrequent, it nonetheless indicated that insight into the consequences of
reduction was not the exclusive hallmark of detached or academic observation. But also note that such explanatory reductions were products of
the institutional discourses locally accepted as sensible ways to construct
grandparents' identities in such terms; other going concerns might very
well construct them in contrasting terms.

Conclusion

When the ageing self is viewed in terms of biographical work, its future
becomes more highly variegated than it otherwise would be. The reductions

we have described are not so much abstract explanatory frameworks as they are useful means of addressing and figuring the self through time which are indigenously employed in the course of everyday life. Such reductions are part of the everyday stock of knowledge or interpretive toolkit, as it were, that can be brought to bear in the construction of future identities.

So, what is the future of the ageing self in practice? The simple answer is 'it depends'. It depends on the interpretive possibilities or identity discourses available to persons addressing issues of self-construction. It depends on the specific interpretive contingencies of the occasions on which questions of self are raised. It depends on the organizational and institutional auspices under which self is considered – which provide the 'conditions of possibility' (Foucault, 1975) for local formations of self.

In our own work on self-construction, we have used the language of narrativity to conceptualize the issues (see Holstein and Gubrium, 2000b). Asked how older persons and others will narrate the contours of ageing lives in the future, we would respond that it depends on the context of consideration. On some occasions, stories of the ageing self are subject to the rather strict confines of formal therapeutic philosophies. Of course, the going concerns surrounding such constructions never determine the ageing selves that come into view once and for all. But on such occasions stories about who and what the older individuals in question have been, are now, and will be in the future are ordinarily accountable in terms of these therapeutic discourses. When we change the interpretive venue and the language of narrativity for framing the ageing self, an overall sense of the the self, itself is likely to change in turn. Even the same venue can make different stories available at different times (see Miller, 2001). Indeed, formal occasions may bring a strict set of self-construction guidelines into play, but they may be relaxed or altogether absent on less formal occasions in the very same setting (see Buckholdt and Gubrium, 1979).

The concept of biographical work offers a sigh of relief for the future of the ageing self, which would otherwise be subject to the inevitabilities of universalized developmental patterning on the one hand, and social, historical and cultural determination on the other. Not that the self in old age 'can be all that it can be', to borrow the theme of a popular US military recruitment advertisement. Rather, the future of the ageing self can be whatever is available for formulating and making good on its realization. Today's world is rife with interpretive opportunities and possibilities, some attractive and some not so attractive. A plethora of going concerns resides between the state or society, on one level, and the person or individual on the other (Gubrium and Holstein, 2000). Their practices of self-definition provide endless occasions for assigning future meaning to experience in the later years – some totalized, some contingent; some felicitous, some daunting. Lived experience is hardly a straightforward matter of what we are likely to become as we age. Ageing selves in the future are subject to the constructive craft of biographical work.

Twelve Ageing and Belief – Between Tradition and Change

Peter G. Coleman, Marie A. Mills and Peter Speck

The growing interest in the subject of spirituality and ageing is a welcome recognition both of older people's central role in the transmission of cultural and religious values and also of the need for a more holistic consideration of the quality of later life. Looked at in retrospect, its neglect has been surprising given the strong link between religion and age identifiable in most cultures. At the same time it has to be recognized that in the western world and in Europe in particular there has been a weakening of allegiance to traditional forms of religious belief. As a result the study of spirituality in Britain and Europe has broadened beyond the limits of the dominant tenets of Judaeo-Christianity to include, not only other world faiths, but the idiosyncratic selection and mixing of elements from different faith traditions (Heelas, 1998). Moreover, the use of the concept of spirituality itself has been broadened to encompass perceptions of personal meaning and significance, including aesthetic sensibilities, which may be largely divorced from religious concepts of the sacred and transcendent. All of these developments need to be touched on in an essay on the future of ageing and belief. Above all it is a mistake to assume that older people are removed from controversies surrounding belief. Some may very well be in the vanguard of those wishing to question previous traditions, whereas others may be as determined to preserve the faith as handed down to them.

In the following account we start first with an examination of the changing context in which ageing and belief need to be considered. We examine the evidence for the view that issues of belief become more salient with age, and the implications for future cohorts of older people of the major changes in religious socialization that they experienced in their youth. We then summarize the results of a study we have recently conducted asking for older people's own views on the support they receive for their spiritual explorations in later life, and examine the consequences of a greater plurality of belief among older people within UK and other European societies.

Ageing, religion and tradition

In popular stereotypes ageing is associated with increasing stability, if not rigidity, of attitudes rather than change. Similarly in traditional religious culture the emphasis has often been on elders' constant and continuing witness to faith by means of which they provide a model and example to younger generations (Gutmann, 1997). If older people have been associated with spiritual revolution it has more often been in resisting change imposed by external authority intent on breaking traditional religious practice. For example, resistance to the Soviet authorities in the 70-year-long persecution of religious practice and education in Russia and Eastern Europe that followed the 1917 revolution was most effectively carried out by older people and particularly by older women, who were less closely monitored and stubbornly persisted in trangressive actions, for example taking children in secret to religious services (Coleman and Mills, 2004).

However, it would be wrong to think that older people are also not capable of new spiritual insights. Prophecy – reading the signs of the time – is associated with age, experience and wisdom. Examples abound in the Old Hebrew Sacred Texts and are echoed in the Christian New Testament in the figures of Simeon and Anna, who recognize the Child Christ as Saviour when he is brought to the Temple by Mary and Joseph. St Luke conveys a powerful message by placing these elderly and pious figures at the beginning of his account. Faithfulness to a tradition is compatible with, and can be argued to require readiness to accept, new insights into that tradition's meaning. It is often older people who have the necessary maturity of mind to integrate the tension between tradition and change (Sinnott, 1998).

It is equally ageist to take older believers' faith for granted. Questioning of long-held beliefs can also come to the fore in late life; sometimes it may seem for the first time. It is interesting that Erik Erikson deliberately places despair as the counterpart to integrity in his description of the culminating challenge of the life cycle. The reality of ageing is often a dialectic between despair and integrity in which the scales hopefully tip decisively in favour of the latter, but not without a struggle (Rosel, 1988). The experience of a long life and the difficulties of maintaining hope in the face of repeated loss, tragedy and disappointment can extinguish even the brightest of once-held faiths. Indeed as churchmen in the UK have commented in the face of the recent tsunami disaster in the Indian Ocean, it is only right that people should question their faith in a benevolent God in the face of such seemingly random destruction. The older person may be the more distressed by the suffering they perceive in the world even when it might be thought they should be inured by long experience. This is not only because they have more time and opportunity to ponder these things but because of the crisis of meaning late life may bring. The same can apply to the experience of personal loss as bereavement (Speck et al., 2005).

Social change, too, poses threats to religious faith. Society, culture and religion are rarely in harmony, because they operate within different time dimensions. Religions develop within particular cultural periods and take from the culture of their time of origin their particular forms of expression, but they also need to preserve the meanings of these forms as the particular culture changes or disappears. For example, the vestments and liturgical gestures of the Roman Catholic and Eastern Orthodox Christian Churches reflect the patterns of the Classical Roman and Byzantine empires, but need to be communicated as expressing eternal realities without being able to rely on the temporal associations they once had. As a result, religious forms of expression can appear alien to people brought up in a changing world, because they appear to be embedded in what has already been uprooted and discarded. This is especially so in a society where religion – and historical understanding – forms such a minimal part of education and personal formation as in most of present-day Europe.

For older people whose upbringing was much more religiously informed, present-day society can appear as the disrupter or enemy of religion and much else of value within their culture. Previous studies of adjustment to social change conducted among older residents of sheltered-housing schemes in Southampton and London have identified significant numbers in states of 'troubled questioning' as well as 'moral siege' about their beliefs and values, including religious teaching (Coleman and McCulloch, 1990). The former no longer knew what to believe and were unsure where to look for guidance. The latter maintained their beliefs and morale but within a closed reference group of fellow believers divorced from the society outside (Jerrome, 1992). Such separation is inimical to Erikson's concept of integrity which is as much about inter-generational as intrapsychic harmony.

Does spiritual interest increase with age?

Nevertheless, the most general impression emerging from gerontological studies into belief and ageing is of the stronger levels of faith and practice of religion (apart from attendance at worship in the oldest groups) demonstrated by older rather than younger people (McFadden, 1996). However, there are two very important qualifications to be made. The first is methodological. On the basis of cross-sectional age comparisons it is not easy to distinguish true developmental change with age from generational shifts in attitudes resulting from changes in education and other societal influences. Nevertheless, the consistent demonstration of David Moberg and other pioneering researchers of age patterns over more than five decades of a rapidly evolving society strongly suggest that in the US at least the ageing process continues to be conducive to deepening of spiritual reflection and belief (Moberg, 2001). At the same time, stronger religious and spiritual responses have been found to be associated with a range of favourable health outcomes from quicker recovery from physical and mental illness to lowered mortality rates. These associations appear stronger in older age groups, suggesting an age-related benefit to continued belief (McFadden and Levin, 1996).

A more fundamental objection is that US data cannot be used as a benchmark for religious belief in other societies, even other western cultures, as has been well demonstrated by Grace Davie (Davie, 2002). Although older people make up an increasing proportion of church attenders in the UK, they appear to be affected by the same trends towards declining religious involvement. Longitudinal analysis of religious identity in participants from the Southampton Ageing Study through the last quarter of the twentieth century has demonstrated a significant decline in its importance, particularly during the 1980s (Coleman et al., 2004). Relatively few studies on religion and ageing have been conducted outside North America and almost none on the health benefits of religion, the major topic of US research in this field. Moreover, doubts have to be expressed about the representativeness of US studies even for North America since most have been carried out in areas with strong particular Christian subcultures, for example the protestant 'Bible Belt' society around Duke University in North Carolina (Koenig, 1997). More studies need to be conducted in areas where religious membership is less homogeneous.

Predictions of the future of belief in Britain and western Europe have to take into account not only decline in the practice of traditional Christian faith, but also the growth in other world faiths, the popularity of new forms of Christianity, and the various forms of 'New Age' spirituality. British society has experienced the waning of church authority, a rise in individual, eclectic beliefs, as well as membership of new sects and movements (Heelas, 1998). As a consequence, 'spirituality' has become a more widely used term than 'religion', especially in the health context.

In our research we use the term 'spiritual' to refer to belief in a transcendent power or reality which is efficacious in the person's own life (Speck, 1988). This trend towards the study of 'spirituality' rather than 'religion' is also evident in America, although the dissociation between the two is deplored by some researchers who point out that religion's prime function is, or at least should be, to facilitate the person's spiritual search (Zinnbauer et al., 1999).

Although many in the present generation of older people are unlikely to have adopted these new ways of viewing religion and spirituality, they will soon be superseded by an older generation not brought up with Sunday school and a tacit acceptance of the authority of Christian culture. Callum Brown has argued that secularization is not the gradual process that it has often been assumed to be but, in Britain and western Europe, a much more recent and dramatic set of events which was set in train in the 1960s (Brown, 2001). The trend towards suspicion of external authority and creeds and preference for individual choice which took root then has meant that there is now a huge discrepancy between, for example, the number of baptized younger and older people in the UK (Voas and Crockett, 2005). As Rob Merchant (2003) points out, in his challenging consideration of the church in an ageing population, the baby-boom generation now in their 50s largely rejected Christianity in young adulthood. They will require a wholly different type of ministry if the churches are to attract them back, even if the ageing process itself leads them in more spiritual directions.

The Saga generation

As a key example of current trends in consumer choice and ageing, Merchant points to the success of the company Saga, which began as a specialist provider of holidays for older people but over the last decade has broadened into a major provider of a range of specialist services and lifestyle products to the over-50s, catering for their increased leisure time, reliability and purchasing power. Its customers are no longer dominated by older people taking coach holiday tours but are now increasingly led by role models from the rock-and-roll generation of the 1960s. This shift is reflected in Saga's advertising. They are catering for an increasingly discriminating audience, who want to maintain many of the features of their previous lifestyles and to be involved in decision making about their lives until its very end.

Saga Magazine has a circulation of one million with a readership probably double this figure. We were fortunate to interest one of its journalists in our research on spiritual beliefs as part of the recent ESRC Growing Older Programme, and received a striking response to the publicity subsequently given our work. As a result we applied successfully to the Nuffield Foundation for funding to enable us to study the spiritual needs of Saga readers. A total of 446 people responded to our survey, predominantly from a white ethnic (73 per cent), Christian (84 per cent) and professional (71 per cent) background. The majority (65 per cent) said that religion meant less to them now than it had in earlier years but wanted greater opportunities for discussion and education on both religious and spiritual matters. As in our previous research (Coleman et al., 2002) a strong degree of spiritual belief was found to be associated with a high sense of personal meaning and the absence of depressive symptoms. The same applied to perceived choice and responsibility in the exercise of spiritual belief.

Although not a representative sample of the current older generation, our participants provide a starting point for considering how churches need to adapt to the changing attitudes of their older members. We asked our participants why they had responded to our enquiry. Their comments echoed the findings of the 2002 *Church Times* survey that there is an urgent need to involve older people in decision making about the Church. The major reasons our participants cited were to seek explanations, find meaning and engage in discussion. Many wrote lengthy and often moving letters to explain their beliefs. They had appreciated the opportunity the survey had given them. For example one man wrote that he had 'found it very valuable to think things over and to try and express my feelings in words for the first time. Because, in a way, all my life has been a search for something which may be God. I have assiduously thought about it. The only way we can come to understanding is through our own experiences.'

Many of the letters confirmed the important role belief played in their lives.

> As I have grown older (and been left alone) I have become increasingly reliant on worship and prayer, both private and collective, to confirm that life still has purpose and meaning, and to help one cope with problems, anxieties and decision making. They have become an essential discipline to control self centredness and help one reach out to others.
>
> We are aware of many people's attitudes towards faith, belief, and *raison d'être* within our age group; and in some instances this is very sad. Yes, we've had our share of bereavements, health problems, aches and pains, and various family situations, but that does not influence our faith - only enhances it and strengthens our beliefs.

But our respondents could also see that the churches needed to change their approaches, specifically to their older members.

These questions ... have helped me to focus more specifically on issues facing the church in general and also in considering local needs in my own locality. There appears to be little creative approach to finding ways of integrating or challenging the rapidly growing group of mature citizens, many of whom are still very active and come with much experience and wisdom they could share, so that they could be a real resource of value to any church. I think this is a reflection on the wider culture of today, and particularly from the media, where ageism is little understood.

We want to be challenged more. So, yes, I will fill in any questionnaire in the hope of change before we have lost everyone. I think the actual kingdom of Jesus totally fascinating. No excuse to be dull in His name! There is no excuse for the clergy.

Churches in general seem to try to please all the people all the time, giving a watered-down interpretation of what Christianity is all about, and so many people who have never really 'got the message' tend to fall into this disillusioned group.

Suggestions were many and varied. Changes should be made to churches and church buildings, making them more accessible and user-friendly, and encouraging use by other organizations when they were empty. It was argued that services should be geared more towards older people, such as having services midweek at a time and in a format more suited to an older generation. Interestingly, many felt that there was a need to create more of a forum to discuss views and create opportunities to learn more about their beliefs and those of others. There was a wish to be useful, to be involved, and not always to be seen as dependent and in need of care. They also wanted greater opportunities to feel part of the community, to know they were wanted and needed – to be missed and contacted if they were unable to attend a service.

Age, exploration and diversity of belief

British as well as American literature indicates that clergy are ill-prepared for the needs of an ageing congregation (Knapp et al., 2002; Merchant, 2003; Webber, 1990). That new forms of ministry are required has been more clearly recognized in hospitals, where many chaplains have adopted the model of following patients in their exploration of spiritual questions wherever the search may take them (Speck, 1988). It is no longer possible to assume that the majority of those in hospital have received a religious upbringing, and therefore they often need sensitive listening to as they reflect on their life's experiences and begin articulating their thoughts and feelings about them.

Moreover, our increasingly pluralistic society means that those who have a religious faith will come from a variety of religious backgrounds. For pastoral care givers this has represented a major challenge. Recent developments within Health Care Chaplaincy (Department of Health,

2003; National Institute for Clinical Excellence (NICE), 2004) recognize the need for a multifaith approach and currently faith leaders of the major world faiths within the UK are beginning to train in how best to care for their people when they become ill. The care of elderly people needs to be part of that training. The NICE guidance on palliative care indicates that all involved in patient care share responsibility for recognizing and responding as appropriate to spiritual need. Staff need to be trained in how best to make this assessment, as many nursing staff feel unsure about what they are assessing in the absence of frank religious need. Ideally assessment should be in the context of an exploratory relationship rather than a 'tick-box' approach. Exploratory questions might be: 'What helps you cope when life is difficult?' and 'Do you have a way of making sense of the things that happen to you in life?'

However, it is not only in hospital settings that older people come to reflect on existential and spiritual questions. The loss of a stable cultural framework for expressing belief means that at every crisis point in life a person needs to find their own particular way of drawing on the various spiritual resources that have become diffused through the culture (Heelas, 1998). We live in a society where – for good or bad – most people have become reluctant to express their beliefs in absolute terms or to give unconditional respect to traditional religious authorities. Rather, they prefer to express what seems reasonable to them to believe and in their own terms. This often means what they see as enabling them to cope with their life situation.

Finding adequate language to express issues of belief is not easy. There are no altogether satisfactory definitions of religion or spirituality (for a fuller discussion of applications to gerontological research see Coleman and O'Hanlon, 2004). Previously they were closely intertwined concepts, but with increased autonomy in belief systems as well as more open critique of the functioning of religious institutions, spirituality has acquired a greater independence of usage. Some have gone so far as to equate spirituality more with personal meaning than with religion. Thus it has been conceptualized, for example by Frankl, as the human drive for meaning and purpose or, more recently, 'the motivational and emotional foundation of the lifelong quest for meaning' (McFadden, 1996: 164).

Gerontologists and others working in closely related fields, for example in healthcare, appear to be turning to the language of spirituality because it raises important questions about well-being, especially in later life. These are issues that tend not to be raised within purely psychological, sociological, economic or political frames of reference (Howse, 1999). The language of spirituality is more holistic, and stresses issues of value, meaning and relationships. It is doubtful, though, that a common definition of spirituality can be constructed on this basis. The concept will necessarily be used differently by those who ground their experiences in a non-material reality, whether defined as transcendent or immanent (i.e. sensing God's presence within creation), and by those who wish to accept them simply as experiences to which humans are inclined.

We therefore think that in the future it is likely that people will come to distinguish more clearly between religious and secular spiritualities. Both deal with heightened experience – seeing 'through' ordinary reality or seeing it in its 'true' or 'valued' nature – but only the former interprets this experience in metaphysical terms. Because of its intrinsic ambiguity the concept of 'spirituality' by itself is of limited use. Probably a more useful generic term for research purposes is 'existential meaning', which can be employed to refer to the perceived purpose of one's own life, whether provided by religious beliefs and/or philosophical, community, family or other principles, values and goals. A major task for the coming years, relevant to both counselling and pastoral work practice with older people, will be facing up to this diversity of view, perhaps differentiating further along a continuum between religious and secular belief, and responding appropriately. This has important implications, for example for the provision of secular spiritual funerals for those who appreciate the benefits of meaningful ritual but are embarrassed by religious language, and for forms of counselling which respect and do not seek to undermine people's religious convictions in the interests of secular psychological ideology.

Conclusion

It is possible to imagine that the present generation of older people in the UK is the last with a major commitment to traditional Judaeo-Christian religion. However, as David Martin (2005) has argued, it is very misleading to conceive of secularization as a standard and inevitable process. What impresses us so much in the decline of religion is mainly the situation of Europe since the eighteenth-century Enlightenment. But the subsequent religious histories of the Americas, Asia and Africa have been quite different. Religion is a field of study which benefits greatly from detailed comparative work.

Desecularization or renewed sacralization is not unimaginable. Believers in traditional religion outside western Europe have shown a much stronger maintenance of religious identity, and this is also evident among immigrant groups to Britain. On present trends they will comprise an increasingly significant number of committed British older believers. The growing confidence and self-expression of older Hindus, Muslims and Sikhs, among others, will inevitably transform the spiritual background of Britain. Moreover, America continues to exert a strong influence on Britain and this includes its powerful charismatic and evangelical Christian churches. The more general interest in spiritual healing and meditation already strongly present in sections of British society will also in time become more widespread among older people as well.

Nevertheless, it is clear that much more note needs to be taken of the views of a large proportion of the current British older population which has remained affiliated to the religion of their upbringing, particularly Christianity, but who remain insufficiently engaged. Their needs are often poorly met by Church organizations that can be surprisingly ageist in their assumptions about what older people require in terms of both spiritual sustenance and challenge. Ministers can seem much more interested in attracting younger people into dialogue with the Church than continuing a serious conversation with their older members about their doubts and concerns. But in neglecting the old, they set a poor example to the young and seriously undermine their evangelical task which is to minister across the whole life span. In our current work we are seeking to explore some current patterns of care-providing by a sample of clergy to elderly members of their community, whether able to attend worship or not. We also wish to develop an understanding as to their knowledge of the ageing process and their attitudes towards their own ageing and that of others.

Part V

The Future for Health and Well-being in Old Age

All humans are susceptible to injury, ill health and disease that risk compromising their well-being and quality of life, but older people have additional, more specific concerns. However, access to supports and services which ameliorate the effects of living with disease is highly variable and different sections of the global population are more or less disadvantaged (World Health Organization, 2001). Part of anticipating the future for health and well-being in old age lies in predicting the forms which health and social care systems will take. The World Health Organization has drawn attention to the inadequacies of existing healthcare systems for ensuring older people with chronic or long-term health conditions attain and retain maximum quality of life and minimal disability. The social response to people with impairments and long-term conditions is crucial. Those living with a long-term condition, be it lung disease, heart disease or a progressive brain disease such as dementia, will need social and health care to be more flexible and better adapted to facilitate maximum participation of older people.

In England, the recent National Service Framework for Older People endorsed a vision of medical care provided in one's own home. This does, however, raise questions about the extent to which technical innovation can be relied upon to achieve care at home? There are both benefits and costs to health and well-being associated with the use of technology to assist personal care and independent living in the home. The medical gaze will extend even further with technological sophistication. Thus telemedicine and other technologies in the home might lead to increased autonomy or alternatively lead to an extended reach by a paternalistic healthcare system. Those who cannot afford an automated door entrance or 'smart' home technologies may be disadvantaged as alternative care options may no longer exist.

Older people currently use a large share of health resources, much of which is reactive and crisis-driven. The potential exists for greater patient and public involvement in health and social care leading to greater self-determination and choice. But will we be expected to become the expert on our own condition, studying its risk factors, signs, symptoms and treatments so that we can be informed consumers of health services? Pessimistically, the rhetoric of choice might simply prove an illusory cover for tightened rationing. Those who fail to adhere to a healthy lifestyle regime in their earlier years could be labelled as undeserving and be denied expensive healthcare. More optimistically, we may see an emphasis on prevention of ill-health and active promotion of well-being.

Will older people with long-term conditions be considered rightful users of health and social services, or will they be considered to be placing an excessive burden on an already overstretched system? One possible pessimistic scenario would involve formalized rationing, such that those in later years of life with long-term conditions may be denied symptomatic or palliative treatment. Medication for older people, with fewer potential years of life, may come to be judged through different criteria from that applied to younger cohorts. The frailest and sickest of older people may continue to be segregated from the rest of society in residential environments with inadequate resources and support. More optimistically, they may become part of multigenerational communities with appropriate input as needed provided by sensitive, informed and well-resourced practitioners.

Those over 80 are now the fastest growing segment of the population and this has led to increased numbers of people living with dementing illnesses, including Alzheimer's disease and vascular dementia. The growth of our understanding of the social side of dementia in parallel with breakthroughs in symptomatic drug treatment has led to a change in how we conceptualize dementia. Increasing recognition is now being given to the role of social and economic circumstances in the person's experience of living with cognitive impairment. In future, much more needs to be done to ensure that the essential humanity and dignity of older people, whatever their ability or disability, is affirmed in interpersonal and institutional contexts.

Everyday health service language betrays a tendency towards 'blaming the victim' when it uses the term 'bed blockers' to refer to older people for whom no appropriate place can be found for discharge. The emphasis on acute care in healthcare systems at end of life persists with a focus on treatment versus palliation. In future, will the palliative care approach, developed largely in response to the inadequacies of the healthcare system in caring for people at the end of life, move from its place on the margins to the centre of mainstream services? Best practice in palliative care for all those with long-term conditions, including those with dementia, is an agenda for the future.

Conceptualizations of health and ill-health will change. Prior to medical technologies, such as pacemakers, and the relative ease with which bypass surgeries are conducted, heart problems held different meaning. Today older people with these conditions can have their bodies reverted back to 'normal'. Many medical conditions which in the past would have disabled older people and led to death can now be treated. With increased commercialization of medicine, medication may become a lifestyle choice and a quick fix to all our ills, or perhaps an essential step in the pursuit of the perfect body and mind.

The current inequities in health and well-being have been persistent despite advances in prevention and treatment. Increased longevity may well see a further growth in disparities in health and well-being. Market systems tend to accentuate social divisions: the rich can make the market work for themselves. It is difficult to spot trends whereby those social groups most vulnerable to ill-health will in the future be able to gain better access to the best care and support.

Thirteen   Will Our Old Age Be Healthier?

Christina Victor

The health of older people is an area of concern for governments throughout the developed world because older people are the main users of health services. Projected increases in the number of older people are seen as posing a considerable challenge to the continued provision of health- and social-care services (McMurdo, 2000). The complexity of the notion of health and the differing ways that it may be defined and measured make debates concerning the health experience of future cohorts of elders highly complex. This chapter examines the physical health status of older people using a population perspective, discusses how the experience of health in later life has changed over the past 150 years and considers what the future health experience of older people might look like.

Rectangularization of mortality

In Britain there has been a massive decrease in overall mortality rates over the past 150 years (Wanless, 2002) that has profoundly changed the distribution and pattern of mortality within society. Whilst there may be debates as to why these changes have happened, there is no doubt as to the reality of the very profound changes in the pattern of deaths within the population. The crude death rate for England and Wales (deaths per 1,000 population) decreased from about 22 per 1,000 population in 1841 to 9 per 1,000 in 2003 (Victor, 2005). Perhaps the most spectacular change has been in terms of infant mortality: deaths in the first year of life have decreased from 153 per 1,000 births (1841) to 5 per 1,000 in 2003. However late-age mortality has also decreased markedly so that death rates for those aged 85 and over decreased by 33 per cent between 1841 and 2003 (the decreases for those aged 65–74 and 75–84 years were 65 per cent and 55 per cent, respectively).

As a result of these reductions in mortality there has been a 'redistribution' of death from the young to the old, massive increases in expectation of life at birth, and increases in the percentage of the population surviving to experience old age. In 2003, 80 per cent of deaths were accounted for by those aged 65 and over, compared with 15 per cent in 1841 (Victor, 2005). Expectation of life at birth has increased from around 40 years to 76 years for men, and 80 years for women. That mortality has become increasingly concentrated into the later phases of life within contemporary western societies is not contested. Rather, it is the consequences of this 'compression' of mortality into the later phases of life which are contested, and there are three major perspectives on the consequences of changes in mortality.

Compression of morbidity

The optimistic perspective argues that as a result of the constriction of mortality into later life, morbidity will also demonstrate a similar trend. Fries (1980, 2003), assuming a 'fixed' biological limit to expectation of life at birth of 85 years, argues that under 'ideal' conditions 95 per cent of deaths would occur between the ages of 77 and 95 years; in Britain in 2003 those aged 75 and over account for currently almost two-thirds of deaths, 64 per cent. His thesis is that morbidity, as well as mortality, would be 'compressed' into the later phases of life because the major causes of morbidity and mortality are similar (or at least are influenced by the same risk factors). Consequently the increase in the numbers of people surviving into 'old age' will be unproblematic because those who survive will be fitter, as the factors that have delayed mortality will also have delayed morbidity and the mean age of onset for chronic disability will be pushed back (Fries, 2003). This theory has very obvious health policy implications. If the compression of morbidity thesis is correct, then expenditure on healthcare could, in theory at least, be reduced (or perhaps contained) and the 'ageing' of the population does not imply any great threat to the provision of health and social welfare.

Expansion of morbidity

Unsurprisingly, this notion has not gone unchallenged and the much less optimistic counter-argument suggests that the result of the compression of mortality will be an increase in morbidity because the factors influencing mortality decline will have minimal impact on morbidity. This thesis has been dubbed the 'failure of success'—lives would be longer but the 'extra' years would be characterized by frailty, disability and ill health because neither the incidence of chronic diseases nor the rate of progression for these conditions would be significantly reduced as a result of reductions in mortality. As a result of decreased death rates, there will be an increase in the morbidity of the population because, although more people will survive into old age, they will do so in much poorer health. Rather than morbidity being compressed into a short period at the end of life, it will be extended across a longer period. This scenario has been termed the 'survival of the unfittest' or the 'expansion of morbidity hypothesis' (Olshansky et al., 1991). This perspective shares with Fries' (1980) the assumption of a fixed maximum average life expectancy of 85 years. However, it assumes that the distribution of age at death will continually shift towards the highest age groups, resulting in an increase in numbers of the oldest old, with a consequent increase in the number of people with (multiple) chronic diseases within the population. This is obviously a pessimistic view as to the implications of more people surviving to older age groups: this will generate a massive increase in the numbers of disabled people experiencing poor quality of life in their later years. The implications for families and societies, especially in terms of healthcare provision, are dire.

Dynamic equilibrium

Manton (1991) offers a hypothesis situated between these two extremes which is usually referred to as the notion of dynamic equilibrium. He suggests that the pattern of mortality in later life is influenced by two interacting sets of factors: the rate of 'natural ageing' and the distribution of risk factors for specific diseases within populations, such as the prevalence of smoking, obesity or alcohol consumption. Interventions and changes to the distribution of risk factors will bring both improvements in mortality and reductions in the severity of disabilities. Hence decreases in mortality and increases in life expectancy will result in more people surviving into 'old age' but they will demonstrate less severe levels of disability because of the improvement in medical interventions and treatments.

Is there a fixed expectation of life?

The hypotheses of both Fries (1980) and Olshansky et al. (1991) rest upon a central assumption of a 'maximum' average life expectancy of 85 years based upon our genetic composition. Using data for the United States, Olshansky et al. (1990) indicate that mortality rates need to decline by approximately 50 per cent (40 per cent for women and 60 per cent for men) for this goal to be achieved. However, in the UK late-age mortality has declined by this amount over the course of the last century. Robine et al. (1996) suggest that some countries will achieve an average life expectancy at birth of 85 years in the next two decades (assuming current trends continue), whilst this will be achieved for the UK by 2050. Furthermore, Manton (1991) has proposed that, for women, if the population demonstrated an 'ideal' risk-factor profile, mortality would be reduced such that life expectancy would increase to 106 years. However, it is not clear whether (a) populations could be persuaded to adopt the 'optimal' lifestyle pattern or (b) mortality rates will continue to decrease significantly from the now low base. The prospects for extended survival remain unclear for the British population; however, maintenance of current trends suggests improvements in mortality and life expectancy at later life for future populations of elders. However, the case of the Soviet Union serves to remind us that life expectancy can decline, so that continuous improvements in life expectancy are neither natural nor inevitable. Given this caveat, current trends across the developed world do not seem to support the notion of a fixed average life expectancy of 85.

Patterns of mortality

A central assumption of the use of mortality data to describe the health status of populations is that they accurately reflect the distribution of disease and disability within that population. There are two distinct aspects to this assumption: demographics (i.e. the age and sex distribution of health problems) and the type of health problems identified. By comparing mortality and morbidity data, we can test the veracity of these assumptions. In terms of mortality the most important causes of death are circulatory disease (accounting for 40 per cent of deaths), respiratory disease (accounting for 19 per cent of deaths) and cancers (23 per cent of deaths), and these disease categories account for 82 per cent of all deaths amongst those aged 65 and over.

There are important variations within the older age groups in the probability of death that largely reflect patterns observed at earlier phases of the life cycle. Mortality increases with age and there are variations in terms of gender, social class and ethnicity which replicate those described at earlier phases of the life cycle. Late-age mortality rates are higher for males than

141

for females and show a marked social class gradient (Khaw, 1999a; Marmot and Shipley, 1996). For example, at age 65 a man from classes 1 and 2 (the professional occupations) could expect to live for another fifteen years, whilst his contemporary from classes 4 and 5 (the unskilled and semi-skilled groups) would live for another 12.4 years (for women the average expectation of life was 18.7 years and 16.7 years, respectively) (Hattersley, 1997). Reductions in both gender- and class-based mortality differentials would clearly have an impact upon overall mortality and, again, hints that mortality rates have not yet 'bottomed out' and that there is still scope within the UK for increases in life expectancy.

Data on changes in life expectancy can be used to test the equity of the 'compression of mortality' hypothesis. Have changes in life expectancy at age 65 been shared equally across the social classes and men and women? Hattersley (1997) reports that between 1971 and 1991 expectation of life at age 65 increased by 0.9 years for men and 1.0 year for women. Hence there seems to be a marginal additional mortality decrease 'advantage' to women, perhaps increasing the well-observed gender differential in mortality in later life. Furthermore, older people from professional backgrounds demonstrate larger 'gains' in life expectancy than do their less occupationally privileged contemporaries. For males from classes 1 and 2 the increase in life expectancy was 0.6 years, compared with 0.4 years for classes 4 and 5 (0.8 years and 0.1 years, respectively for women) (Hattersley, 1997). Hence recent improvements in mortality have not been equally distributed amongst all older people, but rather seem to accentuate existing differentials.

Patterns of morbidity?

Acute health conditions, that is health problems that have restricted normal level of activity in the 14 days before interview, show only a marginal age-related increase in the reported prevalence of acute illness. For example, 20 per cent of males aged 45–64 reported an acute illness episode, compared with 27 per cent of those aged 75 and over. However, the number of days annually estimated to be affected by restricted activity is higher amongst the older age groups, especially the 75-and-over age group, with those aged 65 and over reporting ten days of 'restricted activity' per year. Hence, whilst the prevalence of episodes does not show a great age-related differential, the duration of each episode seems to be greater amongst the oldest age groups. Reported rates of acute illness showed little variation between older people living in the community or those in care home settings (18 per cent for those in the community and 20 per cent for those in care). This affords support for the observation that acute illness varies little with age and that the only major difference seems to be in terms of gender, with females reporting rates of acute illness 10–15 per cent higher than males, perhaps reflecting gender differences in how the question is interpreted.

Chronic health problems are, by definition, long term and not usually characterized by having a cure, although treatment may alleviate some, or all, of the associated symptoms and may halt (or slow) the rate of decline. Data from the 2001 Census that includes both those elders living in the community and those in institutional settings report that 47 per cent of those aged 65–74 have a long-standing limiting disability, as compared with 57 per cent of those aged 75–84 and 74 per cent of those aged 85 years and over. This burden of ill health is not equitably distributed across the population. Women report more chronic illness than do men; rates of long-term illness are higher amongst elders from the Indian subcontinent and those from the manual occupation groups (Bridgwood, 2000; Evandrou, 2000; Khaw, 1999b; Victor, 2005).

When we look at five types of disability – locomotor, personal care, hearing, sight and communication – we find that approximately 60 per cent of those in the community report no disability, compared with 14 per cent of those in institutional settings. Another way of examining disability is to examine older people's ability to perform key activities of daily living such as bathing, shopping, cooking and cleaning: all activities essential for an independent life in the community. The majority of older people can undertake these activities without difficulty; only a minority is unable to undertake them without the assistance of another person. Thus we find that for the task which presented the most difficulty, cutting toenails, 30 per cent were unable to undertake this alone and 70 per cent were totally independent. However, in absolute terms this still represents a large number of people. The ability to undertake these tasks decreases with age. These items can be used to generate an overall index of disability (Melzer et al., 1999) which suggests that 15.7 per cent of people aged 65 and over in England and Wales are severely disabled, a total of 1.3 million people. Females have higher prevalence rates than males, 19.2 per cent compared to 10.6 per cent, and represent 72 per cent of the total severely disabled population. The percentage with no or slight disability decreases with age from 80 per cent of those aged 65–69 to 15 per cent of the 85-plus groups. Melzer et al. (2000) also demonstrate the existence of socioeconomic differentials in both the overall distribution of disability and severe disability which are evident for all age and sex groups.

Data from routine surveys also enable us to establish the major health conditions that are bringing about these chronic health problems in both community and institutional populations. Both the General Household Survey and Health Survey for England demonstrate the importance of musculoskeletal conditions (mostly arthritis), dementia and cognitive impairment, and circulatory diseases in compromising mobility and independence in later life. This pattern of causes of morbidity is somewhat different from that for mortality and we can distinguish three distinct categories of health in problems in old age:

- High mortality and high morbidity (e.g. heart and circulatory diseases)

- High morbidity but low mortality (musculoskeletal disease and dementia)

- High mortality and low morbidity (cancer)

It seems likely that these three categories of health problems will have differential impact upon the relationship between mortality and morbidity and hence future patterns of disability and chronic illness.

Another way of examining this issue is to use combinations of mortality and morbidity data to calculate measures of 'healthy' or 'disability-free' life expectancy. This approach has the merit of combining information about survival rates with data concerning the health status of survivors so that we can determine the number of years or percentage of the life span that individuals can expect to live, on average, free from disability or in good health. For the UK both life expectancy and 'healthy' life expectancy have increased, although the rate of increase has been higher for the former than the latter. Hence there has been a marginal increase in the percentage of life spent in poor health or disability (Kelly et al., 2000). It is not clear if all sections of the population have experienced this direction of change. Given the evidence indicating the differential advantage in terms of life expectancy gained by the most privileged groups, it seems unlikely that the above decreases would be equally distributed (Hattersley, 1997).

Compression or expansion of morbidity?

One method of considering these competing propositions is to examine trends over time in routinely collected data from the General Household Survey from 1972–2002. Clearly there are methodological problems in making such comparisons, including changes in question wording.

Furthermore, changes in the reported prevalence of long-standing limiting illness or the ability to undertake key activities of daily living amongst older people in the community may result from factors linked to the supply and admission to residential/nursing home care and the ability of services to care for more/less disabled/dependent people within the population and not from any changes in overall morbidity. Although the prevalence rates fluctuate, there is no evidence for an increase over time for those aged 65–74 and only a 2 per cent increase in prevalence over 25 years for those aged 75. Constructing a 'pseudo' cohort of those aged 85 and over, there is considerable stability across cohorts. For those aged 85 and over in 1980 (born 1895 or earlier), the prevalence of long-standing limiting illness was 53 per cent for men and 59 per cent for women – remarkably similar to the 51 per cent and 57 per cent, respectively, for the 1916 cohort (85 and over in 2001) (Victor, 2005). This certainly does not suggest any radical changes in disability prevalence over the last 30 years, but these data are derived from the older people who have remained in the community and may, therefore, be biased by the exclusion of the 'sickest' and frailest members of the cohort into long-term care.

International evidence suggests that disability may be decreasing at all severity levels in developed countries. Manton et al. (1997) conclude that disability prevalence in the United States declined by 0.34 per cent per year or by 4.3 per cent for the period 1982–96, whilst Fries (2003) suggests that disability has been decreasing at 2 per cent per year for the period 1982–99, a larger decrease than 1 per cent annual decline in mortality. His thesis is supported by the work of Schoeni et al. (2001). Similar trends have been observed elsewhere (Graham et al., 2004; Hubert et al., 2002; Perenboom et al., 2004), as have inequalities in the distribution of these benefits.

Conclusion: will we be healthier?

Whilst old age is not universally a time of poor health, the reported prevalence of chronic health problems does increase with age, although this observation may reflect the influence of confounding variables such as class or gender. We should also remember the influence that social, environmental and occupational factors have in the genesis of chronic disease. Furthermore, the increase in prevalence rates for chronic illness which we observe with age may, in fact, reflect a cohort, rather than an ageing, effect. Given the harsh circumstances that today's elderly experienced during their formative years, the levels of ill health we have observed may be a reflection of this. Indeed, the Barker hypothesis argues for the 'foetal' origin of disease by suggesting that it is the environment in utero and early infancy which establishes risk factors for disease in middle and later life. Hence, future generations, which have experienced less privation and better health care in infancy and prior to birth, might demonstrate improved health status in later life.

The health status of any specific older person reflects the interaction of numerous factors, including genetic makeup, individual behaviours (such as diet, exercise or smoking), exposure to environmental and occupational hazards, and social factors such as class, gender and ethnicity. Hence, health in old age is the product of a complex interaction between both individual-level and macro-level social and environmental factors, as well as factors concerning the organization of health (and social) care. To date, the debate concerning the health of future cohorts of elders has been conducted at the population level (Fries, 2003). There has been remarkably little research examining the veracity of the compression/expansion of morbidity theses within subgroups of the total populations. Given that mortality and morbidity are not distributed equally within the older population, it seems unlikely that any changes in morbidity would be equitably distributed throughout the population. If morbidity is improving amongst the older populations, then it seems likely that some groups will probably be benefiting from such changes more than others. Hence, if current trends are continued, it seems likely that in the future there will be overall improvements in both mortality and morbidity. However, these improvements are unlikely to be equally distributed and it seems most likely that for some of us old age in the future will be healthy, whilst the less privileged will be less likely to benefit from such improvements.

Fourteen Is there a Better Future for People with Dementia and their Families?

Murna Downs and Errollyn Bruce

The future for people with dementia and their families is of concern to those interested in the future of old age because approximately 5 per cent of those who reach 65 and 20 per cent of those who reach 80 years of age will develop dementia, with similar prevalence rates across urban areas in Europe (Ferri et al., 2005). In 1998 it was estimated that there were nearly half a million people with dementia in the UK, and this figure was predicted to rise to 650,000 by 2021 (Bosenquet et al., 1998). Most people with dementia (60 per cent in 2001) live in developing countries and this percentage is expected to increase to 71 per cent by 2040 (Ferri et al., 2005). Currently dementia represents one of the most stigmatized of the chronic conditions of old age (Graham et al., 2003). In a society which values cognition and reasoning, what Post (2000) refers to as a 'hyper-cognitive' society, the disruption to information processing, memory and language associated with dementia (Ballard, 2000) leaves people especially vulnerable.

The majority of people with dementia will live most of their lives at home in their communities, either alone or with relatives or friends. A significant percentage of people living in residential and nursing homes in the UK have dementia (MacDonald, 2005; Macdonald and Dening, 2002). The quality of these lives will vary. Despite improvements from the postwar warehousing of 'senile dements'[1], we have yet to see people with dementia attain their full rights as citizens, most importantly their rights to social inclusion and adequate health and social care (Innes, 2002).

Our understandings of, and explanations for, dementia differ within and between cultures. In the west, up until the 1970s, dementia was viewed as a normal part of ageing, and terms such a 'senility', 'going senile' or 'senile dementia' were used interchangeably. Today, this view has largely been replaced by the view that dementia is the result of a progressive brain disease, most commonly Alzheimer's disease.

According to the World Health Organization in its International Classification of Diseases (2003), dementia is:

> A syndrome due to disease of the brain, usually of a chronic or progressive nature, in which there is disturbance of multiple higher cortical functions, including memory, thinking, orientation, compre-hensions, calculation, learning capacity, language and judgement. Consciousness is not clouded. The impairments of cognitive function are commonly accompanied, and occasionally preceded, by dete-rioration in emotional control, social behaviour, or motivation. This syndrome occurs in Alzheimer's disease, in cerebrovascular disease, and in other conditions primarily or secondarily affecting the brain.

The World Health Organization (2002) conceptualize disease as having bio-psycho-social elements. Such a conceptualization recognizes that the effect of neurological impairment will be moderated by an individual's health, and psychological, social and economic resources, and by the broader com-munity's and government's response. The bio-psycho-social approach in dementia care is perhaps most easily recognized in Kitwood's (1988) description of the dialectics of dementia, where psychological and social factors in a person's life interact with neurobiological factors, leading to varied experiences of living with dementia and quality of life.

The future for those who develop dementia and their families should include a successful translation into policy and practice of the view that while cognitive changes may be caused by an underlying brain disease, there is much that can be done to maximize quality of life for people living with progressive cognitive impairment (Downs, 2000). Such a future would emphasize social inclusion for people with dementia and their families; successful partnership between users, carers and professionals; and a balance between economics and humanism in dementia care.

Social inclusion for people with dementia and their families

People with dementia experience a variety of forms of social exclusion, predominantly due to stigma (Graham et al., 2003). The consequences of social exclusion can become as, if not more, challenging to cope with than any lapses of memory or difficulty with orientation and planning (Lyman, 1998; Sabat, 2001). People with dementia are excluded not just from society but also from health and social care services. For example, when seeking residential or nursing home care, families may have difficulty placing their relative with dementia. In the UK, Macdonald and Dening (2002) describe an NHS and social-care system which fails to acknowledge the special needs of its clients with what they refer to as 'quiet dementia'. Wilkinson et al. (2002) report that hospitals frequently fail to provide appropriate care for people with dementia. Having dementia is associated with less active treatment in terms of rehabilitation or palliation. Also people with dementia are less likely to receive analgesic medication than are their contemporaries with similar medical conditions, e.g. hip replacement (Cook et al., 1999). In England, the Department of Health's (2001) National Service Framework for Older People tackles ageism within the health service, but there is also a compelling need to tackle 'dementism' (Brooker, 2004). A balanced account of dementia recognizes that people with dementia retain many abilities, including the capacity for emotion and a sense of self in relation to others (Kitwood, 1997; Post, 2000), even though they have a progressive brain disease affecting cognitive functioning.

One response to the social exclusion of people with dementia has been the growth of advocacy and self-help groups set up and run by people with dementia themselves. Increasingly they are taking the platform as conference speakers and authoring publications (e.g. Bryden, 2005; Friedell, 2002; Sterin, 2002). Alzheimer's Societies are giving increased priority to participation by people with dementia in meetings, social groups and outings. Professional caregivers and families are challenging the assumption that people with dementia should be hidden away for fear that they behave inappropriately and are encouraging them to remain socially active. We should expect to find people with dementia in pubs and parks, theatres and swimming pools, and expect staff and public to be accepting of their presence. Indeed many of the so-called anti-dementia drugs emphasize just this aspect of the continuity of ordinary lives in the community (Downs and Bartlett, 2005; Mackenzie et al., 2005).

Perhaps the major challenge to social inclusion is the drive to rid the world of dementing conditions. In the coming years, we need to balance public expectations of the role of science in providing hope for a miracle cure with a strong commitment to equal consideration for those living with the condition and who have no realistic hope of a cure. For example, the 'vision' statement of the US Alzheimer's Association (2005) tries to attain this balance but its first priority is clearly anti-dementia in its focus: 'Creating a world without Alzheimer's disease *while optimizing quality of life for individuals and their families*' (italics added). This is echoed in their mission statement: 'To eliminate Alzheimer's disease through the advancement of research *and to enhance care and support for individuals, their families, and caregivers'* (italics added).

Making the eradication of dementia the primary goal runs the risk of sidelining those who are living with the condition. The value of their experience is potentially marginalized and threatened with illegitimacy by the promise of a dementia-free world. The expectation that science will be able to prevent the onset of the condition or to deliver an effective cure risks diverting attention from the need for skilled support necessary to enable people, now and in the future, to make the most of life with dementia.

Successful partnerships between people with dementia, families and professionals

People with dementia and their families will fare best when their expertise is married to that of professionals to forge powerful partnerships and alliances, but there are obstacles. The view that dementia is a psychiatric condition brought about by brain disease (e.g. Department of Health, 2001) brings with it the same professional paternalism as experienced by other groups of people diagnosed with psychiatric conditions. It has been assumed that people with dementia lack awareness and this has been used as a justification for excluding them from decisions about their care. A growing body of recent evidence challenges these assumptions (Clare and Wilson, 2006; Normann et al., 2002; Norberg et al., 2003). Snyder's (1999) volume and Harris' (2002) edited text provide ample evidence of the capacity of people with dementia to share their experience. The Dementia Advocacy and Support Network International (www.dasninternational. org) is the first international grouping of people with dementia. The public patient forums run by the Department of Health (for England and Wales) provide an obvious avenue for users to influence care; the extent to which people with dementia are encouraged to participate remains to be seen.

The rhetoric of partnership working in health and social care is well established and has been applied to dementia care (Adams and Clarke, 1999). The need for service development for people with dementia and their families has been highlighted in both Audit Commission (2000, 2002) reports on services for older people with mental health problems. Partnership working has the potential to ensure that new developments result in services which people want and from which they will benefit. Evidence suggests that regular review of services from the perspective of people with dementia enhances quality of care (Brooker, 2005).

Involving people with dementia fully in a partnership means slowing down to their pace to allow them time to formulate and express their views. There are potential conflicts of interest between people with dementia and their families, which may require independent advocacy to resolve. For these reasons, there are resource implications if partnership working is to be more than superficial.

Balancing economic and humanitarian interests in dementia care

Dementia care is driven by both economic and humanitarian concerns (Longley and Warner, 2002). People with dementia and their families need appropriate support on humanitarian grounds. We now know that much of the disability and 'suffering' once considered to be inevitable consequences of illness can be avoided. Equally we must not hide from the distress and emotional pain caused to both the person with dementia and their families (Miesen, 2004). Families and carers' organizations and people with dementia themselves are major players in this humanitarian drive. Practitioners and academics have lent support from theoretical, moral and clinical positions (e.g., Brooker, 2004; Gibson, 1999; Kitwood, 1997; Packer, 2000; Post, 2000; Sabat, 2001). Quality dementia care in action is the exception, generally driven by an enlightened professional and supportive team (Ballard et al., 2001). Its adoption as mainstream practice requires political will and economic resources to ensure that the necessary structural supports are put in place (Bender and Wainwright, 2004; Kitwood, 1997; Kitwood and Woods, 1996). These include education and training for managers and frontline staff, adequate staffing levels, supervision arrangements, induction procedures and incentives (Beck et al., 1999; Kitwood, 1997).

The National Service Framework's (NSF) adoption of person-centred care as one of its eight standards (Department of Health, 2001) lends weight to the humanitarian case. In England the NSF for Older People includes a discussion of dementia within its seventh standard on mental health problems. Its main emphasis is on the need for early diagnosis and drug treatment of dementia and the role of specialists in diagnosis and behaviour management. The drive toward diagnosis and behaviour management must be equalled by a similar impetus in service provision, particularly services which have demonstrated efficacy in enhancing quality of life.

Because government policy is inevitably influenced by economic concerns, though couched in humanitarian terms, it is not uncommon for ideas to resurface with a different meaning (Means and Smith, 2003).

151

Economically there is recognition that, given the numbers of people with dementia and the forecasted lack of family carers, cost-effective support solutions need to be identified. Longley and Warner (2002) note the paradox by which on the one hand there is a concern about the epidemic of dementia and on the other hand a lack of policy and resources specifically addressing this condition. This they attribute to the low status of people with dementia and the lack of a cure. In England the contribution that the NSF can make to improvements in dementia care is limited both by the lack of specificity and by the requirement that the standards are met without additional resources.

Unlike pharmacological approaches to managing behaviour, psychosocial approaches have no economic or business-interest drivers. The attention given to the modest gains attained by drug interventions is not equalled in the attention given to studies demonstrating efficacy for psychosocial interventions (Kihlgren et al., 1993; Lawton and Rubinstein, 2000; Moniz-Cook and Woods, 1997; Spector et al., 2003; Teri et al., 1997). However, the costs of implementing quality care need to be set against the costs of custodial care. Custodial care leads to excess disability and iatrogenic care regimes where, through inappropriate medication regimes and enforced immobility, people with dementia become unnecessarily dependent for their daily care. While dependence is a natural consequence of the disease process, premature dependence is not.

What are the obstacles which prevent our moving away from custodial care to the full implementation of quality dementia care? Rehabilitation approaches which support people with impairments to maximize functioning and quality of life are just beginning to be introduced into services used by people with dementia (Clare and Woods, 2001; Marshall, 2004; Perrin and May, 1999). Palliative care services traditionally omit all but those who have been diagnosed with a cancer condition from their remit but this too is changing for the better (Volicer et al., 1994). There is a risk that the excitement over medical advances and the expectation that they will bring effective prevention and treatment will undermine the political will to fund psychosocial interventions.

Conclusion

In the future we will see more people with dementia in our communities. We have the opportunity to ensure that our communities are optimally dementia-friendly. The neurological underpinnings of the experience of dementia, while an important focus of investigation in the search for a cause and cure, provide little in terms of theoretical rationale or practical guidance as to how to maximize quality of life for people living with dementia.

Improved quality of life for people with dementia and their families in future will require action on at least four fronts. First, there will need to be a public education campaign which creates positive public awareness and appropriate understandings of dementia which recognize the subjectivity, individuality, agency and relatedness of people with dementia. Second, we need training and education for practitioners and professionals. This ensures a workforce with the knowledge of all that can be done to promote and support quality of life. Third, we need appropriate services to uphold quality of life for people with dementia and their families. Finally, a better future for people with dementia and their families is possible but requires political will and economic drivers.

Note

1 Term used in the Seebohm Rowntree report, 1947.

Fifteen The Future of Well-being: Quality of Life of Older People in the Twenty-first Century

John Bond and Lynne Corner[1]

'Quality of life' is a concept that is widely used as a 'measure' of well-being in gerontological, health and policy research. In recent years increasing the quality of life of individuals and populations has become a key strategic goal for the UK government, other member states in the European Union, the World Health Organization and the United Nations. 'Quality of life' is also part of the rhetoric of organizations like the World Bank and the World Trade Organization when defending their hegemonic position in the globalized political economy. In everyday life the idea of life quality seems relatively straightforward and self-explanatory. But like many other social science concepts that have been politicized, the concept of 'quality of life' has become increasingly complex and has lost its ability to coherently describe and explain the well-being of individuals and populations. 'Quality of life' nowadays is therefore a heuristic concept used by academics, politicians and global institutions to capture the essence of life for the individual citizen.

In this chapter we will review historical and current perspectives on well-being and quality of life and the implications of cultural, economic, political, social and technological changes in late modernity for the next generations of older people. First, we will briefly examine the meaning of quality of life for individual older citizens within the context of their lived experience and present a framework for understanding well-being or quality of life. Second, we will investigate the implications of our framework for the assessment and measurement of well-being in later life, highlighting the distinction between 'objective' aspects and the 'subjectivity' of the accounts of the 'lived experience' of older people. In the final section we will attempt to forecast the life-course experiences that will influence the quality of life of older people in the next generation in 2040.

A framework for understanding quality of life

There is general consensus amongst researchers that older people report that their own health and that of significant others, family relationships and other social networks, social activity, standard of living, and spirituality are important aspects of their lives (Bowling, 1995a,1995b; Bowling et al., 2003; Farquhar, 1995; Gabriel and Bowling, 2004a, 2004b). The relative importance of any one of these will change across the life course and within the context of time and space. These studies highlight differences between different groups of older people – between men and women, people from different cultural backgrounds, people with different levels of disability and people living in a range of built environments – reflecting the diversity of the lived experience of older people. These aspects of older people's lives have remained important for people across a number of generations and we might therefore assume that upcoming generations of older people will report these aspects as important to them in the future. Given the consistency of older people's reports, it is perhaps not surprising that in policy and politics it is these aspects that dominate thinking about the future.

In understanding quality of life an important distinction can be made between the objective measures of quality of life on the one hand – health status, standard of living, living arrangements and the number of social contacts – and subjective accounts on the other – the meaning of health to the individual, their expectations about incomes and living arrangements and the quality of contact with others. This distinction is critical for understanding the paradoxes of ageing (Westerhof et al., 2003), disability (Albrecht and Devlieger, 1999), loneliness and social isolation (Townsend, 1957), relative deprivation (Runciman, 1966) and poverty (Townsend, 1970). Why is it that older people, people with disability, or people who are socially isolated, deprived or poor do not always present a negative view about their quality of life? To answer this, we need some kind of explanatory framework or model to investigate the complex relationships between experience of life and reported quality of life.

In our book *Quality of Life and Older People* (Bond and Corner, 2004) we developed such a framework (see Figure 15.1). From a broadly constructivist perspective, we argued that quality of life is a subjective lived experience which exists in multiple realities that are constructed and

Figure 15.1 Schematic framework of the role of structure and agency in the development and maintenance of quality of life through life-course experience

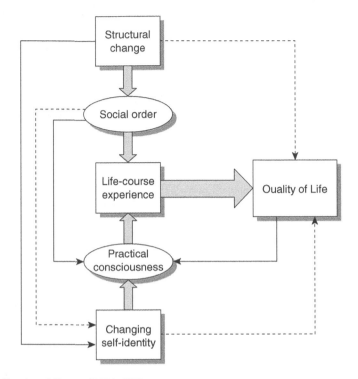

Source: Bond and Corner (2004: 105).

reconstructed by individual older people within the context of their individual lives and life histories. Thus there are many interpretations of quality of life and, from a constructivist perspective, there is no 'scientific' process for establishing the ultimate objective reality. The meaning of quality of life lives in the individual's mind and seeking subjective accounts may be the only way to access it. Building on the work of Hendricks (1999, 2003), our framework attempts to build linkages between agency, as reflected in individual subjectivity, and structure, particularly the nature of social order and structural change (Bond and Corner, 2004). Over time, personal identity is constructed and reconstructed in responses to our experience of the social world in which we are participants. This process is a cognitive one and is captured by individual *practical consciousness* (Hendricks, 1999) – the lens through which the individual gathers the whole range of sensory inputs within interactions and distils them into meaningful social experience. Thus practical consciousness links the individual as a reflexive social actor to the subjectively created 'lived experience' at different points in time and space along the life course and provides the vehicle for explaining the diversity of perspectives and meanings that older people report when providing accounts of their quality of life.

'Measuring' quality of life

Measuring quality of life, particularly health-related quality of life, is now a flourishing research industry. During the last two decades of the twentieth century the concept has had a meteoric rise, as evidenced by books on quality-of-life measures (Bowling, 1995c, 1996; Qureshi, 1994). In the UK, the Economic and Social Research Council (ESRC) has devoted a programme to the study of quality of life in old age (ESRC Growing Older Programme, 2005; Walker and Hennessy, 2004). There are internet websites (for example, www.qolid.org) and a professional society (the International Society of Quality of Life Research) and new texts and articles appear weekly in academic books and journals. The dominant diktats from government, the research councils and the wider scientific community suggest that gerontological researchers will continue to seek to 'measure' quality of life for the foreseeable future. What are the implications of our schematic framework for the future of quality-of-life measurement?

By emphasizing the diversity of later life and the range of changing self-identities that individuals adopt along the life course, our approach poses particular problems for quality-of-life researchers, most of whom use quantitative methods within a post-positivist paradigm (for example, Bowling, 1996). It raises a number of questions. How do we know what is important to someone's quality of life? What makes one person's quality of life better or worse than another's? Who is best suited to judge? Given an individual's changing identity and perspective on what is important in life, how can quality of life be assessed? Increasingly the research community has recognized the importance of gaining the perspective of the older person. It is no longer acceptable for the professional researcher to sit down in an ivory tower creating his or her own measure of quality of life without consulting older people themselves. This recognition of the older person's perspective has only extended to ensuring that older people themselves provide judgements about different domains in quality of life. This post-positivist approach to method, with some notable exceptions (O'Boyle et al., 1994; Ruta et al., 1994), rarely seeks to determine which domains are important for an individual. The usual form of data capture is the structured interview or self-completed questionnaire using 'standardized' instruments that conform to key psychometric properties of appropriateness, reliability, validity, responsiveness to change, precision, interpretability, acceptability and feasibility (Bowling, 1996; McDowell and Newell, 1987). That most instruments do not meet the stringency of these psychometric properties is rarely challenged (Leplege and Hunt, 1997; Rapley, 2003).

Traditional approaches to the assessment of quality of life ignore the symbolic nature and *meaning* of life to the individual. They assume that individual perceptions remain unchanged. Where changes are recognized they are treated technically in terms of 'response shift' (Sprangers and Schwartz, 1999). But quality of life is a personal and fluid concept. For example, models of chronic illness highlight how people adjust to and cope with illness (Anderson and Bury, 1988; Bury, 1991; Charmaz, 2000; Gubrium, 1987; Radley and Green, 1987). What is important to stress is that these illnesses are incorporated into people's lives, as another factor over the life course. The process of adaptation is dynamic. Encouraging participants to discuss these issues in a research context may have implications for an individual's perception of their everyday life. By getting people to think through, conceptualize and articulate their views and beliefs, researchers have to recognize that they may be a part of a process that changes individuals' expectations, judgements they make and the meaning that their circumstances have for them. This may present particular ethical, moral and methodological challenges as to how this is managed within research practice. People's experiences mean that their perceptions, their relationships and roles all change over time and approaches to assessing quality of life need to consider how these huge variations in values and perceptions and rates of adaptation can be incorporated.

In future years we may see greater awareness of the limitations of the traditional approach. In outcome research we expect further development of individualized approaches pioneered by O'Boyle et al. (1994), Ruta et al. (1994) and others to try to overcome the pigeon-hole approach (Murphy et al., 1998).

Looking into the future

Speculation is always hazardous, but here are some initial forecasts about well-being in old age. First we can say that the nature of personal well-being will continue to be at the centre of understandings of the self and self-identity. Second, it is probably also safe to say that life over the next 30 to 40 years will be at least as complex as it is now, with a diversity of everyday life experience. Third, we suggest our framework for under-standing quality of life will stand the test of time. Globalization and large-scale cultural, political and social changes (as discussed throughout this volume) will clearly impact on our future lives, but it is the impact that these may have on our individual lived experiences that will influence the meaning we give to our personal well-being and quality of life.

The sequence of generations and the associated social change for the next generation of older people is a theme throughout this volume and discussed specifically in Part I. Given this volume and complexity of change, how is the baby-boomer generation different from current gen-erations? Their politics is very different (Skidmore and Huber, 2003). It is much more differentiated with less certainty about political affiliation and an experience of radical and unexpected ways of engaging in politi-cal activity. Baby-boomers appear, perhaps as a consequence of increased geographical and social mobility, to be less embedded in social networks and local communities. As Bauman (2003) has emphasized, their lives and relationships are more fluid than traditional patterns. The continuing hegemony of consumerism and the importance of the culture in the development of personal identities are discussed in this volume by, amongst others, Blaikie and Biggs (Chapters 1 and 10, respectively). What we cannot predict is the way that the baby-boomer generation will be treated by younger generations. The history of ageing highlights the ubiq-uitousness of ageism in most cultures (Bytheway, 1995). Social inequali-ties and the presence of dominant social orders will persist, as Walker and Foster argue in their contribution (Chapter 4). It is the way that indi-viduals construct their self-identities in the context of these life experi-ences that will influence the way the baby-boomer generation perceive their personal well-being.

Conclusion

Quality of life is a subjective 'state', one that is strongly influenced by the context in which we each live as individuals and in which we establish our own self-identity. The world in which we all live is constantly chang-ing and we have forecasted some of the expected changes that will influ-ence the meaning we give to our lives as we grow older. We argue that the negative impact of demographic changes has been overstated by politicians and many policy analysts. In the short term they provide a challenge to policymakers, particularly in the provision of pensions, because of the ubiquitous pressures of managing scarce societal resources. We have suggested that we will all experience changes in kinship networks and social relationships and that the world of work and leisure will continue to evolve in unpredictable ways. Finally, we have suggested that technology may not have that profound an influence on the way we create our own self-identities and the way we perceive our future life quality. The paradoxes of ageing (Westerhof et al., 2003), disability (Albrecht and Devlieger, 1999), loneliness and social isolation (Townsend, 1957) and poverty (Townsend, 1970) lead us to believe that although the world around us is constantly changing, the way we construct our own self-identities and our life-course experiences, the meaning we give to our personal well-being and quality of life can be positive in the light of adversity. Although the life-course experience of future generations of older people is likely to be very different from that of current generations, there is no evidence to suggest that their perception of personal well-being will be more or less paradoxical or diverse than it is at present.

Note

1 Ideas developed in this chapter are the result of a fruitful collaboration between the authors made possible by awards to Lynne Corner from the Northern and Yorkshire NHS Executive Fellowship and an Alzheimer's Society Fellowship scheme.

Part VI

The Future of Family and Living Arrangements for Older People

Changing family and living arrangements will have a significant impact on the future of old age. The core values of the family as an intimate domestic arrangement combined with responsibilities between parents and children are unquestioned by most people, but families themselves are changing. Increasingly, couples are living together without forms of religious or legal certification and such partnerships are not always recognized by religious or civil law, most notably same-gender partnerships. Public opinion suggests significant differences between generations in respect to attitudes to pre-marital sex and same-gender relationships (Pilcher, 1998). It is highly likely that the increased diversity in sexual and domestic arrangements through the life course will lead to increasingly diverse household and sexual relationships in old age. An enhanced third age will lead to new forms of intimacy in old age.

Most research on domestic relationships in Britain and the United States indicate that they are still gendered along traditional lines. Increased longevity means that the focus of marriage as primarily an institution for procreation is becoming less appropriate. Couples typically have 30 or 40 years of married life after children have left home. Domestic relationships are broken by bereavement, divorce and separation. There are more widows than widowers because women live longer (in most countries) and tend to marry men older than themselves. Widowers are more likely to remarry than widows. Divorce is more common than in the past, and, among developed countries, it is most frequent in the United States. High rates of divorce are also reflected in increased rates of remarriage and reestablishment of new households. With increased longevity, grandparents and great-grandparents are more likely to have survived to play important roles in extended families.

Families are getting smaller, but fewer married couples are childless and birth spacing is narrowing. The average age of first pregnancy is getting older as working women postpone childbirth into their 30s. In the age of large families older siblings played a key role in bringing up younger children. In later life siblings, particularly sisters, might share elder care. In a society with serial monogamy, divorce can create complex patterns of social relationships. Complex relationships bring with them newly renegotiated commitments and obligations, or their lack. What are the consequences in old age of these complexities? Are there opportunities in old age to find companionship and support or do fragile ties evaporate faced with responsibilities and claims?

Financial flows within the family group vary enormously depending on the family's resources, size and structure and the preferences of each generation. Research suggests an increasingly important role for family financial support and resource-sharing as the number of living generations rises (Arrondel and Masson, 1999). Financial resources and domiciliary support go both up and down the generations.

Traditionally gerontology has been concerned with household arrangements in relationship to care and support of dependent older people. In the UK, and elsewhere, extended family living has declined. Most frequently the prime carer of an older person is their spouse. Although care from the younger generation is most likely to be provided by a daughter, families negotiate the obligations of care and support across the generations and researchers find consistent patterns of preferred carer, which is structured around intimacy, co-residence and gender (Qureshi, 1996; Qureshi and Simons, 1987; Qureshi and Walker, 1989; Wenger, 1984).

The idea of 'care' is strongly gendered. Affective relationships and expressions of emotion are seen to be feminine. The traditional division of labour constructs the domestic duties of person maintenance such as cooking, cleaning and nursing as women's work. Studies of familial attitudes show continuing commitment to provide practical care and emotional support for older members of the household (Finch and Mason, 1992; Qureshi and Walker, 1989). Commentators have noted the rise of the 'sandwich' generation of women who are caring for both children and older parents (Brody, 2004). This phenomenon relates not only to longevity but also to age of childbirth.

An ageing population means that there are expanding proportions of one- and two-person households in the west. Will this result in a greater need for communal care from people without live-in carers? Or will older people seek new forms of household arrangements to supply companionship, social care, and/or new emotional and affective ties?

Non-European and non-nuclear families provide yet another source of diversity in the family circumstances of old people. In many societies daughters-in-law are the prime carers for older people. Concerns in western literature about the future of the family and neglect of old age are paralleled in Asian debates about the decline of filial piety at a time of rapid population ageing. The idea of the patriarchal extended family contains the idea of patriarchy as not only the domination by male members of the household over the females but also of the older (particularly the senior generation) over the younger. What are the right amounts of duty owed and reasonable expectations anticipated from one generation to another?

Older people and their families experience strong emotions when making decisions about continued independent living in the face of increasing frailty. Society's norms can seldom be applied unambiguously to the complexities of individual circumstance. Greater diversity of opinions on moral issues concerning family relationships, gender roles and the right to take risks in old age is to be expected. Greater medical control over the survival of frail and disabled people combined with an increasing diversity in family relationships will see an even greater potential for conflicting expectations about interpersonal support in later life.

Sixteen The Ageing of Family Life Transitions

Sarah Harper

The trends towards falling fertility and mortality and increasing longevity, which have led to the demographic ageing of all western industrialized societies have not occurred in isolation. They are part of wider social, economic and political trends which have impacted upon all aspects of contemporary society. Both the factors encouraging these demographic trends and those associated with demographic ageing are directly influencing other areas of society, while demographic ageing *per se* is also influencing behaviour. Families have not been immune from the influence of such pressures for change.

As Harper (2004a, 2004b) has recently highlighted, we need to understand this change in terms of several interrelated processes. First the factors contributing to demographic ageing – increase in standard of living, education, public health and medical advances – have also had a direct impact on other areas of society. The family mode of social organization, whereby kin groups pooled their resources and related to community as an intact unit, has altered as these ideological, economic and social changes have shifted the locus of control away from the family towards the individual or other social institutions (Waite et al., 2000). Urbanization and technological change have produced new forms of communication, social intercourse and entertainment, reducing the significance of that provided by the family (Burch and Matthews, 1987). In addition, the late twentieth century saw the mass emergence and consolidation of a variety of new kin structures within many industrialized societies – reconstituted or recombinant step-families, ethnic minority families, single-parent families, cohabiting couples.

Second, the factors associated with demographic ageing – falling fertility and mortality and increased longevity – have also impacted upon wider society. The shift to a low mortality–low fertility society results in an increase in the number of living generations, and a decrease in the number of living relatives within these generations. Increased longevity may increase the duration spent in certain kinship roles, such as spouse, parent of non-dependent child, sibling. Marital unions, for example, have the potential to last far longer than historically has been the norm, and this has certainly placed strains on such relationships, contributing to marital breakup, divorce and the formation of complex reconstituted families. A decrease in fertility may reduce the duration of other roles, such as parent of dependent child, or even the opportunity for some roles, such as sibling.

Third, the knowledge of demographic ageing is in itself impacting on social, economic and political decisions and behaviours of both national and international institutions, and individuals themselves. So, for example, we are seeing the ageing of some life transitions, with contemporary ageing societies displaying an increase of age at first marriage, at leaving the parental home, at first childbirth. While public and legal institutions may be lowering the age threshold into full legal adulthood, individuals themselves are choosing to delay many of those transitions which demonstrate a commitment to full adulthood – full economic dependence from parents, formal adult union through marriage or committed long-term cohabitation and parenting. While the reduction in marriage and childbearing and the rapid increase in divorce are clearly related to the tremendous social changes of the last century, it can also be argued that because infant mortality has fallen, and because early death through disease, war, famine, and for women through reproduction is no longer the common experience, individuals feel more comfortable about establishing marital unions later in life, bearing children later and having fewer offspring. The ageing of family transitions in younger life leads to subsequent transition delay for both the individual and other kin members. For example, delayed birth of the first child may lead to long intergenerational spacings, and a transition to both parenthood and grandparenthood at a later age than has been the recent historical norm. Similarly, extended economic dependence on parents not only delays the individual's full transition to independent adulthood, but also the experience of the empty-nest syndrome for the parents themselves.

Family change

The late twentieth century saw the ageing of family life transitions (Harper, 2004a, 2004b). This can be described in terms of three interrelated sets

Table 16.1 Mean age of females at first marriage in the European Union, 1960–2000

	1960	1970	1980	1990	1995	2000[1]
Austria	24.0	22.9	23.2	24.9	26.1	27.2
Belgium	22.8	22.4	22.2	24.2	25.4	26.1
Denmark	22.8	22.8	24.6	27.6	29.0	29.5
Finland	23.8	23.3	24.3	26.0	27.0	28.0
France	23.0	22.6	23.0	25.6	26.9	27.8
Germany	23.5	22.5	22.9	25.2	26.4	27.2
Greece	25.1	24.0	23.3	24.8	25.6	26.6
Ireland	26.9	24.8	24.6	26.6	27.9	
Italy	24.8	23.9	23.8	25.5	26.6	
Luxembourg		22.8	23.0	25.3	26.6	27.1
Netherlands	24.2	22.9	23.2	25.9	27.1	27.8
Portugal	24.8	24.2	23.2	23.9	24.7	25.2
Spain			23.4	25.3	26.8	27.7
Sweden	24.0	23.9	26.0	27.5	28.7	30.2
United Kingdom	23.3	22.4	23.0	25.1	26.4	27.3

[1]For Belgium 1999, France 1999, Germany 1999, Greece 1999, Spain 1999, Ireland 1998, Italy 1999 and for the United Kingdom 1999

Source: Author's analysis of Council of Europe (2001)

of changes that appear to be altering the demographic foundations of family life: the delaying of key life events, the lengthening of life-stage durations, and the increased incidence of variations in family arrangements which this delay and lengthening of durations facilitate.

The delaying of key life events

There has been a consistent delay of age at first marriage or entry into a stable union across the EU (Table 16.1) and of age at the onset of child-bearing (Table 16.2). Alongside this, the age of full economic independence, and indeed residential independence from parents, has been rising. For example, between 1987 and 1996 there was an increase in every EU member state, with the exception of Denmark and the Netherlands, in those aged 20–29 years continuing to live with their parents. The most striking picture emerged from the Southern European countries, with a 50 per cent increase in this same period for those in their late 20s. In 1996, more than 80 per cent of Spanish, Portuguese and Italian men and women aged 20–24 years lived in the parental home, and over 50 per cent of 25–29-year-olds. A range of factors is associated with this delay in flying from the nest, including staying in education, financial uncertainty, peer example and, probably of most significance, delayed marriage.

Table 16.2 Mean age of women at birth of first child in the European Union, 1960–2000

	1960	1970[1]	1980[2]	1990	1995	2000[3]
Austria			24.3	25.0	25.6	26.3
Belgium	24.8	24.3	24.7	26.4		
Denmark	23.1	23.8	24.6	26.4	27.4	
Finland	24.7	24.4	25.6	26.5	27.2	27.4
France	24.8	24.4	25.0	27.0	28.1	28.7
Germany	25.0	24.0	25.0	26.6	27.5	28.0
Greece		24.5	24.1	25.5	26.6	27.3
Ireland		25.5	25.5	26.6	27.3	27.8
Italy	25.7	25.0	25.0	26.9	28.0	
Luxembourg					27.4	28.4
Netherlands	25.7	24.8	25.7	27.6	28.4	28.6
Portugal		24.0	24.9	25.8	26.4	
Spain		25.1	25.0	26.8	28.4	29.0
Sweden	25.5	25.9	25.3	26.3	27.2	27.9
United Kingdom				27.3	28.3	29.1

[1]Ireland and Spain 1975
[2]Austria 1985
[3]France, Germany, Greece and Spain 1999

Source: Author's analysis of Council of Europe (2001)

The lengthening of durations in life stages

The changes identified above also include a lengthening of various life stages. Marriages which are not cut short by divorce are likely to be longer than at any other historical time as a result of increasing life expectancy for both men and women. WHO data suggests, for example, that the great majority of those marriages not terminated by divorce now exceed 40 years. Similarly, despite the delaying of childbirth, increasing longevity is leading to an increase in the duration of relations between parents and adult children. Both these lengthening relationships – that of husband and wife and of child and parent – share similar features. As the common experience of parenthood moves to more than 50 years of shared life, parents and children are adjusting to spending most of their relationship as independent adults. Similarly husbands and wives are spending less of their joint lives as parents of young children. Clearly, the association between marital and parental roles will loosen. Relationships which have been historically based on a hierarchy which existed in part to support successful reproduction must move to greater equality, between both child and parent and husband and wife, as traditional roles based on parenthood give way to 'companionate' relationships. In addition, younger cohorts are now able to enjoy a lengthening of what Ryder

(1965) describes as the period of 'horizontal' freedom between the 'vertical' structure of the 'family of orientation', and vertical structure of the 'family of procreation'.

Interestingly, not only will parents and children spend longer in non-dependent relationships, but the time spent as a child with a dependent parent is also increasing. Within the US, for example, the time spent as the daughter of a parent over 65 now exceeds the time spent as the mother of a child under 18. This must, however, include the caveat that while for much of the last two centuries, a high proportion of those over 65 would be in varying degrees of dependency this is now no longer the case. Indeed, given that it is now not until after age 80 that the crucial stage for relying on children for assistance is reached (Uhlenburg, 1995), an age comparison of 80-plus with under-18 is more appropriate. Under these calculations, adult US women, for example, now spend more time *without* a dependent – albeit a dependent child or potentially dependent parent – than with one.

Changes in family structures

This demographic alteration of family life has led within many western societies to a trend towards the increasing verticalization of family structures (Bengtson, 2001; Hagestad, 1985, 1988; Harper, 2004a) so that most individuals will spend some time as part of a three- or four-generation family. These, however, will have increasingly fewer members, and longer gaps between the generations, and family members will spend longer occupying intergenerational family roles than before. In addition there will be a reduction of horizontal ties or intergenerational contraction, that is, a decrease in the number of members within each generation, and an increase in vertical ties or intergenerational extension, a rise in the number of living generations (Bengtson et al., 1990). However, while the number of living generations will increase, the absolute number of living relatives will decrease. Similarly the increasing delay of first childbirths highlighted above has the potential to create a family structure with long intergenerational spacings.

The impact of these changing family forms on kinship roles and relationships

The contemporary functions of these new demographically altered families may be seen as threefold: to provide mechanisms for intergenerational support, intergenerational solidarity and intergenerational transfers.

Families as mechanisms for intergenerational support

Despite the growth in modern dispersed living arrangements (Grundy, 1987; Grundy and Harrop, 1992; Mason, 1999; McGlone et al., 1996) and individualistic values (Scott, 1999), individuals remain committed to the reciprocal care and support of kin. Families, nuclear and extended, step and reconstituted, still provide the locus of reciprocal care, particularly when there are older adults among the kin network. With the increasing number and proportion of older adults within developed countries, this will increase in significance over the next few decades. Intergenerational transfer of care and services are age-related. The historically accepted picture was that while these generally flow from older to younger generations, they decline during the life course, and those from younger to older generations increase. From a peak of parent-to-child transfers when the parents are in their early 60s, and/or the children are young adults, this declines rapidly so that as the parent reaches the mid-70s child-to-parent transfers begin to dominate. However, we are now beginning to question whether there is sufficient recognition of the full extent of services provided by parents to their children, even in extreme old age. These reciprocal relationships are also dependent on the health and economic resources, commitments and life stage of the individuals, and increasingly on changing family structure and networks.

Families as mechanisms for intergenerational solidarity

Equally important issues are whether contemporary families are able to support the close micro-level intergenerational interaction needed for societies to age successfully, and the importance of understanding intergenerational relations and the family as a means of providing a vital link between the macro and micro experience of change within ageing societies. American research in this area has tended to view issues of solidarity and ambivalence within the context of family dynamics *per se* (Achenbaum, 1978, 1986; Bengtson et al., 2001a, 2001b; Luscher, 2000, 2002). In particular, such research has examined whether multigenerational families can replace maintenance and support roles presently carried out by nuclear families, affected as these are by high rates of divorce and marital breakdown. On the other hand, changes within the family must also be placed within the context of broader institutional developments (for example in the area of public policy) and the way these exert a direct influence on the experience of intergenerational relations (Harper, 2001).

The concern in the mid-1980s, particularly in the US, that demographic ageing, necessitating a considerable shift in resource allocation towards older people, would result in intergenerational age wars has not yet been justified. As Foner (2000) points out, younger cohorts have not risen up to protest against policies which benefit older adults, policies which may seem to operate against the interests of younger and mid-life people. First, younger people have a stake in protecting public programmes for older adults because these programmes relieve them of financial responsibility for the elderly people in their own families. Secondly, as Achenbaum (2004) has argued, younger adults wish to protect these programmes for their own old age.

However, as Harper (2001, 2005) points out, what may be of more significance is the relationship between the macro and micro experience of social relations. For while these public programmes operate at the national level, most people actually experience them at the individual, family or community level. Firsthand knowledge of people of other ages typically comes from local and family settings. Younger people thus do not experience older people as the other – an unknown group of strangers – but as their own kin: parents and step-parents, grandparents and step-grandparents, etc. In other words, within the family there is contact between and knowledge of those of other generations. In addition, most younger people see older members of their own families benefiting from macro-level policies even if they personally do not. Such affective intergenerational ties form important bondings between generations. Furthermore, younger people may receive direct or indirect benefits via their links into families; there is some element of intergenerational transmission within these macro-programmes. However, Harper (2001) argues that ageing societies benefit from strong kin interaction at the very time when intimate kin interactions are changing due to the pressures emanating from and associated with demographic ageing.

Families as mechanisms for intergenerational transfers

The study of intergenerational transfers has broadly fallen into two categories – the transmission of goods and services through, for example, bequests (Hurd, 1987, 1989), and the transmission of values (Bourdieu, 1996). Economists have suggested that bequests are either altruistic (Becker, 1981) or strategic (Bernheim et al., 1985), to induce desired behaviour from descendants through the promise of bequests. However, there is evidence from the Health and Retirement Survey that the bequest motive is stronger through the blood line than through the step-line, which clearly has implications for the new family forms which are emerging. Bourdieu's concept of intergenerational transmissions and cultural capital argues that the family is institutionalized through a variety of ritual and technical mechanisms aimed at creating a shared vision of family goals. During this process kin-based value systems are shared and transmitted from one generation to another. Again there is limited knowledge about how this varies between different generational patterns.

Conclusion

In his thesis on the emergence of the modern life cycle in Britain, the social historian Michael Anderson (1985) highlights a distinctive emerging modern life pattern for most in the late twentieth century which already included many of the factors we have been discussing: most will experience old age, most marry at least once, most will have children, most will have a married child by the time they are in their 50s, and most will have a grandchild before they are 60. However, we need to add to this the ageing of family life transitions which occur as individuals recognize the general lengthening of their own life spans and those of their peers. This thus turns the relationship between fertility and marriage around, and postulates that, for women in particular, ever-lengthening life spans have also allowed them the liberty to delay childbirth, and that the strong association which still remains between marriage and childbearing in most western societies is also contributing to a delay in first marriage. Similarly, marital unions now have the potential to last far longer than historically has been the norm, and this has certainly placed strains on such relationships, resulting in marital breakup, divorce and reconstituted families.

Early work on population ageing and the family focused on the implications of demographic predictions: in other words, increasing longevity equalled increasing numbers of older people requiring care. At the same time, declining fertility was perceived as shrinking the reservoir of family care for the old, and placing increasing pressures on the middle-aged coping both with dependent children and ageing parents. The complexity of the equation is now apparent, as is the recognition that the environments which were producing ageing societies were also producing new family situations, and that the demise or shrinking of the family was too general a concept. Rather, more heterogeneous family forms are emerging, developing their own sets of roles and relationships. Family roles and relationships are being influenced by demography but this must be also placed in the context of wider social and cultural change. There has always been considerable diversity in cultural obligations to family members; even within the same society, these family obligations will continually evolve and change over time.

171

Seventeen Flying Solo in Old Age: Widowed and Divorced Men and Women in Later Life

Kate Davidson

Widowed women are usually the first group considered in discussions of living alone in old age. They constitute the largest category in the population of single householders in later life. There are well-documented biological and cultural explanations for the predominance of female widowhood: men tend to have a shorter life expectancy than women and women tend to marry men who are older than themselves. However, widowhood is not the only reason for solo living – never married and divorced people are also likely to live alone. Indeed, there is also a small minority of married people who return to an empty house because their spouse has entered residential care. This chapter will examine 'flying solo' in a broad context by looking at gender and former marital status differences in social networks for older people. It will focus primarily on the experience of people who are widowed or divorced. The first step is to examine the demographic changes projected over the next two decades for these groups. Second, the experiences of the growing segment of divorced older people will be examined and compared to those of widowed people with particular reference to gender and social networks. The conclusion to the chapter speculates on how, as a result of societal changes brought about by shifting roles, relationships and family dynamics in the twenty-first century, succeeding generations might differently experience solo living.

Demographic shifts

Census data from 2001 reveal that more than half of women aged 75 and over live alone – 53 per cent of those aged 75–84 and 55 per cent of those

Table 17.1 Changes in marital status over time in England and Wales, 2001 and 2021, age 65 and over

	2001	2021	Change 2001–2021
Men			
Married	71	66	–5%
Widowed	17	13	–4%
Divorced	5	13	+8%
Never married	7	8	+1%
All	100%	100%	
N=	3.5m	4.8m	+49%
Women			
Married	40	45	+5%
Widowed	48	35	–13%
Divorced	6	14	+8%
Never married	6	5	–1%
All	100%	100%	
N=	4.8m	5.9m	+23%

Source: http://www.gad.gov.uk/news/marital_projections.htm

aged 85 and over. However, only 26 per cent of men aged 75–84 and 37 per cent of men aged 85 and over live alone (StatBase, 2002). Nevertheless, over one in three very old men living alone at the beginning of the twenty-first century represents a substantial increase on the one in four in 1975 (Davies et al., 1998). Among men currently aged 65 and over living in the community, 17 per cent are widowed, while only 7 per cent are never married and 5 per cent are divorced or separated (StatBase, 2002). By 2021, however, it is projected that the proportion of divorced men over 65 will increase rapidly to 13 per cent while the proportion who are widowed will fall to 13 per cent, and 8 per cent will be never married (Government Actuary's Department, 2001). Women over the age of 65 will similarly experience change in marital status (see Table 17.1).

Comparing 2021 and 2001, more women will be married (45 as opposed to 40 per cent) with a corresponding reduction in widowhood: from 48 to 35 per cent. The proportion of divorced older women is predicted to rise to 14 from 6 per cent, a percentage increase similar to that among men. Never-married status remains stable between the genders. However, what is of particular interest is the increase in men's longevity. In 2021 compared to 2001, almost half as many men again are predicted to survive beyond 65 years, whilst for women this increase is under a quarter. The most recent Continuous Mortality Investigation Report (CMIR 21) predicts that men may well outlive women by the end of this century (Ridsdale,

2004). Interpretation of extrapolating techniques for mortality can be somewhat contentious and should therefore be treated with caution. Nevertheless, if current trends continue, the mortality gap between the genders is likely to be substantially narrowed, even if there is no 'crossover' as predicted. There are therefore far-reaching implications for future generations of men who will be widowed or divorced as they age.

Widowhood in later life has stimulated considerable interest since the 1970s (Lopata, 1973) and, encouragingly, the lived experience of widowed men has been investigated more fully in recent decades (for example, Bennett et al., 2003; Campbell and Silverman, 1987; Davidson, 2002, 2004; Moore and Stratton, 2002; Riggs, 1997; Rubinstein, 1986; van den Hoonaard, 2002). However, as can be identified in Table 17.1, older people who are divorced and have not repartnered (through marriage or cohabitation) are projected to be a rapidly growing segment of the older population in the next decades. To date, little interest has been expressed in this 'rare' population because policy strategies have tended to focus on younger divorcees with reconstituted families and school-age children; court financial decisions tend to be based on child maintenance and marital home allocation and only recently on long-term pension provision for an estranged spouse. As a result, relatively little is known about divorced older people and their social networks and how these might alter in a society which no longer treats divorce with opprobrium.

Love, friendship and support systems

Marital status has been shown to be related to both emotional and social support for older people (Phillipson et al., 2001b). Victor et al. (2002) show that the loss of a spouse in later life is the single most important factor contributing to loneliness and aloneness. In a heterosexual, couple-oriented society, widowed and divorced people can no longer identify themselves as half a pair. It would seem that new partnership formation would help in ameliorating such loss of identity. However, men are much more likely than women to seek actively, and enter into, a new cross-gender relationship (Davidson, 2002; Haskey, 1982) with divorced men even more likely to desire a new partnership than widowed men (de Jong Gierveld, 2003). Interestingly, both marriage and, particularly, remarriage rates are showing a downward trend at all ages (Office of Population Censuses and Surveys, 2002) and it is unhelpful that statistical data on cohabitation combine all people over the age of 55. The apparent dramatic increase in the proportion of divorced older men and women, more than doubling between 2001 and 2021 (Table 17.1), can be partly explained by the increasing legal access and social acceptability of divorce, but also by the downward trend in remarriage rates. The fundamental need for companionship does not wane with age or generation, so we might speculate on alternative social interaction dynamics which have accompanied, and will be influenced by, demographic change.

A new trend in romantic relationships of older people has been identified: the 'living apart together', or LAT, relationship (de Jong Gierveld, 2003; Ghazanfareeon Karlsson and Borell, 2002; Victor et al., 2002). That is, the 'couple' maintain separate homes but visit each other, including overnight, socialize together, and carry out daily routine activities together such as shopping, cooking and eating as well as going on holidays together. In younger couples, this relationship is usually predicated on mate selection, one of the stages towards singling out a partner which usually leads to co-residence, whether marriage or cohabitation (Morgan, 1996). Levin and Trost (1999) report that LAT relationships are entered into by all adult age groups, but the older the individual, the more likely the relationship is to have been preceded by divorce or widowhood. They conclude that the primary reason for the increase in LAT relationships in Norway and Sweden is the virtual disappearance of the social institution of 'housewifery'. Women in particular choose to remain independent and in the labour market and do not wish to have the responsibility of 'keeping house' for anyone but themselves.

It is likely that LAT relationships will become increasingly common, as women may desire a new relationship but also wish to maintain their domestic and financial independence. Older cohorts (especially women) who were socialized into perceiving heterosexual marriage as the only appropriate locus for sexual activity (Gott and Hinchliff, 2003) may not have viewed LAT as an option. In other words, it was 'all or nothing', and as has been demonstrated widely in the literature on widowhood, however distressed and lonely they feel at the death of their spouse, widows are largely reluctant to relinquish the freedom of not having to 'look after' someone. Current societal changes in attitudes towards sexuality will certainly impact upon later generations and their notions of appropriate non-marital sexual behaviour.

Marital status and social networks

Older divorced men report smaller social networks than widowed men, usually as a result of attenuated relationships with adult children and other close family members, compounded by the likelihood that they will have moved from the vicinity of the marital home (Davidson et al., 2003). Perren et al. (2003) found that older divorced men were poorly represented in social organizations and consequently lacked the social interaction stimulated by such membership. As reported elsewhere, they have a higher mortality rate than married, widowed or never married men principally because they are more likely to indulge in risky health behaviours such as poor diet, lack of exercise, smoking and excess alcohol consumption (Davidson and Arber, 2003). With these complex dislocations in later life, older divorced men are likely to face a bleak future. So at a time when married men are living longer, healthier lives, it could be surmised that the growing number of divorcees will need to be targeted for health education and health-promoting strategies. Divorced women tend to keep ties with their adult children, normally stay in the marital home and, like the widowed women, are often supported by longstanding friends and neighbours.

Yet, there is no doubt that becoming 'single again' in later life can be a very negative experience regardless of gender or marital status. Widows and divorced women in particular have described difficulties in adapting to single life for several reasons: reduced financial circumstances, lack of private transport, and the feeling, as Lopata identified, of being a 'fifth wheel' at social gatherings (Lopata, 1979). These women have also seen themselves perceived by married women friends as a sexual threat or as easy sexual prey to married male friends, and this has caused a withdrawal from participating in couple-centred activities. This is primarily the view of younger widowed and divorced women and those without extensive kin and friendship networks, but older women can experience difficulties when they see their still-married friends (Lopata, 1996). Older 'single again' women often maintain their relationships with their married female friends but may renegotiate meeting times and places, for example, during the day and without the husband (Martin-Matthews, 1991).

It is interesting that widowers are more likely than widows to stay in contact with their married couple friends (Rubinstein, 1986), often because the wife of the couple was friendly with the widower's late wife. Because it is the wife of the couple who frequently extends the invitation, widowers are perceived as less of a sexual 'threat' than widowed or divorced women and are made more welcome (Lopata, 1979). Widowers are also more likely than widows to belong to mixed-sex social and sporting clubs and tend not to entertain in the home (Campbell and Silverman, 1987). Men lose the person they have relied on almost exclusively for emotional sustenance and 'gatekeeper' for the infrastructure of intimate friends.

Current older widowers and divorcees may not have acquired many domestic skills, but some widowed men will have had to take responsibility for the domestic labour before the death of their wife because of her illness. Food procurement and preparation tends not to be a big problem for widowers. Frequently, female neighbours, who are termed the 'hot pot brigade' (van den Hoonaard, 2002) cook meals for their widowed neighbour. Adult daughters may do 'batch cooking' for the freezer. Also, many men enjoy the challenge of cooking and learn these skills with great enjoyment and pride in their achievements. Some widowed and divorced men report eating out frequently, or eating principally convenience foods. It is generally the housework that the men dislike, but some are in a position to pay for someone to clean for them (Moore and Stratton, 2002), or again, daughters carry out a periodic 'spring clean'.

Nevertheless, most widows and divorcees live within social and cultural networks from which they receive substantial support (Jenkins, 2003). For both widows and widowers, although family relationships remain an important factor in their support networks, friends and neighbours provide the principal daily interaction. However, the interaction location is highly gendered, with widows more likely to entertain and visit friends in their home, widowers are more likely to meet in public places, such as clubs. Additionally, adult children may not always provide sustained support, after the initial period of mourning. In childhood, the adult children were dependent upon their mother and tended to be the focus of her attention, often to the exclusion of other interests, because she was fulfilling a role as nurturer and carer of her young. Ungerson (1983) found that when this role is reversed, problems may arise because the now-grown children often have families of their own, or are in employment, or may have organized their lives in such a way that an elderly widowed or divorced mother would be an intrusion. Older people themselves are anxious not to be seen as a burden – a perception emphasized by societal expectations and media portrayals of old people (Bytheway, 1995). Most older people want to stay living independently for as long as possible (Healy and Yarrow, 1997; Victor et al., 2002) and this can be achieved, often despite failing heath and sensory abilities, with the presence of friends, neighbours and wider kin networks (Twigg, 1998).

The literature indicates that the loss of a spouse is more likely in the short term to intensify and strengthen social relationships than to decrease them. Several studies reveal that a few years after the death of a spouse, there is an increase in participation in some types of relationships, such as those with friends and neighbours (Morgan, 1989). Most of the decreases in social interaction seem to occur five or more years after the death of a spouse, and this could be the result of any number of factors: economic deprivation, lack of mobility, general ill health. Improved mortality and morbidity rates will mean that these circumstances will be present at later stages in life, and for a shorter period.

Jerrome (1981) investigated the significance of friendship for older women, looking at how middle-class women organized social participation. She found that these women were active and resourceful in the pursuit of interests and pleasures, with or without others, inside or outside the domestic sphere. Only a minority complained of loneliness, and those generally were the very old widowed. Pellman (1992) compared still-married women with widows as to their integration in their community and the effect this had on social support and stress levels. She discovered that there was no significant difference because of marital status, but that age was the greater predictor of stress and loneliness as a result of lack of community integration. Many women have set up patterns of community involvement and multifaceted networks long before they are widowed. For widowed men, this networking may not be consolidated until after retirement, and so his age at the death of his wife, as well as length of residence, is an important factor in neighbourhood relationships. The trend to move out of the large family house into a smaller home, and to a lesser extent the trend to move abroad, may well have detrimental consequences for these older men (and women) for reliance on local support systems.

Conclusion

As identified earlier, by the middle of the twenty-first century, there will be significant population, marital and health-status changes which will result in more men living longer and potentially living alone in later life. The birth rate is falling, and it is predicted that more than a third of adult women will remain childless. If they do have a child, they are more likely to wait until their 30s and then when their children are having children in their 30s, they will be ageing grandparents and perhaps caring for very old parents. The imperative to work longer may hinder intergenerational relationships and so, when future generations become widowed or divorced, they may have even smaller kith and kin networks than current lone elders. However, this is not to say that there will be a substantial reduction in quality of life, or personal and emotional satisfaction.

The current cohort of 'ever married', that is, widowed and divorced older people, will have experienced more gender-segregated roles and responsibilities within marriage. Consequently, earlier literature on widowhood often engaged in the debate as to 'who fares worse': men, because of the loss of their caretaker and nurturer (Ferraro, 1984), or women because of their financially reduced circumstances (Lopata, 1979)? It can be argued that debate is less relevant for future cohorts. Rising generations of men are more likely to be competent domestically and to have had more emotionally based relationships with their friends, adult children and grandchildren. Women are more likely to have experienced longer-term full-time work, have had more control over their finances and be car owners and drivers. For an increasing number of people these altered life-course experiences will narrow the differential skill gap which for previous generations has hampered adjustment to solo living.

Although there is a downward trend in marriage and remarriage rates for men and women at all ages, this may be offset by an increase in cohabitation and LAT relationships. Within one generation, divorce has become more socially acceptable, as has pre-marital sex and cohabitation. It is possible, then, that 'flying solo' in later life may become a social norm, facilitated by better health, financial security and choice to live independently: a liberating rather than debilitating state. This speculation does not ignore the trauma of losing a spouse through death or divorce, rather it acknowledges the substantial social change that has occurred since the middle of the twentieth century.

Eighteen Housing and Future Living Arrangements

Sheila Peace

I've never given it very much thought. We are urban dwellers who like to have easy access to the centre of London through public transport and hope in retirement years to get to the museums and theatres far more than we have ever done. We are also owner-occupiers, who live in a three-bedroomed ground-floor flat as the children are still at home – we're late parents. It would be good to be able to put them up, so some extra rooms would be useful; also good for doing your own thing. We've talked about buying property in France but this would be a second home. We haven't moved house for fifteen years and that wasn't a change of location, we just went up the road. Sharing with non-family? I'm not sure. Obviously I've done that in the past as a student and a single person but at present I want to remain living in the home we've put together like everyone else, having privacy and control over my accommodation and managing for as long as I am able. I think I realize that I have to be used to change. I don't mind paying rent for my accommodation; it might be more sensible ... I also have diabetes and so may have health needs in the future but I don't see why that should make a difference to where I live. (Author's interview with 52-year-old woman)

Sixty, seventy, eighty years of age and more. Time passes and where and with whom we chose to live in later life will be influenced by our past and our present. Across these decades our housing history will evolve through the interplay of a myriad of factors: family history, gender, marital status, education, employment, financial resources, dependents, age of children, health and well-being, network of family and friends, location – the social capital that moulds our decisions. In looking to the future, we have to try to envision the environments in which present-day 45- to 65-year-olds will want to live in retirement and at the end of their lives. For many people this period of at least 30 years may involve several changes of location and/or accommodation; for others there may be no changes at all.

Current living arrangements

It is projected that by 2008 the number of people in the UK who are aged 65 years and over will exceed the number of children under 16 years for the first time, and by 2021 the average age of the population will have risen to 42 years from 37 years in 1998 (Shaw, 2000). Despite some peaks and troughs the ageing of the population that will become increasingly culturally diverse is well researched (Atkin, 1998; Glaser and Tomassini, 2002). In the latter part of the twentieth century a number of trends in living arrangements have emerged reflecting demographic change, marital status and the lifestyles of different age cohorts within a postmodern consumer driven western developed culture. For both young and older adults there has been an increase in the proportion living alone (Evandrou et al., 2001; Grundy, 1996), a trend that is expected to affect successive cohorts of older people (Evandrou and Falkingham, 2000). Living alone in later life is especially common amongst widowed and never-married women. At the same time, given the growth in the post-retirement population, coupledom is a common situation and an experience for most married older men. These situations reflect the decline in the number of people living with relatives, particularly children (Glaser and Tomassini, 2002). There is greater residential independence coupled with the importance of informal care, although it is also more common for the family to offer 'intimacy at a distance' (Grundy et al., 1999).

Given these changing circumstances where are older people living in terms of location and housing? Analysis of census data shows greater concentrations of people over pensionable age living in traditional retirement areas and rural areas than those below pensionable age. Yet while this pattern reflects generational changes in rural/urban living, there are also gender, cohort, cultural and ethnic differences, with more older women living in urban areas than older men, and greater congregations of minority ethnic groups within urban areas (Denham and White, 1998; Hall et al., 1999; www.statistics.gov.uk/CCI). In deprived urban areas, older people are beginning to be recognized as a central part of the community (Phillipson et al., 2001b; Scharf et al., 2004). In later life, migration and repeated relocation are not the concerns of a majority of the older population (Glaser and Tomassini, 2002; Warnes, 1996). The vast majority are community dwellers, living in 'ordinary' housing and many are long-term residents, often reporting high levels of housing satisfaction (Glaser et al., 1998; Warnes and Ford, 1995). If they do move, these are often relatively short distances and may be influenced by the location of family networks or relate to their own concerns regarding health and well-being.

Housing type, housing tenure, housing market

The vast majority of older people in the UK live in mainstream housing: all types of homes – detached houses, semi-detached houses, terraced houses, bungalows and a range of flats. High-rise flats (unless specialized) are not seen as the territory of older people; they are more likely to be found in bungalows and within the smaller number of detached houses than the wider population (Department of the Environment, Transport and the Regions, 1996; Kellaher, 2002). A minority also live in caravans or trailers and hotels. Different types of households exhibit a range of housing tenure: outright owner-occupiers, owner-occupiers with a mortgage, local authority tenants, private tenants and tenants of Registered Social Landlords. Currently around two-thirds of elderly households are owner-occupiers, of which nearly two-thirds own outright (Office for National Statistics, 2000). The remaining households are predominantly social-housing renters while a small number rent privately. This pattern reflects the influence of trends in housing provision and housing policy alongside a diversity of personal financial circumstances (Forrest and Leather, 1998; Peace and Holland, 2001).

In future years owner-occupation is expected to dominate the housing market, and there has been a recognition of the decline of social housing. Location and housing type have become vital to the vagaries of the housing market, which has seen house prices rise exponentially over the past decade. Whilst trends wax and wane, in January 2005 a report by the Halifax bank showed that 'the averaged-priced homes in 548 out of 597 main UK postal towns are now beyond the means of people on average salaries' (http://newsvote.bbc.co.uk/1/hi/uk_politics/4200123.stm). There is enormous regional variation, the highest prices being in the southeast of England. The most expensive area was said to be Gerrards Cross in Buckinghamshire whilst the most affordable town was Lochgelly in Fife. Comments from younger people gave a sense of some of the present housing issues with a bearing on the future:

> As a public-sector employee earning approx. £22,000 a year, I have very little opportunity to get on the property ladder. Private rented accommodation is in excess of £300 per month for a flat and the waiting lists for housing-association accommodation are huge. Council accommodation is non-existent. A rhetorical question, but can people who are just entering the market afford to put a roof over their heads? Mark from Staffordshire (BBC, 2005)

Whilst the older generation may not be struggling as first-time buyers, in later life the 'haves' and 'have nots' in terms of the ownership of housing can greatly influence housing history. The value of property has become a commodity that influences both family inheritance and how and where people live as they reach the end of their lives, affecting resources for specialized accommodation and care.

'Special' housing

Whilst mainstream housing in age-integrated communities is the way of living for most older people, over the last century public bodies in health, social services and housing have developed age-segregated housing (e.g. sheltered housing) and accommodation with care (e.g. residential care homes), originally offering facilities for either those living in social housing whose accommodation no longer suited their needs or for those whose health and well-being led to a need for greater personal and nursing support (Heywood et al., 2002; Peace et al., 1997). Today, the development of a mixed economy and increased privatization has led to a variety of providers: local authority, voluntary (not-for-profit) and private (for profit), with the private sector, increasingly through large companies, being the most common provider of care homes (Laing, 2004) (see Table 18.1). More than 18 per cent of older people over the age of 85 live in accommodation recorded as 'communal establishments' (www.statistics. gov.uk/cci/nugget_print.asp?ID = 876) and whilst the financing of all these forms of accommodation may be supported through state benefits, an assessment of the older person's financial resources will be taken into account including the sale of owner-occupied property (Heywood et al., 2002; Laing, 2004).

The term 'sheltered housing' encompasses a range of accommodation, although flats/bed-sitting rooms in collective settings are the most common. These facilities are managed by a housing manager, with each unit having emergency call systems enabling people to access support services (Heywood et al., 2002). As the physical design of these environments has developed, some accommodation has become 'hard to let' (Tinker et al., 1995) and more recently this housing model has been extended to 'extra-care housing' or 'very sheltered housing', living environments in which people with increasing levels of mental and physical frailty can maintain greater autonomy (Heywood et al., 2002; Oldman, 2000; Tinker et al., 1999). In terms of social policy, extra-care housing is seen as an alternative to care homes and dispersed homecare (Laing, 2005).

Table 18.1   Nursing, residential and long-stay hospital care of elderly and physically disabled people, places by sector, UK, 1970–2001

	Residential places			Nursing home places		(Long-stay geriatric places)
	Local Authority	Private	Voluntary	Private	Voluntary	
1970	108,700	23,700	40,100	20,300		52,000
1980	134,500	37,400	42,600	26,900		46,100
1985	137,100	85,300	45,100	38,000		46,300
1990	125,600	155,600	40,000	112,600	10,500	47,200
1995	79,700	169,300	56,700	193,400	17,900	33,000
2000	60,000	185,000	54,500	186,800	18,000	21,000
2001	57,400	185,100	55,100	178,800	18,000	19,700

Source: Adapted from Laing (2002: 173).

Consequently, these developments are happening in parallel to ongoing changes in the care-home sector, whose future will continue to be influenced by the decline in the provision of long-term geriatric hospital places. At present there are a range of care homes: residential, dual-registered and nursing homes (see Table 18.1). Throughout the twentieth century, recognition of institutionalization within residential living has led to calls for change (Centre for Policy on Ageing, 1984, 1996; National Institute for Social Work, 1988) and the regulation of these facilities has been based on improving the quality of living and dying for residents through person-centred care. However, while some care homes offer a positive life for some people (Mozley et al., 2004), the dependent status of extremely frail older people, many coping with cognitive failure, actively detracts from the creation of valued autonomous lives. Indeed, husbands and wives may live out their days in different places if their needs differ. The setting of national minimum standards for care homes has impacted on costs and charges, and this has been reflected in the changing number of care-home places and has no doubt influenced the decline in the number of residents in these homes over the past decade (Laing, 2004; www.statistics.gov.uk). The quality of end-of-life care still remains an area for increased investment and recognition.

Housing conditions

The condition and dimensions of all forms of housing impact upon lifestyle and well-being. Unsurprisingly, there are reports in the UK that dissatisfaction with the state of housing repair is seen to be more common amongst tenants, challenging the role of landlords, than amongst owner-occupiers (Peace and Holland, 2001). For older people the material environment can take on an added importance, as daily routines may become more confined within the home. A person's well-being may be affected in many ways, for example heating is an important factor and studies in the UK show that in mainstream housing a significant minority of older people do not have central heating or have difficulties meeting fuel expenses (Kellaher, 2002; Wright, 2004). This research points us to the deprivations experienced in some older people's housing. Yet at the other extreme we are conscious that many older people have a more comfortable lifestyle than any previous older generation. For example, they have become proficient users of technology and other ways of facilitating everyday living. The Technology for Living Forum survey shows that many older people are using and value a wide range of technology, e.g. microwave (84.2%), mobile telephone (38.8%), computer (35.2%) (Fisk, 2001: 117), which can be seen as a forerunner to using other forms of assistive technology.

Housing is the stage on which the interactions of every day are played, and Kellaher (2002) considers space as a major consideration when choosing housing, commenting that those with the greatest floor space per person are people who live alone and older owner-occupiers. This has led older households to be seen as 'under-occupied', a view often used when trying to encourage older people to 'free up' family housing. In recent research Hanson and colleagues (2001) have developed a classification of the housing of older people considering both architectural design and everyday living. Utilizing data from 60 older respondents, they are able to reveal not only that older people value their space but also that the more 'specialized' the type of accommodation, the less space is available for everyday activities, a change also reflected in the balance between public and private space (Kellaher, 2002; Willcocks et al., 1987). For example, as the lifestyle of the older person is increasingly supported by others, which may move from informal to formal types of care, the need for cooking, bathing and living space changes, affecting the 'privacy gradient' and the quality of life (see Twigg, 1999).

Views for the future

The discussion so far has outlined trends in housing and living arrangements, recognizing the interaction between aspects of environment that can be seen as material, social and psychological. At present many innovations offering a wider choice in later life are beginning to develop. In terms of the material environment, mention should be made of how architects and designers are seeking to make housing more accessible, visitable and assistive (Peace and Holland, 2001). The Joseph Rowntree Foundation initiative on 'Lifetime Homes' standards has promoted the introduction of a range of requirements (circulation spaces, wheelchair access, door widths, floor strength, window heights) that will all improve quality of life. These standards currently have a small cost premium but their integration into common UK standards is being sought (Hanson et al., 2001; Kelly, 2001). As noted above, middle-aged and older people are already using some forms of 'smart' technology; the question now becomes how soon might they use systems such as temperature monitoring, automatic lighting, property security, cooker safety, and window, blind or curtain control, developments already available but not as yet widespread (Fisk, 2001; Gann et al., 1999). Whilst these innovations enable the home to operate more efficiently, other aspects of 'smart' technology relate specifically to the needs of older people as their health becomes less robust. Older people with dementia may have difficulties with impaired memory, learning or reasoning, leading them to have to depend increasingly on their senses, whilst people with macular degeneration may loose confidence over everyday skills such as pouring a cup of tea. Assistive technology may offer memory joggers, lifestyle monitors and facilities which give people a feeling of independence and enhance their self image as a person with abilities (Judd et al., 1997; Marshall, 1997, 2001).

In terms of the social and psychological environments, research has shown how important many older people find their home environment as a place for meeting and remembering (Gurney and Means, 1993; Sixsmith et al., 2004). In recent research Peace et al. (2006) have considered how older people may constantly reengage with their environment both inside and outside the home, some reaching a point of 'option recognition' where moving may seem preferable to staying put, the place having outstayed its welcome. It is at this point that some people may think outside the boundaries of traditional ways of living. Some older people may have the opportunity and desire to take up residence within a 'granny flat', a separate, private part of their children's housing, offering a different level of interdependence. Other home owners may consider home-sharing, using an agency to offer accommodation to a younger person who will live in their homes and undertake a few tasks that are not seen as personal care (Maitland, 2004).

An alternative decision for homeowners may be to find a group of people with whom to share within a CoHousing scheme, combining their resources and developing their own collective housing. The idea had its roots in Denmark and developed in the Netherlands and the United States. Brenton (2001: 177) comments, 'The CoHousing Community should be seen as a cluster of friends and neighbours in their own homes, loosely associated with each other for a common purpose, rather than as a closed-in institution and in their respect it is a more inclusive model than that of sheltered housing.' (See also Brenton, 1998.) She describes the basic characteristics outlined by Fromm (1991) as:

- Common facilities

- Private dwelling

- Resident structures routines

- Resident management

- Design for social contact

- Resident participation in the development process

- Pragmatic social objectives

and she considers how this may be a particularly useful development to counter 'the growing isolation of single living, especially among older women' (Brenton, 2001: 179). Whilst participants are active members of these developments, an additional corporate response to collective living is the small number of retirement communities just beginning to emerge in the UK (Phillips et al., 2001; Rugg, 1999). Commonly private- or voluntary-sector developments, these communities are seen to offer both an improved physical environment with additional facilities enhancing activity and the maintenance of continuing care. We are yet to see the long-term experience of the balance between activity and frailty in such settings, but recent research highlights the centrality of this issue (Bernard et al., 2004).

These are all social models for ways of living in later life as yet to be fully developed. While social change may be the best way forward for some people, others comment on the importance of 'staying put', continuity in the meaning of home and attachment to their present housing, neighbourhood, town, nation. They see ageing in place as forming a part of 'self' which they do not want to change. Understanding the psychological impact of environment is therefore also essential when considering the future of housing and living arrangements in later life, underpinning the need for people to take time to reestablish patterns if moving.

Conclusion

The views outlined at the beginning of this chapter raise a number of issues that may affect those currently middle-aged: location, migration, attachment to place alongside family, health and ownership. How these are faced will vary. A majority will maintain their mainstream housing, whether as a couple or singly, whilst some will consider more social and extra-familial ways of living through intergenerational arrangements, shared living, seasonal migration to another country, or a hotel lifestyle. Finance will be central and owner-occupation will become a norm. Consequently, the effects of the housing market and its impact on location and relocation will be important. Consultation with an estate agent or housing manager will continue throughout life. However, do estate agents know about some of the issues discussed in this chapter, as people have a need for information about the combination of housing, health and social care? In 20 to 30 years' time, when viewing a property for sale it might be useful to know how others have adapted their housing to install a stair lift or introduce a walk-in shower, where extra-care housing might be sited, or where a home-sharing agency might operate. Will the provision of housing and accommodation and care be so privatized in the UK by this time that estate agents will make the answers to these questions their business? Can the estate agent become the 'one-stop shop'? If so, the balance between individualization and regulation will continue to take centre stage and the importance of housing as a commodity, in dividing the nation between 'haves' and 'have nots', will increase. Innovative social housing and the facility to move between owning and renting needs to lie alongside concerns over family inheritance through property ownership and the recognition that people may require long-term care at the end of life. Understanding the need for a holistic approach to housing, social care and health in later life is essential.

Part VII

Globalization and the Future of Old Age

Opportunities for a prosperous, respected and healthy old age need to be constructed not only at local and national levels but also on a global level. Understanding the future of old age requires an appreciation of the possibilities across the whole world and not merely for those of people in the developed west. One use of the term 'globalization' is to refer to the collective activities of all humans within one worldwide society. A different stance emphasizes the limitations to the role of the nation state and suggests that social change and specific supranational institutions are becoming much more significant to people's lives. Globalization is also frequently used as a gloss for modern multinational capitalism and as part of the critique of the distribution of social and economic inequality across the world. Carefully specified, terms such as 'supranational', 'transnational', 'international' and 'multinational', are frequently better employed than the generic 'globalization'.

There is a great expansion in the volume and diversity of international trade, together with an increasing international division of labour and incorporation of all areas of the world into a single network of trading relationships. New institutions including not only multinational companies but also financial and regulatory regimes, market and brokerage arrangements, as well as local adaptations to these new economic relationships, have developed, as have intergovernmental institutions of considerable influence, such as the United Nations, the World Bank, the Organization of Economic Co-operation and Development, and the G7. These changes have profound effects (both positive and negative) on the quality of life possible for older people, for example through their pension funds, their prospects for work and access to affordable healthcare (see Chapter 9 in this volume).

Technological change has not only fostered these new economic relationships directly, but it has also stimulated communications and the movement of people and ideas as well as goods. These effects are both beneficial and problematic for older people: modern communications spread the SARS virus, which killed vulnerable older people across the world, but it was a supranational institution, the WHO, which organized a containment programme and co-ordinated research which played a major role in combating the threatened epidemic.

We can email, fax and telephone around the world in seconds, journey between the world's major cities within hours, and increasing numbers of people have relocated themselves away from their place of origin in new homes in different cities and countries (Thompson, 2000). Through movement of people and ideas society is becoming more culturally diverse. The music, images and fashions of popular culture have a rapid global reach, such that people around the world are humming the same tunes or expressing outrage or compassion at the events in the lives of the same global celebrities. These trends can represent a challenge to the authority of tradition and the social status of elders, but cultural change can create new possibilities for diversity in old age.

At the same time, there are a series of crises that can be seen to threaten global society and create problems for older people. These include widening inequality, migration issues, and pressures on the environment. Globalization and poverty are interrelated. Access to work and employment that enables people to save or invest for their old age is disproportionately weighted towards people in the affluent West. Older people in the global South, on the other hand, may experience intense poverty and disease (Gorman, 1999; Randel et al., 1999). The first deaths in famine are found amongst the very young and the very old. Insofar as older people require care, there are three basic institutions which can supply financial security in old age: families, states and markets. Globalization is about the spread of markets and thus as market-based institutions become more important the role of states and families as effective sources of financial security diminishes. Globalization redistributes risks in new ways. The cohesion of national and local communities may be threatened and, along with this, their ability to provide welfare. Families disrupted by migration may be less able to provide personal care, although remittances to families 'back home' are a major source of income for many rural elderly people. Can we expect the spread of global markets to exacerbate inequalities in old age in the future?

There have been various demographic crises identified. Rapid growth in world population is identified as one such crisis to which an ageing population is a necessary antidote. Migration is sometimes identified as another. The redistribution of people around the world is a product of poverty and prosperity but is also profoundly influenced by war and famine and the dispersal of refugee populations. Migration has important outcomes for older people. Their children may be absent when the need for support in old age arises. They may have to find a dignified old age away from their native community and the status and relationships found in their home locality. Migration can also be an opportunity for some people to obtain jobs, and migration of young people can slow the ageing of local populations of rich nations.

The world is also seen to be under threat from a variety of human-induced changes to the global environment. Older people on the whole tend to be more vulnerable to such changes insofar as they have fewer resources to deal with them. Scientific knowledge to inform responses to these environmental problems tends to be created in institutions in the developed world. The effective demand for scientific, technical and medical knowledge to manage old age comes from the developed world, and the scientific research effort into 'anti-ageing medicine' is concentrated in the West. Research laboratories in the US and elsewhere research the possibility of extending the human life span, whereas known health technologies that extend human life expectancy remain unobtainable to many old people in the developing world. The future impact of biomedical science and genetic research on ageing needs to be understood, as do the social mechanisms which distribute the cost and benefits of technical manipulation of the ageing process across the world.

191

Nineteen   Anti-ageing Science and the Future of Old Age

John Vincent

Globalization can be seen as a cultural phenomenon: the worldwide spread of ideas, ways of thinking, meaning-systems and symbolic frameworks. The most powerful cultural tools that dominate the way the world understands itself are those of western science (Handlin, 1965). This system of knowledge production, including such institutional features as universities, professional associations, laboratories and academic journals, and such theoretical frameworks as hypothetical deductive reasoning and the logic of experimentation, is worldwide in reach. In parallel to the idea of science, western medicine has also become a global institution. There are other cultural forms of medicine, but the most powerful and the most universal is that derived from medical traditions in Europe, Britain and the United States that legitimize their knowledge by reference to science. The recent history of old age in the west has been one of medicalization (cf. Achenbaum, 1978; Bauman, 1992; Cole, 1992; Estes, 1979; Estes et al., 1984, 2003). This model of ageing sees it as a biological phenomenon of the body and classifies it as something akin to a disease, susceptible to scientific analysis and thus technical control (Katz, 1996; van Tassel and Stearns, 1986). This model has also come to dominate the way in which ageing is conceptualized across the world. What effects of this way of thinking can be discerned for the future of old age?

Knowledge of the fundamental biology of ageing in all living creatures and human beings in particular is making rapid gains (Bloom, 1999; Bramstedt, 2001; Butler et al., 2004; Halliwell and Wong, 2004; Holliday, 2000, 2001; Kirkwood, 1999; *Scientific American*, 2004; Turner, 2004;

Vogel, 1999). Technical control of many features of our bodies, from grey hair and wrinkles to susceptibility to Alzheimer's disease, has been claimed as possible now or in the near future. What social direction will the scientific endeavour follow – will it aim for the perfection of the human body and eradication of the imperfect? If the avoidance of disease becomes a technical possibility, will this return illness again to the category of moral failure on the part of those that let it happen to themselves (or others)? Science is the dominant knowledge system in our globalized world and the meaning of old age constructed in this way will have a profound effect on the long-term future of old age. Will science extend old age, for how long and with what effect? Could ageing be halted or reversed? Is an anti-ageing science to be welcomed?

What do we mean by ageing?

We can distinguish social from biological ageing. Social ageing can be seen as having two elements: first, the life course as a sequence of stages and age statuses to which, secondly, specific age-based normative expectations are attached. The normative expectations of 'old age' as a life stage may change, weaken or strengthen across cultures and through time (Amoss and Harrell, 1981; Holmes and Holmes, 1995; Keith, 1994; Thane, 2000). Social ageing can also be understood in terms of intergenerational relationships. Generations can be understood as birth cohorts, or as familial relationships. New cohorts of older people may be less passive and more independent than their predecessors – an issue examined in Part I of this book. Family relationships will also change, an issue examined in Part VI of this book. Thus 'anti-ageing' can be understood in social terms as the rejection of the normative expectations placed by society on people in the later stages of life. Social movements such as that of the 'third age' seek to challenge such expectations and alter popular understanding of the sequences of life. Scientists' activities are also influenced by these cultural values.

Biological ageing refers to a standard pattern of physiological change over time. In some species, particularly those that reproduce by asexual means of cell division, it is quite difficult to specify what ageing might mean. For humans:

> Caleb Finch offers a good overall definition: 'A nondescript colloquialism that can mean any change over time, whether during development, young adult life, or senescence. Aging changes may be good (acquisition of wisdom); of no consequence to vitality or mortality risk (male pattern baldness); or

adverse (arteriosclerosis).' Unfortunately most studies concentrate on the failures and unpleasant features of ageing. They focus on the processes by which fit people in the 'prime of life' lose vitality and become increasingly vulnerable to illness and death. (International Longevity Center – USA, 2001: v)

Culturally we are very familiar with the bodily identifiers of old age: grey hair, wrinkles, changes in posture, loss of hearing, eyesight and mental acuity. The problem, over and above the key issue of defining someone's humanity by his or her visual appearance, is that these phenomena do not standardize into predictable chronological age with a high degree of accuracy. It is possible for archaeologists to estimate ages for burials in the early years when the sequence of human maturation is reasonably clear from dental and skeletal remains. With the remains of older people, the process is much harder and requires, amongst other things, an understanding of the lifestyle and social conditions of the person whose remains are being studied (Chamberlain, 1994; Mayes, 2000).

What biological features might be chosen to classify people into age groups – to define the 'old' and the 'young'? In America considerable scientific endeavour has gone into finding 'biomarkers' for ageing in mice. Ten years of research funded by the American National Institute on Aging, costing 20 million dollars, has not delivered the desired result:

The fact is, we do not have biomarkers that accurately predict life span in any creatures ... What we would like to find are measures of different biological systems whereby measuring these changes and the rates of change in these systems with age, we can get an idea of the underlying processes and mechanisms that are aging, and get an idea to simplify things – whether your aging clock is running faster or slower. We could use that to not so much predict life span, although that would be the first step, but to actually evaluate treatments that are supposed to do something about aging – either retard the rate of aging, or possibly even reverse it for some types of systems ... We haven't been successful in that, but it's a big order and it is a serious question as to whether we will be successful in it. (Morton Krondracke, Sage Crossroads webcast, www.sagecrossroads.net/public/webcasts/09/index.cfm)

Health, age and disease

Population ageing is worldwide and is largely due to declining fertility rates. Population is also ageing due to a decline in mortality rates – people on average live longer. However, it is life-expectancy gains for babies and young children that is principally behind the rise in life expectancy of the world's population. Scientific knowledge and technical expertise exist to control human fertility and virtually to eliminate child deaths due to infection. The most efficient way to extend human life expectancy with currently available technology would be to devote resources to reducing infant mortality in the developing world. This of course would do nothing for the human life span. However, the scientific study of longevity within biology and medicine tends to be concentrated on the prolongation of life in old age. 'Anti-ageing' from a biological perspective is the means to extend the life span of a species (Olshansky and Carnes, 2001).

Risk factors, the chances of incurring a particular disease, are distributed by age but they are influenced by a wide range of other factors. For example, conditions of the joints, such as arthritis, are age-related but they are also influenced by social and environmental factors such as occupation and housing conditions. Are these phenomena merely unfortunate byproducts of ageing, or are they an intrinsic part of ageing itself? Leading commentators suggest that is not currently reliably possible to separate features related to the genome, individual lifestyles, the impact of the social and natural environment and other idiosyncratic features of personal history from the universal features of human ageing. As a result there are severe problems in understanding human longevity in terms of what is meant by a natural life span. How long it is possible to live a reasonable healthy life without loss of important biological functions is the subject of intense debate. The key questions are: what is disease and what is 'natural' ageing, and to what extent is it possible or sensible to distinguish between them (Kirkwood, 2004; Sage Crossroads, 2004)?

Understanding and control of disease will enable clinicians to develop interventions that extend human life expectancy, but will such disease control extend the human life span? Without a scientific consensus on biomarkers of age it will be very difficult to prove claims to retard or reverse ageing. Biological ageing is being understood with greater precision and degree of control (Robert, 2004). Key areas where knowledge has advanced are in the attempt to identify the genetic basis ageing (but there is no single gene for ageing), understanding of metabolism and oxidation damage (e.g. by free radicals), advances in immunology and cell regulation, cell replication and calorie restriction (Rattan, 2004). Scientific knowledge is contested and there is no single dominant theory of ageing and indeed no consensus on where to look for such a theory (Vaupel et al., 2004).

Many people understand their own ageing in terms of bodily decrements. A colleague argued for anti-ageing medicine, saying 'I must admit I'd far rather not have to wear reading glasses and worry about a dodgy knee myself, and would rather prefer my body as it was ten or twenty years ago.' Of course everyone would rather be healthy than sick, but the healthy/ill contrast is not the same as the young/old distinction (Raikhel, 2000). Would you also want to be in the position of having the knowledge, or lack of it, you had 20 years ago (or have you learned nothing of value in the last 20 years?), and would you want to have missed out on the last 20 years of developing relationships – with lovers, children and friends? These benefits are also aspects of ageing. The critical question is whether you want to be so 'healthy' that you live forever (or even 150 years). Future transplants or stem cell technology might cure knees and eyes, but that won't do much for your individual longevity. These days most gerontologists, whether biologists, medics or social scientists, tend to define their objectives in terms of 'health span', that is to say, the number of illness-free years of life. The widespread consensus among professionals that gerontology is about improving health in old age nevertheless leaves serious unresolved questions about extending life for its own sake (Gems, 2003; Kass, 1971; Mackey, 2003; Moody, 2002; Vincent, 2003a).

What do we mean by anti-ageing medicine?

In recent years the belief in the potential for science and medicine to halt or reverse ageing has seen the rise of 'anti-ageing medicine' (Binstock, 2003, 2004; Gammack and Morley, 2004; Juengst et al., 2003a, 2003b; Millar, 2002; Olshansky et al., 2002, 2004). This term refers to attempts to change the ageing process by intervention based on biological and medical science (Hayflick, 2004; Vincent, 2003b). These attempts can be classified into four types.

Symptom alleviation

These are attempts to hide, postpone or relieve the effects of biological ageing and are not necessarily either modern of scientific in origin but are frequently presented as such. They can be divided into three subcategories: (i) cosmetic – powder and paint or anti-wrinkle cream to disguise the signs of ageing; (ii) prophylactic – exercise and diet to stave off the onset of physical ageing and its signs; and (iii) compensatory – Viagra and HRT, designed to reinvigorate 'failing' functions to a youthful standard. These symptom-alleviation strategies have to be understood in the context of a society that has come to understand body image as the key component of personal identity (Faircloth, 2003; Shilling, 1993; Turner, 1984). New techniques to alleviate the symptoms of ageing are subject to enormous commercialization (Hensley, 2002; Mehlman et al., 2004).

Short-term life extension

Many commentators believe that an increase in life expectancy of approximately three to six years can be achieved relatively soon, by treating or eliminating the diseases which are the proximate causes of death in old age, in particular cancer and heart and lung disease. Some progress is being made in these fields, resulting in recent increases in life expectancy in later life. The main gains in life expectancy made in the twentieth century and across the world are in decreasing infant mortality and infectious disease, particularly through public health measures. Some gains in late life expectancy have been made in recent years through lifestyle change, particularly through stopping smoking, eating a good diet and exercising. However, some authorities argue that only relatively limited gains to life expectancy (3–6 years to the mid-80s in the UK and other developed countries) would be made even if all cancer and all heart disease are eliminated. This is because people will die of something else or of 'old age' within a relatively short period even if they escape cancer or heart disease (cf. Hayflick, 2004).

Long-term life extension

This category covers research and intervention designed to increase longevity by between 20 and 60 years. To achieve these gains in longevity requires an increase in the life span which can be achieved only by fundamentally changing the ageing process itself. Genetic manipulation or chemical interventions, perhaps to increase the duration and efficiency of cell maintenance mechanisms, might increase life span by this amount. The use of stem cells to replace senescent organs is another candidate for such life-span-changing technology. The understanding of the genetics and biochemistry of cellular ageing has progressed to the point where the age span of mice and other creatures can be manipulated. This is not currently a possibility for humans, but is frequently predicted and assumed by many to be a feasible, if not readily achievable, goal (*The Gerontologist*, 2002).

Eliminating ageing (immortality)

This is not a new objective; it has been the implicit goal of post-Enlightenment science and its attempts to perfect humans through progress. It is subject not only to biological speculation but also to philosophical and cultural debate. Scientists with serious academic credentials consider it to be within the bounds of technical possibility in the near future, although understandably they have been met with great scepticism (Benecke, 2002; de Grey, 2003; de Grey et al., 2002; Fukuyama, 2002; Shostak, 2002).

We can speculate on what might happen if any of these enterprises are successful. What would happen if everyone could look younger? Would this reinforce the cult of youth? Or would it merely set in train new methods of differentiation based on bodily appearance, in particular distinctions based on generation and fashion? One might anticipate comments by the cognoscenti – 'Your body is so 1990 – full of piercings', or perhaps 'Large breasts came back in by 2030 only to be passé by 2040.' The existing multimillion-dollar industry in such products would in this view expand still further – and develop more specialist niche markets, e.g. repairing the damage caused by cosmetic surgery. Postmodern trendspotters stress that increasing diversity and thus increasing diversity of appearance within chronological age groups might reasonably be anticipated. In future will you be less able to judge people's ages? Or, will there be a cultural reaction, a rejection of artificiality, a reversal of symbols, a claim to liberation by the assertion that grey is beautiful – 'Wear your wrinkles with pride'? To liberate old age status, reaffirming strategies of other devalued identities could be followed – 'Black is beautiful, grey is great'. If fat is a feminist issue, is it also an ageist one (Friedan, 1993)? There already exist small groups who proclaim themselves 'raging grannies', or 'wrinklies', examples of 'feisty' old (usually) women who use their appearance to challenge political and cultural attitudes (Great Old Broads, 2005; Martyn and Goodridge, 2001; Raging Grannies of Seattle, 2003).

What would happen if cancer and heart disease were eliminated? If high-tech, heroic surgery, transplants and expensive drug regimes could remove these causes of death, who would benefit? It would depend on the structure of healthcare and medicine – access to the technologies would determine the nature of an individual's old age. In global terms, current patterns suggest the world's poor in Africa and Asia are unlikely to have access to such longevity. If healthier lifestyles could prevent such deaths and the constraints were knowledge rather than resources, would we all then die of old age? Or how else would we die? If simple preventative measures and lifestyle changes could ensure a healthy longevity, this would remove many of the anxieties of ageing and increase the sense of personal control and individual responsibility for ageing.

What would happen if we could slow down cellular ageing? Would this lead to a fitter and healthier old age? This would also depend on the technology and the social control of the technology. Would this new longevity be concentrated in a few highly affluent areas of the West? If it were, it would likely have to be serviced by the mortal labour of 'others' from less advantaged sectors of the world community. If the elixir of life turned out to be a cheap once-a-day pill which altered the ageing consequences of metabolism (Lane et al., 2002), this might be widely available but give enormous power to those holding the patent or otherwise able to control the science (Rose, 1997).

In the past, death could come at any age; only in the modern world have death and age been so tightly linked. Will anti-ageing procedures separate them again? Immortality, as currently discussed by biologists usually depends on genetic modification of humans and thus is not within the one generation time span around which this volume is framed. Human genetic modification, even with the necessary knowledge and technical ability, would need several generations to make a significant impact on human longevity. Most thought experiments with immortality portray it as a dystopia (Kirkwood, 1999, 2004). It is seen as a technological nightmare (pollution, poverty or pain from unanticipated effects), an aesthetic desert (nothing new or valuable) or a spiritual void (being against nature or God) (Williams, 1973). If the solution to ageing is seen as the battle to conquer nature, then old age remains a cultural desert. Death is always the consequence and always viewed as a failure.

Conclusion: utopian visions?

Globalization will impact on old age over the next 30 years through the domination of a medical model of ageing. It will affect the social distribution of good health. Who in the world will be able to access healthy lifestyles and good healthcare and thus a reasonable old age? In turn an ageing population will impact on the global environment. On spaceship

Earth, we share a single environment in which one person's pollution, climate-changing activities and resource depletion know no boundaries and affect everyone. Hence, it is impossible to conceive of a habitable world in which population keeps growing indefinitely – unlimited life extension would impact on the environment and arguably make the world uninhabitable.

Twenty   Ageing and Globalization

Chris Phillipson

What are the challenges raised by the combination of globalization and population ageing? The theme of globalization became highly influential in the social sciences during the 1990s, notably in sociology and political science (Held et al., 1999) and subsequently in social policy (George and Wilding, 2002) and social gerontology (Estes and Phillipson, 2002; Estes et al., 2003; Vincent, 2003a). Globalization is now seen as an influential force in the construction of old age, most notably in the framing of social and economic policies designed to manage and regulate population ageing. Research on ageing can no longer be confined to local or national cultures, as it is shaped by a transnational context, with international organizations (such as the World Bank and International Monetary Fund) and cross-border migrations creating new conditions and environments for older people.

This chapter explores the implications of globalization for theorizing about the nature of growing old in the twenty-first century. Globalization confirms the importance of locating individuals within social and economic structures, these being increasingly subject to forces outside of the nation state. However, it is also linked to the abandonment of those routines and institutions established in what is referred to as 'the first phase of modernity'. Giddens (1991) and Beck (1992) argued that we are now living in a 'post-traditional society', where in comparison with the past there is greater emphasis on developing new lifestyles and making fresh choices about the conduct of daily life.

Defining globalization

In this chapter the term 'globalization' is taken to refer to those mechanisms, actors and institutions which link together individuals and groups across different nation states. David Held et al. (1999: 49) identify globalization in the following terms:

> Far from this being a world of 'discrete civilisations' or simply an international order of states, it has become a fundamentally interconnected global order, marked by intense patterns of exchange as well as by clear patterns of power, hierarchy and unevenness.

Globalization brings forth a new set of actors and institutions influencing public policy for old age. For example, the increasing power of global finance and private transnational bodies raises significant issues about the nature of citizenship, and associated rights to health and social care, in old age. In the period of welfare-state construction, rights were defined and negotiated through various manifestations of nation-state-based social policy. Globalization, however, transfers citizenship issues to a transnational stage, this driven by a combination of the power of inter-governmental structures, the influence of multinational corporations, and the pressures of population movement and migration.

Drawing on the work of Bauman (2000) and Beck (1992), it might also be argued that rights, in the period of late modernity, have become more fragmented as well as individualized. At one level, the risks associated with ageing are relatively unchanged – the threat of poverty, the need for long-term care, the likelihood of serious illness. What has changed, as Bauman (2000) argues in a more general context, is that the duty and the necessity to cope with these have been transferred to individual families (women carers in particular) and individual older people (notably in respect of financing for old age). The new social construction (and contradiction) of ageing is, on the one hand, the focus upon growing old as a global problem and issue and on the other hand, the individualization of the various risks attached to the life course. The tension between these different elements is likely to set the broad parameters around which the future of old age is constructed.

The impact of globalization

Three aspects of globalization have particular relevance for their likely effect on older people: first, its influence on the ideological terrain around which ageing is constructed; second, its identification of ageing as a new form of 'risk'; and third, its role in creating new structures through which ageing is controlled and managed.

The impact of globalization on ideologies relating to ageing has been a highly significant development. A key aspect of this has been the move from debates that focused on ageing as a burden for national economies to perspectives that view population ageing as a worldwide social problem. The report of the World Bank (1994), *Averting the Old Age Crisis*, was a crucial document in this regard, but more recent contributions have included those from the Central Intelligence Agency (CIA, 2001) and documents such as *The Global Retirement Crisis*, produced by the Washington-based Center for Strategic and International Studies (Jackson, 2002). There is insufficient space in this chapter to deal with the particular arguments raised by these papers (see, however, the discussions in Blackburn, 2002; Stiglitz, 2002, 2003; Vincent, 2003a) but the general point raised concerns what amounts to a politicization of ageing generated by the intensification of global ties.

The above development has arisen from at least three factors. First, the growth of neoliberalism is one obvious dimension, propagating hostility towards collective provision by the state or at the very least a view that private provision is inherently superior to that provided by the public sector (Walker and Deacon, 2003; Yeates, 2001). Second, politicization has also arisen from the way in which globalization fosters awareness about the relative economic position of one nation state compared with another. George and Wilding (2002: 58) make the point that 'globalization has created an economic and political climate in which national states become more conscious of the taxes they levy and their potential economic implications. Neoliberal ideology feeds and justifies these concerns.' Third, the ideological debate has been promoted through key supranational bodies such as the OECD, the WTO, the World Bank, and the IMF, along with transnational corporations (notably pharmaceutical companies) all of which contribute to a distinctive world view about the framing of policies for old age.

Globalization has also played an influential role in the production of new forms of risk associated with the privatization of social policy. On the one hand, growing older seems to have become *more* secure, with longer life expectancy, rising levels of economic well-being (Disney and Whitehouse, 2002) and enhanced lifestyles in old age. Set against this, the pressures associated with the *achievement* of security are themselves generating fresh anxieties among older as well as younger people. Risks once carried by social institutions have now been displaced onto the shoulders of individuals and/or their families (Bauman, 2000; O'Rand, 2000). Dannefer (2003b: 270) summarizes this process in the following way:

> ... corporate and state uncertainties are transferred to citizens - protecting large institutions while exposing individuals to possible catastrophe in the domains of health care and personal finances, justified to the public by the claim that the pensioner can do better on his or her own, and that Social Security can do better diversified into equity markets.

More generally, Stiglitz (2003) argues that risk has been turned into 'a way of life' through a combination of changes in the labour market (with the erosion of jobs for life) and reliance on private pension arrangements, which are subject to the volatility of the global stock market (see Chapter 9 in this volume).

Finally, globalization – through both the spread of worldwide communications and the power of global organizations – has elevated ageing to an issue that transcends individual societies or states. Gerontology, for much of the twentieth century, was preoccupied with issues affecting older people in advanced capitalist societies (Dannefer, 2003b). Indeed, disengagement theory and modernization theory took the view that the western model of ageing would ultimately be diffused across all cultures of the world (Fennell et al., 1988). Globalization has provided a fundamental challenge to vestiges of this approach. Global interests may indeed continue to be subject to US hegemony and/or western imperialism in various guises, but globalization also illustrates the emergence of new social and political forms at international, national, regional and local levels (Held and McGrew, 2002). Cerny and Evans (2004: 63) make this point in the following way:

> The central paradox of globalization, the displacement of a crucial range of economic, social and political activities from the national arena to a cross-cutting global/transnational/domestic structured field of action, is that rather than creating one economy or one polity, it also divides, fragments and polarizes. Convergence and divergence are two sides of the same process. Globalization remains a discourse of contestation that reflects national and regional antagonisms and struggles.

Globalization and the future of ageing

How will globalization influence the future lives of older people? The broad area of pensions for older people is clearly one major area, highlighted in this volume in Part III and discussed extensively elsewhere by Blackburn (2002), Estes and Phillipson (2002) and Vincent (2003a). But three additional areas of change can be identified from current thinking in this area: first, the impact of globalization on issues of governance and citizenship; second, the likely emergence of a new 'global geography of the life course'; and third, the role of migration and transnational communities.

The first issue to be addressed concerns that of global governance and its impact on ageing. This issue is complex. On the one side, the negative effects are well-known: corporations that appear to trample over the rights and needs of individuals and communities; intergovernmental organizations (IGOs) that put debt repayment before maintaining or improving schemes of social protection; and forms of crisis construction that emphasize the costs associated with issues such as ageing populations. Yet contrary trends may also be identified. Deacon (2000: 13), for example, notes what appears to be the emergence of a 'new politics of global social responsibility'. He writes:

> Orthodox economic liberalism and inhumane structural adjustment appear to be giving way to a concern on the part of the [World Bank] and the IMF with the social consequences of globalization. International development assistance is concerned to focus on social development. United Nations agencies are increasingly troubled by the negative social consequences of globalization ... [there is a shift] away from a politics of liberalism to a global politics of social concern.

At the same time, the ability of corporations or other organizations to evade their responsibilities may be constrained by different forms of transnational governance. In the European context, avoidance by successive UK governments of age-discrimination legislation has been challenged by a European Union directive outlawing discrimination in the workplace on grounds of age, race, disability or sexual orientation. Similarly, national legislation, following the European Convention on Human Rights has the potential to be used to challenge age discrimination in areas such as service provision and employment, as well as fundamental issues relating to the right to life, the right not to be subject to inhumane treatment, and the right to a fair hearing. Both examples illustrate the way in which international law may be used to challenge discrimination against the old. They further illustrate the need for new approaches to theorizing about age that can integrate the continuing power and influence of the nation state with the countervailing powers of global institutions (Phillipson, 2002).

The second area reflects the transformation of the life course which has emerged as a byproduct of globalization (Dannefer, 2003b). For much of its history, social gerontology – at least in its focus on older people in western societies – was built around the idea of the progressive emergence of an orderly life course developed through phases of education, work and retirement (Riley and Riley, 1994). Globalization, however, poses a challenge to this notion of a 'normal biography' constructed around a linear model of the life course. The causal elements here include: the impact of de-traditionalization; the increase in the magnitude and intensity of risks through the life course; the collapse of lifetime jobs, hastened by the globalization of finance and the mobility of capital (Beck, 2000); and increased rates of human migration (albeit only a return to the levels of population movement characteristic of the late nineteenth century).

The challenge for studies in ageing lies in acknowledging the way in which the life course may, as a result of the above processes, assume a 'non-linear' shape, with features of so-called 'normal ageing' occurring earlier or later in life depending upon a particular sequence of biographical events (Hoerder, 2001). By extension, an additional issue concerns greater variability in respect of images and definitions of ageing. In the context of accelerated movement of populations, interlaced with powerful global networks, ideas about the meaning of old age, when old age begins, and normative behaviours for later life, will almost certainly demonstrate greater variation within any one society than has historically been the case.

The future of ageing will also be determined through the influence of transnational communities, and the role of migration in reshaping nation states (Winder, 2004). In this context, if what might be called 'the first phase of ageing' (which lasted for much of the twentieth century) was about growing old as a reinforcement of national identity and citizenship, the second phase will involve to a much greater extent the development of 'hybrid identities'. Growing old in the first phase – or ageing in the twentieth century – was partly a celebration of community, or of lives lived within particular communities with unique histories (Phillipson, 2002). In the second phase, however, which we have now entered, belonging and identity is becoming detached from particular places. Ulrich Beck (2000: 169) argues, 'People are expected to live their lives with the most diverse and contradictory transnational and personal identities and risks.' And Martin Albrow (1996: 151) makes the point that '[u]nder globalized conditions it becomes less easy for individuals to affirm their identity within the strict confines of nation, gender, age or any other categorical distinctions'.

Clearly, there will be losers and winners in this process, but the increasing importance of migration and mobility is raising substantial questions for gerontological research in a global context. A world of greater mobility will in the long term bring a number of benefits associated with cultural diversity. But in the short term an increase in racism and associated forms of oppression also seems evident and may well create further divisions within the population of older people. This appears especially evident in hard-pressed inner city areas where pressures on resources and services may produce conflict between the white population and minority ethnic groups (Scharf et al., 2002).

Finally, transnational communities bring major issues for social policy, with the development of groups mutually sharing care tasks or financial responsibilities that may be strung across continents. Moreover, the experience of migration – with people in middle and older age settling into new cultures or bearing the strain of moving from one culture to another – raises questions about the adequacy of support in areas such as housing, income and social services. On the one hand, migrant groups bring new forms of social capital to hard-pressed urban areas (indeed they may be said to revitalize such communities in significant respects). On the other hand, they may represent a significant challenge for traditional models of delivering health and social care (Phillipson et al., 2001a). A successful response to the latter will require a more sensitive understanding of the distinctive histories of particular ethnic minority groups, as well as improved mechanisms for incorporating their views on ways of improving the delivery of community care services (Phillipson and Scharf, 2004). A critical task over the next decade will be to respond to the diversity of care needs among the multicultural and multiethnic populations generated by the social dynamics of globalization (Urry, 2000).

Conclusion

The types of changes globalization will bring to the lives of older people are easy to predict in some respects, much less clear in others. Older people will certainly be living in a culturally and socially diverse world, increasingly aware not only of the ageing of their own society but the impact of growing old on different communities across the globe. An additional change will be the growing impact of supranational bodies in determining policies for older people: progressively more people will find crucial aspects of their daily lives influenced by intergovernmental organizations of different kinds. A major concern must be the extent to which older people are themselves active within movements that challenge the power of multinational corporations (Klein, 2000). Struggles over low pay, decent living standards and human rights affect all age groups and need to be fully incorporated into pensioners' movements within and across nation states.

Globalization – as one constituent of the 'risk society' – will generate new forms of insecurity, of which anxieties and fears about ageing may represent a significant dimension. But other aspects are less easy to predict: will a new cohort of older people (e.g. the postwar baby-boom generation) give a different voice and meaning to the nature of growing old? If they do, to what extent will this be determined by social networks that embrace global as well as national contexts? To what extent will globalization undermine the social, economic and cultural threads (tenuous at best given the role of class, gender and ethnicity) linking together people identified only through biological age? Globalization has certainly transformed the world, but it is changing growing old as well – and in equally radical ways.

Twenty-one   The Future Life Course, Migration and Old Age

Tony Warnes

This final chapter attempts to envisage the most likely changes over the next three decades in the final stages of the life course, as will be lived by the majority of people in the world's most affluent countries. The account is primarily an exercise in extrapolation, and the intention is to synthesize and reflect upon long-term societal and experiential change, partly to inform research priorities (though not to produce forecasts with operational utility). The second aim is to show that migrations (within and between countries) are simultaneously a response to and symptom of the changing life course, and important modifiers of the consequences for society and for the lives of older people. In one sense, migrations are the visible and traceable indicators of 'expressed' residential preferences and strategies; they reflect both people's aspirations and the ability to achieve them, and therefore manifest the population's changing social and material resources, activities and roles at different stages of life. The great diversity of migrations is also an indicator of differentials and inequalities in society.

Long-term change in the life course

Thinkers and writers in all literate societies have made generalizations about the 'stages of life', from infancy to the decrepitude that some suffer in advanced old age. Until the later twentieth century, these representations had the character more of religious tracts or imaginative literature than of scientific or evidence-based writing, and most were framed around metaphors of the 'journey of life' and its states, change or metamorphosis (Cole and Winkler, 1994; Eastman, 1996). They featured development and decline and thus physical states and capacities, with a secondary interest in the subjective or experienced life course; or with behaviour, its motivations and psychological states.

The life course became prominent in both family sociology and developmental psychology during the 1960s (Neugarten and Datan, 1973). It 'provided a way of examining the interrelationship between individual development and the family's development as a collective unit ... under changing historical and social contexts .... Unlike the [concepts of the] individual "life cycle" and the "family cycle", the life course paradigm ... emphasizes the timing by which individuals make their transitions into and out of various roles and development tasks in relation to "social time clocks"' (Hareven, 1996: 31).

Life course approaches in sociology focus on the socially-constructed roles and positions of people at different ages, both within families and in relation to society. It is these, rather than the individual's physical or mental states, that have been transformed by urbanization, industrialization and postmodernization processes (Thomas, 1972). To exemplify, infancy is a physiological constant, but 'childhood' was the product of late industrialism, as the period of life during which a person is socialized, educated and trained for later economic roles. Similarly, old-age frailty, while modifiable, is in the end inescapable, but mass 'retirement', when paid work ceases and people are supported by savings, pensions and the productive efforts of younger people, was created by state social protection (Clark and Spengler, 1980; Macnicol, 1998; Townsend, 1981; Vincent, 1999).

Put most simply, contemporary highly developed or postmodern societies display three successive life course stages, characterized successively by socialization, economic and family production, and retirement. For ease of reference, some apply the terms 'the first, second and third ages' of the contemporary life course (for the adoption of the schema, see Laslett, 1987, 1989 and Midwinter, 2005). The transformation of the typical life course since the 1870s (at about which time the compulsory elementary education of pre-teen children became widespread in western Europe) has been radical, intricate and pervasive – the last because many of the changes have been the product of either massive declines in fertility and mortality, or enforced by statutes and public funding, neither of which many in the population could resist. The main features of the changed life course are familiar to social gerontologists, including the spread of early-retirement since the 1960s (Kohli et al., 1991), but less widely appreciated are the massive transformations in the chronology of the changes and the growing differentiation of the first and third stages.

To pursue this point, it is useful to examine in more detail the changed durations and activities of the life course over the last 150 years. While a full exposition would require extensive references to demographic,

209

social and economic history, the main features have been summarized in Figure 21.1. This represents five situations that can be placed both in a chronology for the most developed countries, say in Europe or North America, and in a global framework of the level of economic development. The topmost diagram represents the life course as experienced by the majority of men and women in mid-nineteenth-century Europe. Average life expectancy at birth was little more than 40 years (as in the poorest countries today). This low figure was and is strongly influenced by the very high rate of infant mortality: in the worst industrial cities during the 1840s, as many as 25 per cent of all infants died in the first year of life.

Infectious diseases, malnutrition and industrial accidents contributed to mortality at all adult ages, and few survived beyond 70 years of age. Compulsory schooling had not been introduced, and most children contributed to household production, farm or factory work from a very young age (commonly 8 to 12 years). Only the children of the most affluent received school education or experienced a modern childhood. Nor had pensions been introduced, except for senior government, army and naval officers. Modern retirement for the majority did not exist, and the life course was dominated by the 'second age'. These conditions broadly continue in the least developed countries of the contemporary world.

The second diagram represents the situation in Europe during the 1930s. By then, longevity had increased substantially, compulsory elementary education was widespread, and retirement-pensions had been introduced, although by no means universally. Many other details can be interpreted from this diagram and from those for later years. The underlying trend was for the duration of the first and third ages to increase, and for the second age to contract. By the late twentieth century, the occupational structure had lost most unskilled manual jobs (although routine and personal, service occupations were still numerous). To equip the population for the more demanding and skilled occupations, not only had secondary education become universal, but also a majority of young people entered college-based further education or vocational training. The period of 'socialization' had extended, for most, to 18 years of age, and for many for several years more. The overall effect of 150 years of economic and social development has been to transform the life course, once dominated for men by paid work and, for women, by child-rearing and domestic and paid work, into a much more clearly staged and appreciably less gender-differentiated progression.

The final, lowest diagram is a speculative attempt to represent the life-course stages in the most developed countries three decades from now. Most observers would agree that the period of education and training will continue to increase, into the mid-20s for more and more young

Figure 21.1 The changing life course in Britain, 1850s–2030s

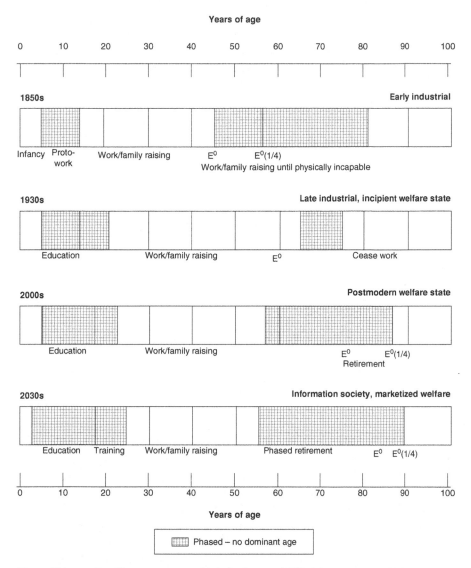

Notes: E⁰ is average life expectancy at birth (both sexes). E⁰(¼) is the age to which one quarter of the birth cohort is expected to survive. E⁰ in England and Wales in 1930–32 was 58.7 years for men and 62.9 years for women. In 2000–02 the comparable figures were 78.7 and 83.3 years. By 2001, one quarter of males in that year's birth cohort would attain 85 years, and one quarter of females would attain 89 years. The Government Actuary's 2003-base projections forecast a male E⁰ of 81.3 years in 2035 and a female E⁰ of 85.3 years: see http://www.gad.gov.uk/

people (although life-long retraining and learning will also become more extensive) (Evandrou, 1997). There is, however, considerable uncertainty about the future relative durations of the second and third ages. On the one hand, governments are increasingly persuaded that early retirement should be suppressed and replaced by phased withdrawal from the labour force; on the other hand, most waged and salaried workers continue to prefer early retirement if their retirement income prospects are thought satisfactory. Only the self-employed show a strong inclination to continue paid work through their 60s and beyond, and although the shift from routine to managerial and developmental occupations has established the conditions for the growth of 'locum' and 'consultancy' employment, as yet there is scant evidence of the trend.

The consequences for old age of the succession of life course stages

As longevity and the duration of retirement have increased in the most developed societies, so the accumulation of material and social resources during working age has increasingly conditioned quality of life in old age. The concept of 'human capital' has recently mainly been applied to the skills, knowledge, assets and contacts that a young adult acquires from their upbringing and education, and which condition their competition for employment and status through early- and mid-adult life. It is, however, readily adaptable to the circumstances of a person on the threshold of old age or retirement, and usefully illuminates the long-term or old-age consequences of the earlier life course. Figure 21.2 encapsulates the general principle, that the accumulation (or lack of it) through the successive life stages of savings, assets, social contacts and entitlements conditions a person's material, social and instrumental support resources in old age.

During the last few years, analyses of 'human capital' have mainly been by labour and health economists, and only two concerned specifically with the 'older' population are known, one on the (in)portability of acquired entitlement and knowledge resources (Friedberg, 2000), the other on attitudes towards education and acquiring new credentials among employed people aged 50 or more years (Simpson et al., 2002). 'Human capital' should be distinguished from 'social capital', which has recently attracted much attention from communitarian theorists, politicians and public-health analysts as a factor in community cohesion and health (Haezewindt, 2003). The interest in variations in social capital applies more to neighbourhoods and local areas than to individuals.

Figure 21.2   The accumulation of human capital through the life course

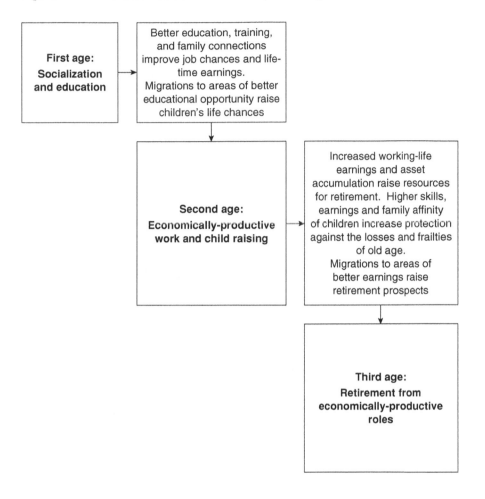

Many components of comparative advantage or of accumulated human capital at the two major life transitions, from the first to the second ages, and from the second to the third, are the same. Assets and income condition the material standard of life at all life stages, but both *a priori* reasoning and observation suggest that other dimensions of human capital have markedly different weights at the two transitions. Social networks (or 'who you know') are less likely to influence the quality of life in retirement than occupational positioning and progress, while health, wealth and current and deferred income (or pension) endowments are considerably more variable among those in the seventh and later decades of life than among those aged in their 20s.

Life-course stages, 'optimal' residential locations and migration

There is an intrinsic relationship between the staging of the life course and residential moves or migration. In most contemporary societies, people are most likely to move when they cease being dependent on their parents and establish their own households and sexual unions and have children. There are, in addition, many secondary stimuli of residential mobility or migration, particularly in more affluent countries, such as the birth of a (or another) child, career promotions and increased income, retirement, bereavement of a spouse, the onset of a limiting illness, and an adult child's domestic crises and personal reverses (Warnes, 1983, 1992). The general connection is readily understood. In the language of micro-economic science, the optimal locations for each stage of life are not the same, e.g. the world or country regions that maximize job and earnings opportunities differ from those that maximize the material standard of living and quality of life in retirement (largely because of the high costs and poor like-for-like value of housing in the former). As individuals and households progress from one stage to the next, their 'residential location requirements' change, and the transitions stimulate many to migrate.

The connection was recognized by the pioneering British student of (internal) migration, E. G. Ravenstein (1885), when he found that young adults predominated among migrants and inferred the dominance of the economic motive with the statement, 'they move to improve themselves in material respects'. While he noted differences in migration propensities between men and women, he made no comment about the age at which migration takes place or about 'life-cycle' influences. The pioneer study of rural–urban migration in industrializing Britain confirmed the dominance of very young adults in the flows (Redford, 1926).

More subtle connections between life-course stages and migration arise because the calculation of where it is best to live is not simply for one day or the next month, but to a greater or lesser extent a prospective assessment (Figure 21.2). Migrants are of course concerned with their short-term earnings and standard of living, but they are also motivated by the prospects in the years to come for themselves and, among many, for their wives, partners and dependants. It is not rare for the decision to move to be influenced by the children's opportunities, even beyond the parents' lifetimes. Evidently not all migrations succeed in raising life chances or human capital; indeed, the chances of a single migration making a radical change in a person's life chances are probably quite small. Some migrants fail in even their immediate goals, say to find a well-paid job or a high-quality residential setting for retirement, and

214

therefore reverse their decision and return. Others realize (or knew all along) that the migration entails losses as well as gains. Many distance themselves from close relatives and friends; many go to countries in which they cannot speak the language or have little knowledge of the local job and housing markets or of social and health services; and many become aliens, with fewer rights and entitlements than citizens, and subject to discrimination, exploitation, exclusion and abuse.

Variations in the resources that a migrant has accumulated arise in several ways. Aspects of a person's migration and family histories, particularly the ages at which they moved and took up permanent residence, and where they married and had children, influence the locations of and the relationships with their close and extended kin – and therefore the availability of both routine and 'crisis' informal social and instrumental support. Then, the migrant's personal history interacts with the national policy towards immigrants to determine their state welfare entitlements, as to pensions, income benefits, health and personal social services, and social or subsidized housing and long-term care.

As in the general population, a migrant's educational and occupational backgrounds correlate with their lifetime earnings and income and assets in old age. Their socioeconomic background also strongly influences the migrant's knowledge of the host country's welfare institutions and their ability to make use of the available services, especially through their language skills. These capacities are modified by information received from their relatives and friends, and by whether the migrant can turn to a community association for advice. Access to, and the utilization of, services is also strongly influenced by the receptiveness of the country's housing, health and personal social services agencies and their staff to foreigners and cultural minorities. In short, for young economic or labour migrants, and for retirement-amenity seeking older migrants too, there are complex relationships between their migration history, current social position, national policies, and their access to social security and housing entitlements and to informal and formal care (Warnes, 2004; Warnes et al., 2004).

Multiple affiliations and residences

The radical improvements in international transport and travel in recent decades, combined with the spread of high incomes and wealth, have recently introduced another complication in the relationships between the life course, migration and the circumstances of old-age lives – and not only for the most affluent. There are multiplying reports from northern

European countries, specifically The Netherlands, Belgium, Norway, Sweden and Switzerland (Ahmadi and Tornstam, 1996; Bolzman et al., 2004; Hoeksma, 2004; Lie, 2002; Torres, 2004), that long-term international labour migrants who reach retirement have maintained and established links and residences (or residential opportunities) in both their adopted and their origin countries – and some in third countries too. This has been shown by Poulain and Perrin (2002: 79, Figure 3.6) from Belgium's continuous-registration data. Many Turks migrate to and from Belgium at all ages, with the inward and the departure flows both showing the 'adolescent' and 'retirement' transition peaks. Many other long-term labour migrants in retirement 'shuttle' at least once a year between the two countries. They have inherited from their distinctive life course the exceptional 'capital' for old age of access to both Turkey's low living costs and Belgium's superior health and social services. Maintaining dual residences (with the help of relatives and friends) enables the group to maximize their social and family contacts and quality of life. Such transnational residential patterns are replicated by an increasing number of affluent northern Europeans who acquire second homes in, and retire to, southern European countries (Huber and O'Reilly, 2004; King et al., 2000).

Conclusion

On a global scale, large differentials in levels of development and economic opportunities associate with the forms and durations of the life course. International migrants who move from the least-developed to the most-developed world regions not only move (by definition) between countries and levels of economic development, but also into socio-demographic and welfare environments that are quite different from those they leave. The long-term consequences for their social position and welfare are profound. Similarly, affluent retirement migrants who move to another country or continent simultaneously extend and compromise their 'capital' resources for later life. The migrant's achievement is not only to accumulate material advantages, but also to create residential opportunities and actual and latent sources of formal and informal support, and all strongly condition the quality of the successive stages of their later lives.

What are the implications for future gerontological research of setting migration decisions in a life-course framework? One is that migration must be conceived not as a single relocation decision by an individual at a moment in time, for this neglects important aspects of the formative and decision-making processes, and pays scant attention to the outcomes and consequences in both the short and long terms. Migrations and later life need to be understood in their household, family and temporal contexts. As the main life-course stages have elaborated, and particularly the period of retirement has extended, a post-adolescent migrant's calculus must increasingly be influenced by his or her prospects and opportunities, not only during the second age but also through the third. We need a deeper ethnography of migration decision-making, with studies that consider the influence and interest of the closest relatives of the migrant cross-sectionally and in the future. Moreover, migration policies will increasingly need to be informed not only by the labour market and economic growth implications for the attraction country, but also by considerations of the extent to which the social welfare and quality of the life of the migrants when they reach the third age are protected and raised to the national norms.

It may be that the sharpest differentiation of the first, second and third ages was during the third quarter of the twentieth century, and that the little variation then in the chronological ages of the stage transitions is already breaking down. If so, people's life courses have and will become more variable, and a more overt symptom and cause of inequalities (and be more difficult to research). Contrary to the media image of low-skilled, poorly-educated migrant workers, migrations have timelessly been selective of the better-educated and more enterprising. Both occupational success and a supportive family network would normally be markers of a good outcome of a migration; the combined effect will be to compound the successful migrant's relative advantages.

The recent spread of owning multiple homes and of transnational residential patterns manifests not only increased affluence and the revolution in transport technology, but also rising inequalities on the regional, national, continental and global scales. From a north-Atlantic political perspective, it appears most likely that a person's 'welfare' and 'quality of life' in old age will increasingly reflect their individual life course and their achieved material, knowledge, social and entitlement resources. The complement is that an older person's welfare situation will be less and less a function of the welfare regime in their country or countries of residence. Over the next three decades, if we are to understand the material, social and welfare circumstances of older people, it will increasingly be necessary to have knowledge of their biographies or individual life courses, for neither their country of residence nor their birth dates or last occupation will be as reliable predictors of their social and experiential positions as they were in the recent past.

217

References

AARP (American Association of Retired Persons) (2002) 'Census 2000 Number and Percentage Change since 1990. Children under 18 Living in Grandparent-headed Households', Washington DC: AARP Grandparent Information Center, retrieved March 2002 from: www.aarp.org/confacts/grandparents/grandfacts.html.

AARP (2004) *Baby Boomers Envision Retirement II*, Washington DC: Knowledge Management.

Abramson, A. and Silverstein, M. (2004) *Images of Aging in America: Report of Findings*, Washington DC: AARP and the University of Southern California.

Achenbaum, W. A. (1978) *Old Age in a New Land: The American Experience since 1790*, London: Johns Hopkins University Press.

Achenbaum, W. A. (1986) *Social Security: Visions and Revisions,* Cambridge: Cambridge University Press.

Achenbaum, W. A. (2004) 'One Happy Family? Sources of Intergenerational Solidarity and Tension as Contemporary US Society Ages', in S. Harper (ed.), *Families in Ageing Societies: A Multi-Disciplinary Approach,* pp. 53–63, Oxford: Oxford University Press.

Acheson, D. (1998) *Inequalities in Health*, London: The Stationery Office.

Adams, T. L. and Clarke, C. L. (1999) *Dementia Care: Developing Partnerships in Practice*, Bailliere Tindall in association with the Royal College of Nursing.

Agulnik, P. and Le Grand, J. (1998) 'Tax Relief and Partnership Pensions', *Fiscal Studies* 19: 403–28.

Ahmadi, F. and Tornstam, L. (1996) 'The Old Flying Dutchmen: Shuttling Immigrants with Double Assets', *Journal of Aging and Identity* 1 (3): 191–210.

Albrecht, G. L. and Devlieger, P. J. (1999) 'The Disability Paradox: High Quality of Life Against All the Odds', *Social Science and Medicine* 48: 977–88.

Albrow, M. (1996) *The Global Age,* Cambridge: Polity Press.

Alwin, D. F. and McCammon, R. J. (2003) 'Generations, Cohorts, and Social Change', in J. T. Mortimer and M. J. Shanahan (eds) *Handbook of the Life Course*, New York: Kluwer Academic/Plenum.

Alzheimer's Association (2005) *Position Statements*, www.alz.org/AboutUs/PositionStatements/overview/asp, accessed 31 March 2005.

Amoss, P. T. and Harrell, S. (eds) (1981) *Other Ways of Growing Old : Anthropological Perspectives,* Stanford, CA : Stanford University Press.

Anderson, M. (1985) 'The Emergence of the Modern Life Cycle in Britain', *Social History* 10 (1): 69–87.

Anderson, R. and Bury, M. (1988) *Living with Chronic Illness: The Experience of Patients and their Families*, London: Unwin Hyman Ltd.

Arber, S. and Cooper, H. (1999) 'Gender Differences in Health in Later Life: A New Paradox?', *Social Science and Medicine* 48: 61–76.

Arber, S. and Evandrou, M. (eds) (1993) *Ageing, Independence and the Life Course*, London: Jessica Kingsley Publishers.

Arber, S. and Ginn, J. (1991a) *Gender and Later Life: a Sociological Analysis of Resources and Constraints*, London: Sage.

Arber, S. and Ginn, J. (1991b) 'Gender, Class and Income Inequalities in Later Life', *British Journal of Sociology* 42: 369–96.

Arber, S. and Ginn, J. (1993) 'Class, Caring and the Life Course', in S. Arber and M. Evandrou (eds) *Ageing, Independence and the Life Course*, London: Jessica Kingsley Publishers.

Arber, S. and Ginn, J. (1998) 'Health and Illness in Later Life', in D. Field and S. Taylor (eds) *Sociological Perspectives on Health, Illness and Health Care*, Oxford: Blackwell Science.

Arber, S. and Ginn, J. (2004) 'Ageing and Gender: Diversity and Change', in C. Summerfield and P. Baab (eds) *Social Trends 2004 Edition, No. 34*, Office for National Statistics, London: The Stationery Office.

Arber, S. and Thomas, H. (2001) 'From Women's Health to a Gender Analysis of Health', in W. C. Cockerham (ed.), *The Blackwell Companion to Medical Sociology*, Oxford: Blackwell.

Arber, S., Price, D., Davidson, K. and Perren, K. (2003) 'Re-examining Gender and Marital Status: Material Well-being and Social Involvement', in S. Arber, K. Davidson and J. Ginn (eds) *Gender and Ageing: Changing Roles and Relationships*, Maidenhead: Open University Press.

Arrondel, L. and Masson, A. (1999) 'Intergenerational Transfers: The State, the Market and the Family', *Futuribles* 247 (Nov): 5–40.

Atkin, K. (1998) 'Ageing in a Multi-racial Britain: Demography, Policy and Practice', in M. Bernard and J. Phillips (eds) *The Social Policy of Old Age*, London: Centre for Policy on Ageing.

Atkinson, A. (2004) 'Social Security in a Long Life Society', *Ageing Horizons* 1.

Attias-Donfut, C. (2000) 'Cultural and Economic Transfers between Generations: One Aspect of Age Integration', *The Gerontologist* 40: 270–2.

Attias-Donfut, C. (2003) 'Family Transfers and Cultural Transmissions between Three Generations in France', in V. L. Bengtson and A. Lowenstein (eds) *Global Aging and Challenges to Families*, New York: Aldine de Gruyter.

Audit Commission (2000) *Forget Me Not: Mental Health Services for Older People*, London: Audit Commission www.audit-commission.gov.uk

Audit Commission (2002) *Forget Me Not 2002: Developing Mental Health Services for Older People*. London: Audit Commission, www.audit-commission.gov.uk.

Baars, J., Dannefer, D., Phillipson, C. and Walker, A. (eds) (2006) *Aging, Globalisation and Inequality: The New Critical Gerontology*, Amityville, NY: Baywood.

Bajekal, M., Blane, D., Grewal, I., Karlsen, S. and Nazroo, J. (2004) 'Ethnic Differences in Influences on Quality of Life at Older Ages: A Quantitative Analysis', *Ageing and Society* 24: 709–28.

Balchin, S. and Shah, P. (eds) (2004), *The Pensioners' Incomes Series 2002/3*, DWP London: The Stationery Office.

Bales, K. (2000) *Disposable People: New Slavery in the Global Economy*, Berkeley: University of California Press.

Ballard, C. (2000) 'Criteria for the Diagnosis of Dementia' in J. O'Brien, D. Ames and A. Burns (eds) *Dementia*, London: Arnold.

Ballard, C., Fossey, J., Chithramohan, R., Howard, R., Burns, A., Thompson, P., Tadros, G. and Fairbairn, A. (2001) 'Quality of Care in Private Sector and NHS Facilities for People with Dementia: Cross Sectional Survey', *British Medical Journal* 323: 426–7.

Baltes, P. and Smith, J. (2002) 'New Frontiers in the Future of Aging: From Successful Aging of the Young Old to the Dilemmas of the Fourth Age', retrieved 5 July 2004, from the Valencia Forum website: www.valencia forum.com/Keynotes/pb.html

Bardasi, E. and Jenkins, S. (2002) *Income in Later Life: Work History Matters*, Bristol: The Policy Press.

Barot, R. (ed.) (1996) *The Racism Problematic: Contemporary Sociological Debates on Race and Ethnicity*, Lewiston: The Edwin Mellen Press.

Barr, N. (1998) *The Economics of the Welfare State*, Oxford: Oxford University Press.

Bauman, Z. (1992) *Mortality, Immortality and Other Life Strategies*, Cambridge: Polity Press.

Bauman, Z. (1998) *Work, Consumerism and the New Poor*, Buckingham: Open University Press.

Bauman, Z. (2000) *Liquid Modernity*, Cambridge: Polity Press.

Bauman, Z. (2003) *Liquid Love*, Cambridge: Polity Press.

BBC (British Broadcasting Corporation) (2005) 'Are you priced out of the housing market?', online discussion, http://news.bbc.co.uk/1/hi/talking_pointh/4197581.stm 26 January 2005.

Beck, C., Ortigara, A., Mercer, S. and Shue, V. (1999) 'Enabling and Empowering Certified Nursing Assistants for Quality Dementia Care', *International Journal of Geriatric Psychiatry* 14: 197–211.

Beck, U. (1992) *The Risk Society*, London: Sage Books.

Beck, U. (2000) *The Brave New World of Work*, Cambridge: Polity Press.

Becker, G. S. (1981) *A Treatise on the Family*, Cambridge, MA: Harvard University Press.

Bender, M. and Wainwright, T. (2004) 'So Sad to See Good Care Go Bad—But is it Surprising?', *Journal of Dementia Care* 12 (5): 27–9.

Benecke, M. (2002) *The Dream of Eternal Life: Biomedicine, Aging, and Immortality*, trans. Rachel Rubenstein, New York: Columbia University Press.

Bengtson, V. L. (1993) 'Is the "Contract across Generations" Changing? Effects of Population Aging on Obligations and Expectations across Age Groups', in V. L. Bengtson and W. A. Achenbaum (eds) *The Changing Contract across Generations*, New York: Aldine de Gruyter.

Bengtson, V. L. (2001) 'Beyond the Nuclear Family: The Increasing Importance of Multi-generational Bonds', *Journal of Marriage and the Family,* 63: 1–16.

Bengtson, V. L. and Harootyan, R. A. (1994) *Intergenerational Linkages: Hidden Connections in American Society*, New York: Springer Publishing Company.

Bengtson, V. L., Rosenthal, C. and Burton, L. (1990) 'Families and Aging: Diversity and Heterogeneity', in R. H. Binstock and L. K. George (eds) *Handbook of Aging and the Social Sciences,* 3rd edn, pp. 263–87, San Diego: Academic Press.

Bengtson, V. L., Marti, G. and Roberts, R. E. L. (1991) 'Age Groups Relations: Generational Equity and Inequity', in K. Pillemer and K. McCartney (eds) *Parent-child Relations across the Lifespan*, Hillsdale, NJ: Lawrence Erlbaum Associates.

Bengtson, V. L., Rosenthal, C. J. and Burton, L. M. (1996) 'Paradoxes of Families and Aging', in R. H. Binstock and L. K. George (eds) *Handbook of Aging and the Social Sciences,* 4th edn, San Diego: Academic Press.

Bengtson, V. L., Mabry, J. B. and Schmeeckle, M. (2001a) 'Intergenerational Relations', in G. L. Maddox (ed.), *The Encyclopedia of Aging,* 3rd edn, New York: Springer.

Bengtson, V. L., Silverstein, M., Giarrusso, R. and Schmeeckle, M. (2001b) 'The Longitudinal Study of Generations', in G. Maddox (ed.), *The Encyclopedia of Aging,* 3rd edn. New York: Springer.

Bengtson, V. L., Biblarz, T. J. and Roberts, R. E. L. (2002) *How Families Still Matter: A Longitudinal Study of Youth in Two Generations*, New York: Cambridge University Press.

Bennett, K., Hughes, G. and Smith, P. (2003) '"I Think a Woman Can Take It": Widowed Men's Views and Experiences of Gender Differences in Bereavement', *Ageing International* 28 (4): 408–24.

Bernard, M., Bartlam, B., Biggs, S. and Sim, J. (2004) *New Lifestyles in Old Age: Health, Identity and Well-being in Berryhill Retirement Village*, Bristol: The Policy Press.

Bernheim, B. D., Shleifer, A. and Summers, L. H. (1985) 'The Strategic Bequest Motive', *Journal of Political Economy* 93 (6): 1045–76.

Berrington, A. (2004) 'Perpetual Postponers? Women's, Men's and Couple's Fertility Intentions and Subsequent Fertility Behaviour', *Population Trends* 117: 9–19.

Best, F. (1980) *Flexible Life Scheduling: Breaking the Education-Work-Retirement Lockstep*, New York: Praeger.

Beveridge, S. W. (1942) *Social Insurance and Allied Services* (Rep. No. Cmd 6404), London: HMSO.

Biggs, S. (1999) *The Mature Imagination*, Buckingham: Open University Press.

Biggs, S. (2004) 'New Ageism: Age Imperialism, Personal Experience and Ageing Policy', in S. O. Daatland and S. Biggs (eds) *Ageing and Diversity*, Bristol: The Policy Press.

Binstock, R. H. (2003) 'The War on "Anti-Aging Medicine"', *The Gerontologist* 43: 4–14.

Binstock, R. H. (2004) 'Anti-aging Medicine and Research: A Realm of Conflict and Profound Societal Implications', *Journals of Gerontology Series A – Biological Sciences and Medical Sciences* 59: 523–33.

Binstock, R. H. and Post, S. G. (eds) (1991) *Too Old for Health Care? Controversies in Medicine, Law, Economics, and Ethics*, Baltimore, MD: Johns Hopkins University Press.

Black, H. K. (2003) 'Narratives of Forgiveness in Old Age', in J. F. Gubrium and J. A. Holstein (eds) *Ways of Aging*, Boston, MA: Blackwell.

Blackburn, R. (2002) *Banking on Death*, London: Verso Books.

Blaikie, A. (1999) *Ageing and Popular Culture*, Cambridge: Cambridge University Press.

Blaikie, A. (2004) 'It's a Wonderful Life? Cultures of Ageing', in E. B. Silva and T. Bennett (eds) *Contemporary Culture and Everyday Life*, Durham: Sociology Press.

Blakemore, K. and Boneham, M. (1994) *Age, Race and Ethnicity: A Comparative Approach*, Buckingham: Open University Press.

Bloom, F. E. (1999) 'Breakthroughs 1999', *Science* 286: 2267.

Bollas, C. (1987) *The Shadow of the Object*, London: Free Association Books.

Bolzman, C., Poncioni-Derigo, R., Vial, M. and Fibbi, R. (2004) 'Older Labour Migrants' Well-being in Europe: The Case of Switzerland', *Ageing and Society* 24: 411–30.

Bond, J. and Corner, L. (2004) *Quality of Life and Older People*, Buckingham: Open University Press.

Bonoli, G. and Gay-des-Combes, B. (2003) 'Adapting Pension Systems to Labour Market Changes in Western Europe', in C. Bochel, N. Ellison and M. Powell (eds) *Social Policy Review 15: UK and International Perspectives*, Bristol: The Policy Press.

Borell, K. and Ghazanfareeon Karlsson, S. (2003) 'Reconceptualizing Intimacy and Ageing: Living Apart Together', in S. Arber, K. Davidson and J. Ginn (eds) *Gender and Ageing: Changing Roles and Relationships*, Maidenhead: Open University Press.

Bosenquet, N., May, J. and Johnson, N. (1998) *Alzheimer's Disease in the United Kingdom: Burden of Disease and Future Care*, London: Imperial College of Science and Technology. (Health Policy Review paper 12.)

Bottero, W. (2004) 'Class Identities and the Ideology of Class', *Sociology* 38: 985–1003.

Bourdieu, P. (1996) *The State Nobility: Elite Schools in the Field of Power*, Cambridge: Polity Press.

Bowl, R. (1986) 'Social Work with Old People', in C. Phillipson and A. Walker (eds) *Ageing and Social Policy: A Critical Assessment*, Aldershot: Gower Publishing Company Ltd.

Bowling, A. (1995a) 'The Most Important Things in Life: Comparisons Between Older and Younger Population Age Groups by Gender: Results from a National Survey of the Public's Judgements', *International Journal of Health Sciences* 6 (4): 169–75.

Bowling, A. (1995b) 'What Things are Important in People's Lives? A Survey of the Public's Judgements to Inform Scales of Health Related Quality of Life', *Social Science and Medicine* 41 (10): 1447–62.

Bowling, A. (1995c) *Measuring Disease*, Buckingham: Open University Press.

Bowling, A. (1996) *Measuring Health*, 2nd edn, Buckingham: Open University Press.

Bowling, A., Gabriel, Z., Dykes, J., Marriot-Dowding, L., Fleissig, A., Evans, O., Bannister, D. and Sutton, S. (2003) 'Let's Ask Them: A National Survey of Definitions of Quality of Life and its Enhancement Among People Aged 65 and Over', *International Journal of Aging and Human Development* 56 (4): 269–306.

Bramstedt, K. A. (2001) 'Scientific Breakthroughs: Cause or Cure of the Aging "Problem"', *Gerontology* 47: 52–4.

Breeze, E., Grundy, C., Fletcher, A., Wilkinson, P., Jones, D. and Bulpitt, C. (2002) *Inequalities in Quality of Life Among People Aged 75 Years and Over in Great Britain*, GO Findings 1, Sheffield: Growing Older Programme, University of Sheffield.

221

Brenton, M. (1998) *'We're in Charge': Cohousing Communities of Older People in the Netherlands: Lessons for Britain?*, Bristol: The Policy Press.

Brenton, M. (2001) 'Older People's Cohousing Communities' in S. M. Peace and C. A. Holland (eds) *Inclusive Housing in an Ageing Society: Innovative Approaches*, Bristol: The Policy Press.

Brewer, M., Goodman, A., Shaw, J. and Shephard, A. (2005) *Living Standards, Inequality and Poverty: Election Briefing 2005*, London: Institute of Fiscal Studies.

Bridgwood, A. (2000) *People Aged 65 Years and Older*, London: Office of National Statistics.

Brodie, J. (1996) *Perspectives on Poverty and Ethnic Minority Elders*, London: Age Concern.

Brody, E. M. (2004) *Women in the Middle: Their Parent Care Years*, 2nd edn, New York: Springer Publishing Company.

Brokaw, T. (1998) *The Greatest Generation*, New York: Random House.

Brooker, D. (2004) 'What is Person-centred Care for People with Dementia?', *Reviews in Clinical Gerontology* 13: 212–22.

Brooker, D. (2005) 'Dementia Care Mapping (DCM): A Review of the Research Literature', *The Gerontologist*, 45 Special No. 1 (1) 11–18.

Brown, C.G. (2001) *The Death of Christian Britain*, London: Routledge.

Brown, R. (1992) 'World War, Women's Work and the Gender Division of Paid Labour', in S. Arber and G. Gilbert (eds) *Women and Working Lives: Divisions and Change*, Basingstoke: Macmillan.

Brückner, H. and Mayer, K. U. (2005) 'De-standardization of the Life Course: What it Might Mean? And if it Means Anything, Whether it Actually Took Place', in R. Macmillan (ed.), *The Structure of the Life Course: Standardized? Individualized? Differentiated?* (Vol. 9, pp. 27–54), Amsterdam: Elsevier.

Bryden, C. (2005) *Dancing with Dementia: My Story of Living Positively with Dementia*, London: Jessica Kingsley Publishers.

Buckholdt, D. R. and Gubrium, J. F. (1979) *Caretakers: Treating Emotionally Disturbed Children*, Beverly Hills, CA: Sage.

Buenos Aires Herald (2005) 'Nation at a Glance', 17 January.

Burch, T. K. and Matthews, B. J. (1987) 'Household Formation in Developed Societies', *Population and Development Review*, 13 (3): 495–511.

Burgo, E. (2004) 'Argentina's Miraculous Recovery', *The Guardian*, 13 December: 23.

Bury, M. (1991) 'The Sociology of Chronic Illness: A Review of Research and Prospects', *Sociology of Health and Illness* 13 (4): 451–68.

Butler, R. N., Warner, H. R., Williams, T. F., Austad, S. N., Brody, J. A., Campisi, J., Cerami, A., Cohen, G., Cristofalo, V. J., Drachman, D. A., Finch, C. E., Fridovich, I., Harley, C. B., Havlik, R. J., Martin, G. M., Miller, R. A., Olshansky, S. J., Pereira-Smith, O. M., Smith, J. R., Sprott, R. L., West, M. D., Wilmoth, J. R. and Wright, W. E. (2004) 'The Aging Factor in Health and Disease: The Promise of Basic Research on Aging', *Aging – Clinical and Experimental Research* 16: 104–11.

Bytheway, B. (1995) *Ageism*, Buckingham: Open University Press.

Bytheway, B. (2003) 'Positioning Gerontology in an Ageist World', in L. Andersson (ed.), *Cultural Gerontology*, Westport, CT: Greenwood.

Bytheway, B. (2005) 'Ageism and Age Categorization', *Journal of Social Issues* 61 (2): 361–74.

Campbell, S. and Silverman, P. (1987) *Widower: When Men are Left Alone*, New York: Prentice Hall.

Caspi, A. and Moffitt, T. E. (1993) 'When do Individual Differences Matter? A Paradoxical Theory of Personality Coherence', *Psychological Inquiry,* 4: 247–71.

Castles, F. (2004) *The Future of the Welfare State: Crisis Myths and Crisis Realities*, Oxford: Oxford University Press.

Centre for Policy on Ageing (CPA) (1984) *Home Life: A Code of Practice for Residential Care*, report of a Working Party sponsored by the Department of Health and Social Security and convened by the Centre for Policy on Ageing under the Chairmanship of Kina, Lady Avebury, London: Centre for Policy on Ageing.

Centre for Policy on Ageing (CPA) (1996) *A Better Home Life*, London: Centre for Policy on Ageing.

Cerny, P. G. and Evans, M. (2004) 'Globalization and Public Policy under New Labour', *Policy Studies* 25 (1): 51–65.

Chamberlain, A. (1994) *Human Remains*, London: British Museum.

Charmaz, K. (2000) 'Experiencing Chronic Illness', in G. L., Albrecht, R. Fitzpatrick and S. C., Scrimshaw (eds) *Handbook of Social Studies in Health and Medicine*, pp. 277–92, London: Sage.

Cherlin, A. J. (1999) *Public and Private Families: An Introduction*, 2nd edn, New York: McGraw-Hill.

Cheston, R. and Bender, M. (1999) *Understanding Dementia: The Man with the Worried Eyes*, London: Jessica Kingsley Publishers.

Chudacoff, H. (1989) *How Old Are You? Age Consciousness in American Culture*, Princeton: Princeton University Press.

CIA (Central Intelligence Agency) (2001) *Long Term Global Demographic Trends: Reshaping the Geo-political Landscape*, July 2001, obtainable from: www.odci.gov/cia/reports/index.html.

Claramunt, C. Orchando (2004) 'Assessing Pension System Reforms in Latin America', *International Social Security Review* 57 (2): 25–42.

Clare, L. and Wilson, B. A. (2006) 'Longitudinal Assessment of Awareness In Early-stage Alzheimer's Disease Using Comparable Questionnaire-based and Performance-based Measures: A Prospective One-year Follow-up Study', *Ageing and Mental Health* 10 (2): 156–65.

Clare, L. and Woods, R. (2001) *Cognitive Rehabilitation in Dementia*, Sussex: Psychology Press.

Clark, G. L. (2000) *Pension Fund Capitalism*, Oxford: Oxford University Press.

Clark, R. L. and Spengler, J. J. (1980) *The Economics of Individual and Population Ageing*, Cambridge: Cambridge University Press.

Clark, T. and Emmerson, C. (2002) *The Tax and Benefit System and the Incentive to Invest in a Stakeholder Pension, IFS Bulletin 28*, London: Institute for Fiscal Studies.

Clausen, J. (1993) *American Lives: Looking Back at the Children of the Great Depression*, New York: Free Press.

Cohen, N. (2004) 'When You're 64', *Financial Times* Special Report: 'Reinventing Retirement', 17 November.

Cole, T. R. (1992) *The Journey of Life: A Cultural History of Aging in America*, Cambridge: Cambridge University Press.

Cole, T. R. and Winkler, M. G. (eds) (1994) *The Oxford Book of Aging*, Oxford: Oxford University Press.

Coleman, P. G. and McCulloch, A. W. (1990) 'Societal Change, Values and Social Support: Exploratory Studies into Adjustment in Late Life', *Journal of Aging Studies* 4: 321–32.

Coleman, P. G. and Mills, M. (2004) 'Memory and Preservation of Religious Faith in an Atheistic Society: Accounts of the Practice of Religion in the Former Soviet Union', *Proceedings of the International Oral History Association Conference* (editor A. Portelli), Rome.

Coleman, P. G. and O'Hanlon, A. (2004) *Ageing and Development: Theories and Research*, London: Hodder Arnold.

Coleman, P. G., McKiernan, F., Mills, M. and Speck, P. (2002) 'Spiritual Belief and Quality of Life: The Experience of Older Bereaved Spouses', *Quality in Ageing: Policy, Practice and Research* 3: 20–6.

Coleman, P. G., Ivani-Chalian, C. and Robinson, M. (2004) 'Religious Attitudes among British Older People: Stability and Change in a 20 year Longitudinal Study', *Ageing and Society* 24: 167–88.

Commission of the European Communities (2005) *Communication from the Commission: Green Paper 'Confronting Demographic Change: A New Solidarity between the Generations.'*, retrieved April 2005 from: http://europa.eu.int/comm/employment_social/news/2005/mar/comm2005-94_en.pdf.

Concialdi, P. (2004) 'An Alternative Policy on Pensions; Some Issues and Remarks', paper presented to the meeting of the EPOC network, Barcelona, February 2004.

Connidis, I. (2003) 'Bringing Outsiders In: Gay and Lesbian Family Ties over the Life Course', in S. Arber, K. Davidson and J. Ginn (eds) *Gender and Ageing: Changing Roles and Relationships*, Maidenhead: Open University Press.

Cook, A., Niven, K. and Downs, M. (1999) 'Assessing the Pain of People with Cognitive Impairment', *International Journal of Geriatric Psychiatry* 14: 421-5.

Cooley, C. H. (1964 [1902]) *Human Nature and the Social Order*, New York: Schocken.

Council of Europe (2001) *Recent Demographic Developments in Europe*, Strasbourg: Council of Europe Publishing.

Coupland, D. (1991) *Generation X: Tales for an Accelerated Culture*, New York: St Martin's Press.

Coupland, N., Coupland, J. and Giles, H. (1991) *Language, Society and the Elderly*, Oxford: Blackwell.

Craig, G. (2004) 'Citizenship, Exclusion and Older People', *Journal of Social Policy* 33 (1): 95-114.

Cronin, A. (2004) 'Sexuality in Gerontology: A Heteronormative Presence, a Queer Absence', in S. O. Daatland and S. Biggs (eds) *Ageing and Diversity*, Bristol: The Policy Press.

Crosnoe, R. and Elder, G. (2004) 'From Childhood to the Later Years: Pathways of Human Development', *Research on Aging* 26 (6): 623-54.

Crystal, S. and Shea, D. (1990) 'Cumulative Advantage, Cumulative Disadvantage, and Inequality among Elderly People', *Gerontologist* 30 (4): 437-43.

Crystal, S. and Shea, D. (2002) *Annual Review of Gerontology and Geriatrics 2002: Focus on Economic Outcomes in Later Life: Public Policy, Health, and Cumulative Advantage*, New York: Springer Publishing Company.

Curry, C. and O'Connell, A. (2003) *The Pensions Landscape*, London: Pensions Policy Institute.

Cutler, T. and Waine, B. (2001) 'Social Insecurity and the Retreat From Social Democracy: Occupational Welfare in the Long Boom and Financialisation', *Review of International Political Economy* 8 (1): 96-118.

Dale, A. (2004) 'A Non-Occupationally Based Classification (NOC) for Surveys and the Census', www.ccsr.ac.uk/publications/newsletters/10/nocpap.htm.

Dannefer, D. (1984) 'Adult Development and Social Theory: A Paradigmatic Reappraisal', *American Sociological Review,* 49: 100-16.

Dannefer, D. (1987) 'Accentuation, the Matthew Effect, and the Life Course: Aging as Intracohort Differentiation', *Sociological Forum,* 2: 211-36.

Dannefer, D. (1988) 'Differential Aging and the Stratified Life Course: Conceptual and Methodological Issues', Ch. 1 in P. Lawton and G. Maddox (eds) *Annual Review of Gerontology & Geriatrics, Vol. 8,* New York: Springer Publishing.

Dannefer, D. (1993) 'When does Society Matter for Individual Differences? Implications of a Counterpart Paradox', *Psychological Inquiry,* 4: 281-4.

Dannefer, D. (1999) 'Freedom isn't Free: Power, Alienation, and the Consequences of Action', in J. Brandtstadter, and R. M. Lerner (eds) *Action and Development: Origins and Functions of Intentional Self-Development,* New York: Springer.

Dannefer, D. (2000) 'Paradox of Opportunity: Education, Work and Age Integration in the United States and Germany', *The Gerontologist* 40: 282-6.

Dannefer, D. (2003a) 'Cumulative Advantage/Disadvantage and the Life Course: Cross-Fertilizing Age and Social Science Theory', *Journal of Gerontology* 58 (B): S327-37.

Dannefer, D. (2003b) 'Toward a Global Geography of the Life Course', in J. Mortimer and M. Shanahan (eds) *Handbook of the Life Course*, pp. 647-59, New York: Kluwer Academic/Plenum Publishers.

Dannefer, D. and Uhlenberg, P. (1999) 'Paths of the Lifecourse: A Typology', in V. L. Bengtson, and K. W. Schaie (eds) *Handbook of Theories of Aging: In Honor of Jim Birren,* pp. 306-26, New York: Springer Publishing Company.

Davey Smith, G., Wentworth, D., Neaton, J., Stamler, R. and Stamler, J. (1996) 'Socioeconomic Differentials in Mortality Risk among Men Screened for the Multiple Risk Factor Intervention Trial: II. Black Men', *American Journal of Public Health* 86 (4): 497-504.

Davidson, K. (2002) 'Gender Differences in New Partnership Choices and Constraints for Older Widows and Widowers', *Ageing International* 27 (4): 43–60.

Davidson, K. (2004) 'Why Can't a Man Be More Like a Woman? Marital Status and Social Networking of Older Men', *The Journal of Men's Studies* 13 (1): 25–43.

Davidson, K. and Arber, S. (2003) 'Older Men's Health: A Lifecourse Issue?', *Men's Health Journal* 2 (3): 72–5.

Davidson, K. and Fennell, G. (eds) (2004) *Intimacy in Later Life*, New Brunswick, NJ: Transaction Publishers.

Davidson, K., Daly, T. and Arber, S. (2003) 'Exploring the Worlds of Older Men', in S. Arber, K. Davidson and J. Ginn (eds) *Gender and Ageing: Changing Roles and Relationships*, Maidenhead: Open University Press/McGraw Hill.

Davie, G. (2002) *Europe: The Exceptional Case. Parameters of Faith in the Modern World*, London: Darton, Longman and Todd.

Davies, M., Falkingham, J., Love, H., McCleod, T., McKay, A., Morton, O., Taylor, L. and Wallace, P. (1998) *Next Generation*, London: The Henley Centre.

de Beauvoir, S. (1970) *Old Age*, London: Penguin.

de Grey, A. (2003) 'The Foreseeability of Real Anti-aging Medicine: Focusing the Debate', *Experimental Gerontology* 38 (9): 927–34.

de Grey, A., Ames, B., Andersen, J., Bartke, A., Campisi, J., Heward, C., McCarter, R. and Stock, G. (2002) 'Time to Talk SENS: Critiquing the Immutability of Human Aging', *Annals of the New York Academy of Sciences* 959: 452–62.

de Jong Gierveld, J. (2003) 'Social Networks and Social Well-being of Older Men and Women Living Alone', in S. Arber, K. Davidson and J. Ginn (eds) *Ageing and Gender: Changing Roles and Relationships*, Maidenhead: Open University Press/McGraw Hill.

Deacon, B. (2000) *Globalization and Social Policy: The Threat to Equitable Welfare*. Occasional Paper No.5, Globalism and Social Policy Programme (GASPP), UNRISD.

Denham, C. and White, I. (1998) 'Differences in Urban and Rural Britain', *Population Trends* 91: 23–35.

Department of the Environment, Transport and the Regions (DETR) (1996) *English Housing Condition Survey*, London: DETR.

Department of the Environment, Transport and the Regions (DETR) (2000) *Index of Deprivation, 2000: Regeneration Research Summary, Number 31*, London: DETR.

Department of Health (2001) *National Service Framework for Older People*, Department of Health, London: Crown Copyright. www.doh.gov.uk/nsf.

Department of Health (2003) *NHS Chaplaincy: Meeting the Religious and Spiritual Needs of Patients and Staff*, Document 32413, London: Department of Health.

Department of Social Security (DSS) (2000) *The Changing Welfare State: Pensioner Incomes*, Department of Social Security, Paper No. 2, London: DSS.

Department of Social Security (DSS) (1998) *A New Contract for Welfare: Partnership in Pensions* CM.4179, London: The Stationery Office.

Department for Work and Pensions (DWP) (2002) *Simplicity, Security and Choice: Working and Saving for Retirement* CM.5677, London: The Stationery Office.

Department for Work and Pensions (DWP) (2003a) *The Future of UK Pensions: Reply by the Government to the Third Report of the Work and Pensions Select Committee Session 2002-03* (HC92-1), London: The Stationery Office.

Department for Work and Pensions (DWP) (2003b). *Income Related Benefits: Estimates of Take-up 2000/2001*, London: DWP.

Diamond, P. A. and Orszag, P. R. (2004) *Saving Social Security: A Balanced Approach*, Washington DC: Brookings Institution Press.

Disney, R. and Emmerson, C. (2005) 'Public Pension Reform in the United Kingdom: What Effect on the Financial Well-being of Current and Future Pensioners?', *Fiscal Studies* 26: 55–81.

Disney, R. and Whitehouse, E. (2002) 'The Economic Well-Being of Older People in International Perspective: A Critical Review', in S. Crystal and D. Shea (eds) *Economic Outcomes in Later Life: Public Policy, Health and Cumulative Advantage*, New York: Springer Publishing Company.

Donkin, A., Goldblatt, P. and Lynch, K. (2002) 'Inequalities in Life Expectancy by Social Class, 1972–1999', *Health Statistics Quarterly* 15 (Autumn): 5–15.

Dowd, J. J. (2002) '*Die Bildung* of the Warrior Class: Socialization and the Acquisition of Cultural Resources', in R. A. Settersten and T. J. Owens (eds) *New Frontiers in Socialization,* pp. 393–431, New York: JAI Press.

Downs, M. (2000) 'Dementia in a Socio-cultural Context: An Idea whose Time has Come', *Ageing and Society* 20 (3): 369–75.

Downs, M. and Bartlett, R. (2005) 'Images of Coping with Dementia in Advertisements for Anti-Dementia Drugs', paper presented at the Gerontological Society of America's annual conference, 2005, Orlando, FL.

Easterlin, R., Schaeffer, C. and Macunovich, D. (1993) 'Will the Baby Boomers be Less Well Off than their Parents? Income, Wealth and Family Circumstances over the Life Cycle in the United States', *Population and Development Review* 19 (3): 497–522.

Eastman, R. M. (1996) 'Literary Representations of Aging', in J. E. Birren (ed.), *Encyclopedia of Gerontology*, San Diego: Academic.

Ebrahim, S. (1996) 'Ethnic Elder', *British Medical Journal* 313: 610–13.

Ekerdt, D. J. (1986) 'The Busy Ethic: Moral Continuity between Work and Retirement', *The Gerontologist* 26: 239–44.

Elder, G. (1974) *Children of the Great Depression*, Chicago: University of Chicago Press.

Elder, G. (1994) 'Time, Human Agency, and Social Change: Perspectives on the Life Course', *Social Psychology Quarterly* 57: 4–15.

Elder, G. (1999) *Children of the Great Depression: Social Change in Life Experience,* Chicago: University of Chicago Press.

Elder, G. and Liker, J. (1982) 'Hard Times in Women's Lives: Historical Differences Across 40 Years', *American Journal of Sociology,* 58: 241–69.

Erens, B., Primatesta, P. and Prior, G. (2001) *Health Survey for England 1999: The Health of Minority Ethnic Groups*, London: The Stationery Office.

Erikson, E. H. (1963) *Childhood and Society*, New York: Norton.

Erikson, E. H. (1976) 'Reflection's on Dr. Borg's Life Cycle', *Daedalus* 105: 1–28.

Erikson, E. H. (1986) *The Life Cycle Completed*, New York: Norton.

Ermisch, J. and Francesconi, M. (2000) 'Cohabitation in Great Britain: Not for Long but Here to Stay', *Journal of the Royal Statistical Society Series A* 163: 153–72.

ESRC Growing Older Programme (2005) www.shef.ac.uk/uni/projects/gop/, accessed 21 March.

Estes, C. (1979) *The Aging Enterprise*, San Francisco: Jossey-Bass.

Estes, C. (1991) 'The New Political Economy of Aging: Introduction and Critique', in M. Minkler and C. Estes (eds) *Critical Perspectives on Aging: The Political and Moral Economy of Growing Old*, New York: Baywood Publishing Company Inc.

Estes, C. (2004) 'Social Security Privatisation and Older Women: A Feminist Political Economy Perspective', *Journal of Aging Studies* 18: 9–26.

Estes, C. and Minkler, M. (1984) *Reading in the Political Economy of Aging,* New York: Baywood Publishing Company Inc.

Estes, C. and Phillipson, C. (2002) 'The Globalization of Capital, the Welfare State and Old Age Policy', *International Journal of Health Services* 32 (2): 279–97.

Estes, C., Gerard, L., Zones, J. and Swan, J. (1984) *Political Economy, Health and Aging*, Boston: Little Brown.

Estes, C., Biggs, S. and Phillipson, C. (2003) *Social Theory, Social Policy and Ageing: A Critical Introduction*, Maidenhead: Open University Press.

Evandrou, M. (ed.) (1997) *Babyboomers: Ageing in the 21st Century*, London: Age Concern Books.

Evandrou, M. (2000) 'Social Inequalities in Later Life: The Socio-economic Position of Older People from Ethnic Minority Groups in Britain', *Population Trends* 101: 11-18.

Evandrou, M. and Falkingham, J. (2000) 'Looking Back to Look Forward: Lessons from Four Birth Cohorts for Ageing in the 21st Century', *Population Trends* 99: 21-36.

Evandrou, M. and Falkingham, J. (2001) 'What Future for the Baby Boomers in Retirement?', *Insurance Trends* 31: 1-14.

Evandrou, M. and Falkingham, J. (2005) 'A Secure Retirement for All? Older People and New Labour', in J. Hills and K. Stewart (eds) *A More Equal Society? New Labour, Poverty, Inequality and Exclusion*, pp. 167-88, Bristol: Polity Press.

Evandrou, M. and Victor, C. (1989) 'Differentiation in Later Life: Social Class and Housing Tenure Cleavages', in B. Blytheway (ed.) *Becoming and Being Old: Sociological Approaches to Later Life*, London: Sage.

Evandrou, M., Falkingham, J., Rake, K. and Scott, A. (2001) 'The Dynamics of Living Arrangements in Later Life: Evidence from the British Household Panel Survey', *Population Trends* 105: 37-44.

Faircloth, C. A. (2003) *Aging Bodies: Images and Everyday Experience*, Walnut Creek: AltaMira.

Falkingham, J. and Rake, K. (2001) 'Modelling the Gender Impact of British Pension Reforms', in J. Ginn, D. Street and S. Arber (eds) *Women, Work and Pensions: International Issues and Prospects*, Buckingham: Open University Press.

Farquhar, M. (1995) 'Elderly People's Definitions of Quality of Life', *Social Science and Medicine* 41 (10): 1439-46.

Featherstone, M. and Hepworth, M. (1986) 'New Lifestyles in Old Age?', in C. Phillipson, M. Bernard and P. Strang (eds) *Dependency and Interdependency in Old Age*, Beckenham: Croom Helm.

Featherstone, M. and Hepworth, M. (1989) 'Ageing and Old Age: Reflections on the Post-modern Life Course', in B. Bytheway (ed.), *Becoming and Being Old: Sociological Approaches to Later Life*, London: Sage.

Fennell, G., Phillipson, C. and Evers, H. (1988) *The Sociology of Old Age*, Milton Keynes: Open University Press.

Ferraro, K. (1984) 'Widowhood and Social Participation in Late Life: Isolation or Compensation?', *Research on Aging* 6: 451-68.

Ferri, C. P., Prince, M., Brayne, C., Brodaty, H., Fratiglioni, L., Ganguli, M., Hall, K., Hasegawa, K., Hendrie, H., Huang, Y., Jorm, A., Mathers, C., Menezes, P. R., Rimmer, E. and Scazufca, M. (2005) 'Global Prevalence of Dementia: A Delphi Consensus Study', *Lancet* 366 (9503): 2112-17.

Field, F. (2002) 'A Universal Protected Pension: Harnessing Self-Interest to the Collective Good', in A. Deacon (ed.), *Debating Pensions Self-Interest Citizenship and the Common Good*, London: Civitas.

Financial Times (2004) 'Pension Loss Toll Could Top 65,000', 21 Sept.: 5.

Finch, J. and Mason, J. (1992) *Negotiating Family Responsibilities*, London: Routledge.

Firebaugh, G. and Goesling, B. (2004) 'Accounting for the Recent Decline in Global Income Inequality', *American Journal of Sociology* 110 (2): 283-312.

Fisk, M. J. (2001) 'The Implications of Smart Home Technologies', in S. M. Peace and C. A. Holland (eds) *Inclusive Housing in an Ageing Society: Innovative Approaches*, Bristol : The Policy Press.

Foner, A. (2000) 'Age Integration or Age Conflict as Society Ages?', *Gerontologist* 40 (3): 272-6.

Forrest, R. and Leather, P. (1998) 'The Ageing of the Property Owning Democracy', *Ageing and Society* 18: 35-63.

Foucault, M. (1975) *The Birth of the Clinic*, New York: Vintage.

Friedan, B. (1993) *The Fountain of Age*, London: Vintage.

Friedberg, R. (2000) 'You Can't Take it with You? Immigrant Assimilation and the Portability of Human Capital', *Journal of Labor Economics* 18: 221-51.

Friedell, M. (2002) 'Awareness: A Personal Memoir on the Declining Quality of Life in Alzheimer's', *Dementia: The International Journal of Social Research and Practice* 1 (3): 359-66.

Fries, J. F. (1980) 'Aging, Natural Death and the Compression of Morbidity', *New England Journal of Medicine* 303: 130–5.

Fries, J. F. (2003) 'Measuring and Monitoring Success in Compressing Morbidity', *Annals of Internal Medicine* 139 (5): 455–63.

Fromm, D. (1991) *Collaborative Communities: Cohousing, Central Living and Other Forms of New Housing with Shared Facilities*, New York: Van Nostrand Reinhold.

Fukuyama, F. (2002) *Our Posthuman Future: Consequences of the Biotechnology Revolution*, New York: Farrar, Straus and Giroux.

Fussell, P. (1983) *Class, A Guide Through the American Status System*, New York: Summit Books.

Gabriel, Z. and Bowling, A. (2004a) 'Quality of Life from the Perspectives of Older People', *Ageing and Society* 24 (5): 675–91.

Gabriel, Z. and Bowling, A. (2004b) 'Quality of Life in Old Age from the Perspectives of Older People', in A. Walker and C. H. Hennessy (eds) *Growing Older: Quality of Life in Old Age*, pp. 14–34, Maidenhead: Open University Press.

Galland, O. (1997) 'Leaving Home and Family Relations in France', *Journal of Family Issues* 18: 645–70.

Gammack, J. K. and Morley, J. E. (2004) 'Anti-aging Medicine – the Good, the Bad, and the Ugly', *Clinics in Geriatric Medicine* 20: 157–79.

Gann, D., Barlow, J. and Venables, T. (1999) *Digital Futures: Making Homes Smarter*, Coventry: Chartered Institute of Housing.

Gems, D. (2003) 'Is More Life Always Better? The New Biology of Aging and the Meaning of Life', *Hastings Center Report* 33 (4): 31–9.

George, V. and Wilding, P. (2002) *Globalization and Human Welfare*, London: Palgrave.

Gerontologist, The (2002) *Aging and Issues of End of Life* (Special Issue), 42.

Ghazanfareeon Karlsson, S. and Borell, K. (2002) 'Intimacy and Autonomy, Gender and Ageing: Living Apart Together', *Ageing International* 27 (4): 11–26.

Gibson, F. (1999) 'Can We Risk Person-centred Communication?', *Journal of Dementia Care* 7 (2): 20–4

Giddens, A. (1991) *Modernity and Self-Identity*, Cambridge: Polity Press.

Giddens, A. (1998) *The Third Way*, Cambridge: Polity Press.

Gill, I., Packard, T. and Yermo, J. (2004) *Keeping the Promise of Social Security in Latin America*, Palo Alto: Stanford University Press.

Gilleard, C. and Higgs, P. (2000) *Cultures of Ageing: Self, Citizen and the Body*, Harlow: Pearson Education.

Gilleard, C. and Higgs, P. (2002) 'The Third Age: Class Cohort or Generation?', *Ageing and Society* 22: 369–82.

Gilleard, C. and Higgs, P. (2005) *Contexts of Ageing: Class, Cohort and Community*, Oxford: Polity.

Gimlin, D. (2002) *Body Work: Beauty and Self Image in American Culture*, Berkeley: University of California Press.

Ginn, J. (2003) *Gender, Pensions and the Lifecourse: How Pensions Need to Adapt to Changing Family Forms*, Bristol: The Policy Press.

Ginn, J. and Arber, S. (1993) 'Pension Penalties: The Gendered Division of Occupational Welfare', *Work, Employment and Society* 7 (1): 47–70.

Ginn, J. and Arber, S. (1999) 'Changing Patterns of Pension Inequality: A Shift From State to Private Sources', *Ageing and Society* 19: 319–42.

Ginn, J. and Arber, S. (2001a) 'A Colder Pension Climate for British Women', in J. Ginn, D. Street and S. Arber (eds) *Women, Work and Pensions*, Buckingham: Open University Press.

Ginn, J. and Arber, S. (2001b) 'Pension Prospects of Minority Ethnic Groups: Inequalities by Gender and Ethnicity', *The British Journal of Sociology* 52: 519–39.

Ginn, J. and Arber, S. (2002) 'Degrees of Freedom: Do Graduate Women Escape the Motherhood Gap in Pensions?', *Sociological Research Online* 7 (2).

Ginn, J., Street, D. and Arber, S. (2001) *Women, Work and Pensions: International Issues and Prospects*, Buckingham: Open University Press.

Gjonca, E. and Calderwood, L. (2003) 'Socio-Demographic Characteristics' in M. Marmot, J. Banks, R. Blundell, C. Lessof and J. Nazroo (eds) *Health, Wealth and Lifestyles of the Older Population in England: The 2002 English Longitudinal Study of Ageing*, London: Institute for Fiscal Studies.

Glaser, K. and Tomassini, C. (2002) 'Demography: Living Arrangements, Receipt of Care, Residential Proximity and Housing Preferences among Old People in Britain and Italy in the 1990s', in K. Sumner (ed.), *Our Lives, Our Homes: Choice in Later Life Living Arrangements*, London: Centre for Policy on Ageing/The Housing Corporation.

Glaser, K., Hancock, R. and Stuchbury, R. (1998) *Attitudes in an Ageing Society* (Research sponsored by Age Concern England for the Millennium Debate of the Age), London: Age Concern Institute of Gerontology.

Goodman, A. and Webb, S. (1994) 'For Richer, for Poorer: The Changing Distribution of Income in the United Kingdom, 1961–91', *Fiscal Studies*, 15 (4): 29–62.

Goodman, A., Shaw, J. and Shephard, A. (2005) 'Understanding Recent Trends in Income Inequality', in S. Delorenzi, J. Reed and P. Robinson (eds) *Maintaining Momentum: Promoting Social Mobility and Life Chances from Early Years to Adulthood*, London: Institute for Public Policy Research.

Gorman, M. (1999) 'Development and the Rights of Older People', in J. Randel, T. German and D. Ewing (eds) *The Ageing and Development Report: Poverty, Independence and the World's Older People*, London: Earthscan.

Gott, M. (2005) *Sexuality, Sexual Health and Ageing*, Maidenhead: Open University Press.

Gott, M. and Hinchliff, S. (2003) 'Sex and Ageing: A Gendered Issue', in S. Arber, K. Davidson and J. Ginn (eds) *Gender and Ageing: Changing Roles and Relationships*, Maidenhead: Open University Press/McGraw-Hill.

Government Actuary's Department (2001) *Marital Projections: England and Wales*, Accessed 20 September 2004.

Graham, N., Lindesay, J., Katona, C., Bertolote, J., Camus, V., Copeland, J., de Mendonca Lima, C., Gaillard, M., Gely Nargeot, M, Gray, J., Jacobsson, L., Kingma, M., Kuhne, N., O'Loughlin, A., Rutz, W., Saraceno, B., Taintor, Z. and Wancata, J. (2003) 'Reducing Stigma and Discrimination against Older People with Mental Disorders: A Technical Consensus Statement', *International Journal of Geriatric Psychiatry* 18: 670–8.

Graham, P., Blakely, T., Davis, P., Sporle, A. and Pearce, N. (2004) 'Compression, Expansion or Dynamic Equilibrium? The Evolution of Health Expectancy in New Zealand', *Journal of Epidemiology and Community Health* 58 (8): 659–66.

Great Old Broads (2005) *Great Old Broads for Wilderness* www.greatoldbroads.org/about_us.htm (accessed 21 April 2005).

Grewal, I., Nazroo, J., Bajekal, M., Blane, D. and Lewis, J. (2004) 'Influences on Quality of Life: A Qualitative Investigation of Ethnic Differences among Older People in England', *Journal of Ethnic and Migration Studies* 30 (4): 737–61.

Grundy, E. (1987) 'Household Change and Migration among the Elderly in England and Wales', *Espace, Population, Societies* 1: 109–23.

Grundy, E. (1996) 'Population Review: (S) The Population Aged 60 and Over', *Population Trends* 84: 14–20.

Grundy, E. and Harrop, A. (1992) 'Co-Residence between Adult Children and their Elderly Parents in England and Wales', *Journal of Social Policy* 21: 325–48.

Grundy, E. and Sloggett, A. (2003) 'Health Inequalities in the Older Population: The Role of Personal Capital, Social Resources and Socio-economic Circumstances', *Social Science and Medicine* 56: 935–47.

Grundy, E., Murphy, M. and Shelton, N. (1999) 'Looking Beyond the Household: Intergenerational Perspective on Living Kin and Contacts with Kin in Great Britain', *Population Trends* 97: 19–27.

Gubrium, J. (1987) 'Structuring and Destructuring the Course of Illness: The Alzheimer's Disease Experience', *Sociology of Health and Illness* 9: 1–24.

Gubrium, J. (1992) *Out of Control: Family Therapy and Domestic Disorder*, Thousand Oaks, CA: Sage.

Gubrium, J. (2000) 'Deconstructing Self and Well-being in Later Life', in K. Warner Schaie and J. Hendricks (eds) *The Evolution of the Aging Self: Societal Impact on the Aging Process*, New York: Springer Publishing Company.

Gubrium, J. and Holstein, J. (2000) 'The Self in a World of Going Concerns', *Symbolic Interaction* 23: 95–115.

Gubrium, J. and Holstein, J. (eds) (2001) *Institutional Selves: Troubled Identities in a Postmodern World*, New York: Oxford University Press.

Gubrium, J. and Holstein, J. (eds) (2003) *Ways of Aging*, Boston, MA: Blackwell.

Gubrium, J. and Wallace, J. (1990) 'Who Theorizes Age?', *Ageing and Society* 10: 131–49.

Gullette, M. (2004) *Aged by Culture*, Chicago: University of Chicago Press.

Gurney, C. and Means, R. (1993) 'The Meaning of Home in Later Life', in S. Arber and M. Evandrou (eds) *Ageing, Independence and the Life Crises*, London: Jessica Kingsley.

Gutmann, D. L. (1997) *The Human Elder in Nature, Culture and Society*, Boulder, CO: Westview Press.

Haezewindt, P. (2003) 'Investing in Each Other and the Community: The Role of Social Capital', *Social Trends* 33: 19–27.

Hagestad, G. O. (1985) 'Continuity and Connectedness', in V. L. Bengtson, and J. F. Robertson, (eds) *Grandparenthood,* Beverly Hills, CA: Sage.

Hagestad, G. O. (1988) 'Demographic Change and the Life Course: Some Emerging Trends in the Family Realm', *Family Relations,* 37: 405–10.

Hagestad, G. and Dannefer, D. (2001) 'Concepts and Theories of Aging: Beyond Microfication in Social Science Approaches', Ch. 1 in R. Binstock, and L. George, (eds) *Handbook of Aging and the Social Sciences,* 5th edn, New York: Academic.

Hales, C. and Gough, O. (2003) 'Employee Evaluations of Company Occupational Pensions HR Implications', *Personnel Review* 32 (3): 319–40.

Hall, R., Ogden, P. and Hill, C. (1999) 'Living Alone: Evidence from England and Wales and France for the Last Two Decades', in S. McRae (ed.), *Changing Britain: Families and Households in the 1990s*, Oxford: Oxford University Press.

Halliwell, B. and Wong, P. (2004) 'Special Section – Papers from: Asia Pacific Conference and Exhibition on Anti-ageing Medicine (8–11 Sept. 2003)', *Mechanisms of Ageing and Development* 125: 283.

Handlin, O. (1965) 'Science and Technology in Popular Culture', in G. Holton (ed.), *Science and Culture* (reprinted in B. Barnes (ed.), (1972) *Sociology of Science*), Harmondsworth: Penguin.

Hanson, J., Kellaher, L. and Rowlands, M. (2001) *Profiling the Housing Stock for Older People: The Transition from Domesticity to Care*, Final Report of the EPSRC EQUAL Research study, University College London.

Hareven, T. K. (1996) 'The Life Course', in J. E. Birren (ed.), *Encyclopedia of Gerontology,* San Diego: Academic.

Harkin, J. and Huber, J. (2004) *Eternal Youths: How the Baby Boomers are Having Their Time Again*, London: Demos.

Harper, S. (2001) 'Family Roles, Relationships and Transitions', in S. Harper (ed.), *Families in Ageing Societies*. Oxford: Oxford University Press.

Harper, S. (2004a) 'The Challenge for Families of Demographic Ageing', in S. Harper, (ed.), *Families in Ageing Societies: A Multi-Disciplinary Approach,* pp. 6–30, Oxford: Oxford University Press.

Harper, S. (2004b) 'The Implications of Ageing Societies', in B.-M. Oberg (ed.), *Changing Worlds and the Ageing Subject: Dimensions in the Study of Ageing and Later Life,* Burlington, VT: Ashgate.

Harper, S. (2005) 'Understanding Grandparenthood', in M. L. Johnson and V. L. Bengtson (eds) *The Cambridge Handbook of Age and Ageing,* New York: Cambridge University Press.

Harris, J. (2005) 'Beveridge and Pensions', paper presented to 'Why Has it All Gone Wrong? The Past, Present and Future of British Pensions', 15 June 2005, British Academy, London.

Harris, P. B. (ed.) (2002) *The Person with Alzheimer's Disease: Pathways to Understanding the Experience*, Baltimore: Johns Hopkins University Press.

Haskey, J. (1982) 'Widowhood, Widowerhood and Remarriage', *Population Trends* 30: 15–20.

Hattersley, L. (1997) 'Expectation of Life by Social Class', in M. Whitehead and F. Driver (eds) *Health Inequalities*, London: Stationery Office.

Hayflick, L. (2004) '"Anti-aging" is an Oxymoron', *Journals of Gerontology Series A-Biological Sciences and Medical Sciences* 59: 573–8.

Healy, J. and Yarrow, S. (1997) *Parents Living with Children in Old Age*, Bristol: The Policy Press.

Heaphy, B. (forthcoming) 'Ageing, Sexualities and Social Change', *Current Sociology*.

Heaphy, B., Yip, A. and Thompson, D. (2004) 'Ageing in a Non-heterosexual Context', *Ageing and Society* 24: 881–902.

Heath, A. and Ridge, J. (1983) 'Social Mobility of Ethnic Minorities', *Journal of Biosocial Science* supplement, 8: 169–84.

Heelas, P. (1998) *Religion, Modernity and Postmodernity*, Oxford: Blackwell.

Held, D. and McGrew, A. (2002) *Governing Globalization: Power, Authority and Global Governance*, Cambridge: Polity Press.

Held, D., McGrew, A., Goldblatt, D. and Perraton, J. (1999) *Global Transformations*, Oxford: Polity Press.

Hen Co-op (1995) *Disgracefully Yours*, London: Piatkus Publishers.

Hendricks, J. (1999) 'Practical Consciousness, Social Class, and Self-concept: A View from Sociology', in C. D. Ryff and V. W., Marshall (eds) *The Self and Society in Aging Processes*, pp. 187–222, New York: Springer Publishing.

Hendricks, J. (2003) 'Structure and Identity – Mind the Gap: Toward a Personal Resource Model of Successful Ageing', in S., Biggs, A. Lowenstein, and J., Hendricks (eds) *The Need for Theory: Critical Approaches to Social Gerontology*, pp. 63–87, Amityville, NY: Baywood Publishing Company, Inc.

Hensley, S. (2002) 'Drug Costs Start in Labs Desperate for Discoveries', *The Wall Street Journal*, 2 May.

Heywood, F., Oldman, C. and Means, R. (2002) *Housing and Home in Later Life*, Buckingham: Open University Press.

Higgs, P. and Gilleard, C. (2004) 'Class, Power and Inequality in Later Life', in S. O. Daatland and S. Biggs (eds) *Ageing and Diversity*, Bristol: The Policy Press.

Hilal, J., Malki, M., Shalabi, Y. and Ladadweh, H. (1998) *Towards a Social Security System in the West Bank and Gaza Strip*, Ramallah: Palestine Economic Policy Research Institute (MAS).

Hills, J. (2004) 'Heading for Retirement? National Insurance, State Pensions, and the Future of the Contributory Principle in the UK', *Journal of Social Policy* 33 (3): 347–71.

Hinterlong, J., Morrow-Howell, N. and Sherraden, M. (2001) 'Productive Ageing; Principles and Perspectives', in N., Morrow-Howell, J. Hinterlong and M. Sherraden (eds) *Productive Ageing: Concepts and Challenges*, pp. 3–19, Baltimore: Johns Hopkins.

Histadrut (2004) 'Pensions in Israel', internal mimeograph, Histadrut: Tel Aviv, Israel.

Hochschild, A. R. (1983) *The Managed Heart*, Berkeley: University of California Press.

Hockey, J. and James, A. (2003) *Social Identities across the Life Course*, Basingstoke: Palgrave MacMillan.

Hoeksma, J. (2004) 'The Needs for Care of Older Chinese Migrants in Rotterdam', in A. M. Warnes, M. Casado-Díaz and U. Lundh (eds) *Older Migrants in Europe: Sources, Case Studies and a Guide to Research*, Sheffield: Sheffield Institute for Studies on Ageing.

Hoerder, D. (2001) 'Reconstructing Life Courses: A Historical Perspective on Migrant Experiences', in V. Marshall, W. Heinz, H. Kruger and A. Verma (eds) *Reconstructing Work and the Life Course*, Toronto: University of Toronto Press.

Hofman, R., Rocca, W., Brayne, C., Breteler, M., Clarke, M., Cooper, B., Copeland, J., Dartigues, J., da Silva Droux, A. and Hagnell, O. (1991) 'The Prevalence of Dementia in Europe: A Collaborative Study of 1980–1990 Findings', *International Journal of Epidemiology* 20: 736–48.

Hogan, D. (1981) *Transitions and Social Change: The Early Lives of American Men,* New York: Academic Press.

Holliday, R. (2000) 'Ageing Research in the Next Century', *Biogerontology* 1: 97–101.

Holliday, R. (2001) 'Aging and the Biochemistry of Life', *Trends in Biochemical Sciences* 26 (1): 68–71.

Holmes, E. R. and Holmes, L. D. (1995) *Other Cultures, Elder Years*, 2nd edn, Thousand Oaks, CA: Sage Publications.

Holstein, J. and Gubrium, J. (2000a) *Constructing the Life Course*, Walnut Creek, CA: AltaMira.

Holstein, J. and Gubrium, J. (2000b) *The Self We Live By: Narrative Identity in a Postmodern World*, New York: Oxford University Press.

Holstein, J. and Gubrium, J. (2004) 'Context: Working it Up, Down, and Across', in C. Seale, G. Gobo, J. Gubrium and D. Silverman (eds) *Qualitative Research Practice*, London: Sage.

House of Commons (2003) *The Future of UK Pensions, Work and Pensions Committee Third Report of Session 2002-03, Volume 1*, London: The Stationery Office.

House of Commons (2005) *House of Commons Hansard Debates for 4 April 2005*, the Minister for Pensions, Malcom Wicks, Part 4, Col 1116.

House of Lords (2003) *Aspects of the Economics of an Ageing Population. Volume I - Report*, Select Committee On Economic Affairs, Session 2002-03, 4th Report, London: The Stationery Office, HL Paper 179-I.

Howse, K. (1999) *Religion and Spirituality in Later Life: A Review*, London: Centre for Policy on Ageing.

Howse, K. (2004) 'What has Fairness Got to Do with It? Social Justice and Pension Reform', *Ageing Horizons* 1: 1-16.

Huber, A. and O'Reilly, K. (2004) 'The Construction of Heimat under Conditions of Individualised Modernity: Swiss and British Elderly Migrants in Spain', *Ageing and Society* 24: 327-51.

Huber, J. and Skidmore, P. (2003) *The New Old*, London: Demos.

Hubert, H., Bloch, D., Oehlert, J. and Fries, J. (2002) 'Lifestyle Habits and Compression of Morbidity', *Journal of Gerontology A - Biological and Medical Science* 57 (6): M338-42.

Hurd, M. D. (1987) 'Savings of the Elderly and Desired Bequests', *The American Economic Review*, 77 (3): 298-312.

Hurd, M. D. (1989) 'Mortality Risks and Bequests', *Econometrica*, 57 (4): 779-813.

Innes, A. (2002) 'The Social and Political Context of Formal Dementia Care Provision', *Ageing and Society*, 22 (4): 483-99.

International Longevity Center - USA (2001) *Biomarkers of Aging: From Primitive Organisms to Man,* ILC Workshop Report, Tuscon, Arizona: International Longevity Centre - USA.

Jackson, R. (2002) *The Global Retirement Crisis*, Center for Strategic and International Studies, Washington DC: Citigroup/CSIS.

Jackson, W. A. (1998) *The Political Economy of Population Ageing*, Cheltenham: Edward Elgar.

Jamieson, L. (1998) *Intimacy: Personal Relationships in Modern Societies,* Cambridge: Polity Press.

Jenkins, C. L. (ed.) (2003) *Widows and Divorcees in Later Life: On Their Own Again,* New York: Howarth Press Inc.

Jenkins, R. (1996) *Social Identity*, London: Routledge.

Jennings, B. (2004) 'Alzheimer's Disease and Quality of Life', in K. Doka (ed.), *Living with Grief: Alzheimer's Disease*, Washington DC: Hospice Foundation of America.

Jerrome, D. (1981) 'The Significance of Friendship for Women in Later Life', *Ageing and Society* 1: 175-97.

Jerrome, D. (1992) *Good Company: An Anthropological Study of Old People in Groups*, Edinburgh: Edinburgh University Press.

Jochim, J. (1997) 'Generation X Defies Definition', *Nevada Outpost*, 6 January.

Johnson, P. and Falkingham, J. (1992) *Ageing and Economic Welfare*, London: Sage Publications.

Johnson, P., Conrad, C. and Thomson, D. (eds) (1989) *Workers versus Pensioners*, Manchester: Manchester University Press.

Judd, S., Marshall, M. and Phippen, P. (1997) *Design for Dementia*, London: Hawker Publications.

Juengst, E. T., Binstock, R .H., Mehlman, M. J. and Post, S. G. (2003a) 'Enhanced: Antiaging Research and the Need for Public Dialogue', *Science* 299: 1323.

Juengst, E. T., Binstock, R. H., Mehlman, M. J., Post, S. G. and Whitehouse, P. (2003b) 'Biogerontology, "Anti-aging Medicine,"' and the Challenges of Human Enhancement', *Hastings Center Report* 33 (4): 21-31.

Jung, C. (1967 [1934]) *Collected Works: Vol. 9*, London: Routledge.

Kass, L. R. (1971) 'Death as an Event: A Commentary on Robert Morison', *Science* 173 (3998): 698-702.

Katz, S. (1996) *Disciplining Old Age: The Formation of Gerontological Knowledge*, London: University Press of Virginia.

Kawachi, I., Kennedy, B. P., Lochner, K. and Prothrow-Stith, D. (1997) 'Social Capital, Income inequality, and Mortality', *American Journal of Public Health* 87 (9): 1491–8.

Keith, J. (1994) *The Aging Experience: Diversity and Commonality Across Cultures,* London: Sage Publications.

Kellaher, L. (2002) 'Is Genuine Choice a Reality? The Range and Adequacy of Living Arrangements Available to Older People', in K. Sumner (ed.), *Our Lives, Our Homes: Choice in Later Life Living Arrangements,* London: Centre for Policy on Ageing/The Housing Corporation.

Kelly, M. (2001) 'Lifetime Homes', in S. M. Peace and C. A. Holland (eds) *Inclusive Housing in an Ageing Society: Innovative Approaches*, Bristol : The Policy Press.

Kelly, S., Baker, A. and Gupta, S. (2000) 'Healthy Life Expectancy in Great Britain 1980–1996', *Health Statistics Quarterly* 7: 16–24.

Khaw, K. T. (1999a) 'Inequalities and Health: Older People', in D. Gordon, M. Shaw, D. Dorling and G. Davey-Smith (eds) *Inequalities in Health: The Evidence*, Bristol: The Policy Press.

Khaw, K. T. (1999b) 'How Many, How Old, How Soon?', *British Medical Journal*, 319: 1350–52.

Kiernan, K. and Smith, K. (2003) 'Unmarried Parenthood: New Insights from the Millennium Cohort Study', *Population Trends* 114: 26–33.

Kihlgren, M., Kuremyr, D., Norberg, A., Brane, G., Karlsson, I., Engstrom, B. and Melin, E. (1993) 'Nurse-patient Interaction after Training in Integrity-promoting Care at a Long Term Ward: Analysis of Video-recorded Morning Care Sessions', *International Journal of Nursing Studies* 30: 1–13.

Kimmel, D. C. and Sang, B. E. (1995) 'Lesbians and Gay Men in Midlife', in A. R. D'Augelli and C. J. Patterson (eds) *Lesbian, Gay and Bisexual Identities over the Lifespan: Psychological Perspectives*, New York: Oxford University Press.

King, R., Warnes, A. M. and Williams, A. M. (2000) *Sunset Lives: British Retirement Migration to the Mediterranean*, Oxford: Berg.

Kinsella, K. (1988) *Aging in the Third World*, Washington DC: Africa and Latin America Branch, Center for International Research, Bureau of the Census, U. S. Department of Commerce.

Kinsella, K. and Taeuber, C. M. (1993) *An Aging World II*, Washington DC: US Department of Commerce, Economics and Statisitcs Adminstration, Bureau of the Census.

Kirkwood, T. (1999) *Time of Our Lives: The Science of Human Ageing*, London: Weidenfeld and Nicolson.

Kirkwood, T. (2004) 'Review of Benecke: The Dream of Eternal Life', *Ageing and Society* 24: 482–4.

Kitwood, T. (1988) 'The Technical, the Personal, and the Framing of Dementia', *Social Behaviour* 3: 161–80.

Kitwood, T. (1997) *Dementia Reconsidered: The Person Comes First*, Buckingham: Open University Press.

Kitwood, T. and Woods, R. T. (1996) *Training and Development Strategy for Dementia Care in Residential Settings*, Bradford: Bradford Dementia Group.

Klein, N. (2000) *No Logo: Taking Aim at the Brand Bullies,* London: Flamingo Books.

Knapp, J. L., Beaver, L. M. and Read, T. D. (2002) 'Perceptions of the Elderly Among Ministers and Ministry Students: Implications for Seminary Curricula', *Educational Gerontology* 28: 313–24.

Koenig, H. G. (1997) *Is Religion Good for Your Health? The Effects of Religion on Physical and Mental Health,* Binghamton, NY: The Haworth Press.

Kohli, M. (1986) 'Social Organization and Subjective Construction of the Life Course', in A. B., Sørensen, F. Weinert and L. Sherrod (eds) *Human Development: Multidisciplinary Perspectives*, Hillsdale, NJ: Lawrence Erlbaum.

Kohli, M. (1988) 'Ageing as a Challenge for Sociological Theory', *Ageing and Society* 8: 367–94.

Kohli, M. (2004) 'Intergenerational Transfers and Inheritance: A Comparative View', in M. Silverstein and K. W. Schaie (eds) *Annual Review of Gerontology and Geriatrics, Vol. 24: Focus on Intergenerational Relations Across Time and Place*, New York: Springer Publishing Company.

Kohli, M. and Meyer, J. W. (1986) 'Social Structure and the Social Construction of Life Stages', *Human Development* 29: 145-9.

Kohli, M., Rein, M., Guillemard, A.-M. and von Gunsteren, H. (eds) (1991) *Time for Retirement: Comparative Studies of Early Exit from the Labor Force,* Cambridge: Cambridge University Press.

Kotlikoff, L. J. and Burns, S. (2004) *The Coming Generational Storm*, Cambridge, MA: MIT Press.

Kübler-Ross, E. (1961) *On Death and Dying*, New York: Macmillan.

Kyriakides, C. and Virdee, S. (2003) 'Migrant Labour, Racism and the British National Health Service', *Ethnicity and Health* 8 (4): 283-305.

Laing, W. (2002) *Healthcare Market Review, 2001-2,* London: Laing and Buisson.

Laing, W. (2004) *Healthcare Market Review, 2003-4,* London: Laing and Buisson.

Laing, W. (2005) *Extra-Care Housing Markets 2005*, London: Laing and Buisson.

Lane, M. A., Ingram, D. K. and Roth, G. S. (2002) 'The Serious Search for an Anti-aging Pill', *Scientific American* August: 36.

Langer, J. (1969) *Theories of Development*, New York: Holt, Rinehart and Winston.

Laslett, P. (1987) 'The Emergence of the Third Age', *Ageing and Society* 7 (2): 133-60.

Laslett, P. (1989) *A Fresh Map of Life: The Emergence of the Third Age,* London: Weidenfeld and Nicolson.

Lawton, M. P. and Rubinstein, R. (2000) *Interventions in Dementia Care: Toward Improving Quality of Life*, New York: Springer Publishing Company.

Leplege, A. and Hunt, S. (1997) 'The Problem of Quality of Life in Medicine', *Journal of the American Medical Association* 278 (1): 47-50.

Levin, I. and Trost, J. (1999) 'Living Apart Together', *Community, Work and Family.* 2: 279-94.

Levy, F. and Michel, R. (1991) *The Economic Future of American Families,* Washington DC: The Urban Institute Press.

Lie, B. (2002) *Immigration and Immigrants 2002*, Oslo: Statistics Norway.

Longley, M. and Warner, M. (2002) 'Alzheimer's Disease: An Introduction to the Issues', in M., Warner, S., Furnish M. Longley and B. Lawlor *Alzheimer's Disease, Policy and Practice across Europe,* Oxford: Radcliffe Medical Press.

Lopata, H. Z. (1973) *Widowhood in an American City*, Cambridge, MA: Schenkman.

Lopata, H. Z. (1979) *Women as Widows: Support Systems*, New York: Elsevier.

Lopata, H. Z. (1996) *Current Widowhood: Myths and Realities,* Thousand Oaks, CA: Sage.

Lucas, S. R. and Good, A. D. (2001) 'Race, Class, and Tournament Track Mobility', *Sociology of Education* 74 (2): 139-56.

Luscher, K. (2000) 'Ambivalence: A Key Concept for the Study of Intergenerational Relations', in European Observatory on Family Matters (ed.) *Family Issues Between Gender and Generations,* pp. 111-50, Luxemburg: European Commission.

Luscher, K. (2002) 'Intergenerational Ambivalence: Further Steps in Theory and Research', *Journal of Marriage and Family* 64 (3): 585.

Lyman, K. A. (1998) 'Living with Alzheimer's Disease: The Creation of Meaning among Persons with Dementia', *Journal of Clinical Ethics* 9 (1): 49-57.

MacDonald, A. (2005) 'Care Homes and Dementia', *Aging and Mental Health* 9 (2): 91.

Macdonald, A. and Dening, T. (2002) 'Dementia is Being Avoided in NHS and Social Care', *British Medical Journal* 324: 548.

Mackenzie, J., Downs, M. and Bartlett, R. (2005) 'Moving Towards Culturally Competent Dementia Care: Have we been Barking up the Wrong Tree?', *Reviews in Clinical Gerontology*, Published Online, 9 November 2005.

Mackey, T. (2003) 'An Ethical Assessment of Anti-aging Medicine', *Journal of Anti-Aging Medicine* 6: 187-204.

Macnicol, J. (1998) *The Politics of Retirement in Britain, 1878-1948*, Cambridge: Cambridge University Press.

Maitland, N. (2004) Personal conversations with Nan Maitland, Chair of Homeshare International, www.home-share.org.uk

Mann, K. (2001) *Approaching Retirement - Social Divisions, Welfare and Exclusion,* Bristol: The Policy Press.

Mannheim, K. (1952) 'The Problems of Generations', in D. Kecskemeti (ed.), *Essays on the Sociology of Knowledge,* London: Routledge and Kegan Paul. (Original work published 1922.)

Manton, K. (1991) 'New Biotechnologies and Limits to Life Expectancy', in W. Lutz (ed.), *Future Demographic Trends in Europe and North America,* New York: Academic Press.

Manton, K., Corder, L. and Stallard, E. (1997) 'Chronic Disability Trends in Elderly United States Populations: 1982-1984', *Proceedings National Academy of Science USA* 94: 2593-8.

Marmot, M. and Shipley, M. (1996) 'Do Socioeconomic Differences in Mortality Persist After Retirement?', *British Medical Journal* 313: 117-80.

Marr, A. (2004) BBC News, 12 October.

Marshall, M. (1997) 'Design and Technology for People with Dementia', in R. Jacoby and C. Oppenheimer (eds) *Psychiatry in the Elderly,* 2nd edn, Oxford: Oxford University Press.

Marshall, M. (2001) 'Dementia and Technology', in S. M. Peace and C. A. Holland (eds) *Inclusive Housing in an Ageing Society: Innovative Approaches,* Bristol: The Policy Press.

Marshall, M. (2004) *Perspectives on Rehabilitation and Dementia,* London: Jessica Kingsley.

Martin, D. (2005) *On Secularization: Towards a Revised General Theory,* London: Ashgate.

Martin-Matthews, A. (1991) *Widowhood in Later Life,* Toronto and Vancouver: Butterworth.

Martyn, R. and Goodridge, K. (2001) *Outrageous Agers: An Exhibition of Photography and Video Installations Addressing Stereotypes of Women and Ageing,* www.var.ndirect.co.uk/outrageous/ex_index.html (accessed 21 April 2005).

Mason, D. (ed.) (2003) *Explaining Ethnic Differences: Changing Patterns of Disadvantage in Britain,* Bristol: The Policy Press.

Mason, M. A. (1999) *The Custody Wars,* New York: Basic Books.

Mayes, S. (2000) *The Archaeology of Human Bone,* London: Routledge.

Mayhew, V. (2003) *Pensions 2002: Public Attitudes to Pensions and Saving for Retirement,* Department for Work and Pensions Research Report No. 193, Leeds: Corporate Document Services.

Mays, N. (1983) 'Elderly South Asians in Britain: A Survey of the Relevant Literature and Themes for Future Research', *Ageing and Society* 3: 71-97.

McDowell, I. and Newell, C. (1987) *Measuring Health: A Guide to Rating Scales and Questionnaires,* New York: Oxford University Press.

McFadden, S. H. (1996) 'Religion, Spirituality and Ageing', in J. E. Birren and K. W. Schaie (eds) *Handbook of the Psychology of Aging,* 4th edn, San Diego: Academic Press.

McFadden, S. H. and Levin, J.S. (1996) 'Religion, Emotions and Health', in C. Magai and S. H. McFadden (eds) *Handbook of Emotion, Adult Development and Aging,* San Diego: Academic Press.

McGlone, F., Park, A. and Roberts, C. (1996) 'Relative Values: Kinship and Friendship', in R. Jowell, R., Curtice, J., Park, A., Brook, L. and Thomson, K. (eds) *British Social Attitudes, The 13th Report,* Aldershot: Dartmouth Publishing Co.

McMurdo, M. E. T. (2000) 'A Healthy Old Age: Realistic or Futile Goal?', *British Medical Journal* 321: 1149-51.

Mead, G. H. (1934) *Mind, Self and Society,* Chicago: Chicago University Press.

Mead, M. (1973) *Coming of Age in Samoa: A Psychological Study of Primitive Youth for Western Civilization,* New York: American Museum of Natural History.

Means, R. and Smith, R. (2003) *Community Care: Policy and Practice,* Basingstoke: Palgrave Macmillan.

Mehlman, M. J., Binstock, R. H., Juengst, E. T., Ponsaran, R. S. and Whitehouse, P. J. (2004) 'Anti-aging Medicine: Can Consumers be Better Protected?', *Gerontologist* 44: 304-10.

Melzer, D., McWilliams, B., Brayne, C., Johnson, T. and Bond, J. (1999) 'Profile of Disability in Elderly People: Estimates from a Longitudinal Study', *British Medical Journal* 318: 1108-11.

Melzer, D., McWilliams, B., Brayne, C., Johnson, T. and Bond, J. (2000) 'Socio-economic Status and the Expectation of Disability in Old Age: Estimates for England', *Journal of Epidemiology and Community Health* 54: 286-92.

Merchant, R. (2003) *Pioneering the Third Age: The Church in an Ageing Population*, Carlisle: Paternoster Press.

Midwinter, E. (2005) 'How Many People are there in the Third Age?', *Ageing and Society* 25: 9-18.

Miesen, B. (2004) 'Towards a Psychology of Dementia Care: Awareness and Intangible Loss', in G. M. M. Jones, and B. M. L. Miesen, (eds) *Caregiving in Dementia: Research and Applications*, Vol. 3, pp. 183-213, Hove: Brunner-Routledge.

Millar, R. A. (2002) 'Extending Life: Scientific Prospects and Political Obstacles', *The Millbank Quarterly* 80 (1): 155-74.

Miller, D. (1991) *Modernity and Self-identity*, Cambridge: Polity Press.

Miller, G. (2001) 'Changing the Subject: Self-construction in Brief Therapy', in J. Gubrium and J. Holstein (eds) *Institutional Selves: Troubled Identities in a Postmodern World*, New York: Oxford University Press.

Minkler, M. and Robertson, A. (1991) 'The Ideology of Age/Race Wars: Deconstructing a Social Problem', *Ageing and Society* 11: 1-22.

Minns, R. (2001) *The Cold War in Welfare: Stock Markets versus Pensions*, London: Verso.

Moberg, D. O. (2001) *Aging and Spirituality: Spiritual Dimensions of Aging Theory, Research, Practice and Policy*, Binghamton, NY: The Haworth Press.

Modell, J. (1989) *Into One's Own: From Youth to Adulthood in the United States, 1920-1975*, Berkeley: University of California Press.

Modood, T., Berthoud, R., Lakey, J., Nazroo, J., Smith, P., Virdee, S. and Beishon, S. (1997) *Ethnic Minorities in Britain: Diversity and Disadvantage*, London: Policy Studies Institute.

Modood, T., Berthoud, R. and Nazroo, J. (2002) '"Race", Racism and Ethnicity: A Response to Ken Smith', *Sociology* 36: 419-27.

Moniz-Cook, E. and Woods, R. T. (1997) 'The Role of Memory Clinics and Psychosocial Intervention in Early Stages of Dementia', *International Journal of Geriatric Psychiatry* 12: 1143-5.

Moody, H. (2001) 'Productive Aging and the Ideology of Old Age', in N. Morrow-Howell, J. Hinterlong and M. Sherraden (eds) *Productive Aging Concepts and Challenges*, Baltimore: Johns Hopkins University Press.

Moody, H. (2002) *Aging Concepts and Controversies*, 4th edn, London: Sage Publications.

Moore, A. and Stratton, D. (2002) *Resilient Widowers*, New York: Springer Publishing Company.

Morgan, D. (1989) 'Adjusting to Widowhood: Do Social Networks Really Make It Easier?', *The Gerontologist*, 29: 101-7.

Morgan, D. (1996) *Family Connections*, Cambridge: Polity Press.

Mozley, C., Sutcliffe, C., Bagley, H., Cordingley, L., Challis, D., Huxley, P. and Burns, A. (2004) *Towards Quality Care: Outcome for Older People in Care Homes* (Personal Social Services Research Unit), Aldershot: Ashgate.

Mueller, K. (2004) 'The Political Economy of Pension Reform in Central and Eastern Europe', in OECD *Reforming Public Pensions: Sharing the Experiences of Transition and OECD Countries*, Paris: OECD.

Mullan, P. (2002) *The Imaginary Time Bomb: Why an Ageing Population is Not a Social Problem*, London: I.B. Tauris.

Murphy, E., Dingwall, R., Greatbatch, D., Parker, S. and Watson, P. (1998) 'Qualitative Research Methods in Health Technology Assessment: A Review of the Literature', *Health Technology Assessment* 2 (16).

National Institute for Clinical Excellence (NICE) (2004) *Guidance on Cancer Services: Improving Supportive and Palliative Care for Adults with Cancer*, London: NICE.

National Institute for Social Work (1988) *Residential Care: A Positive Choice*, London: HMSO.

Nazroo, J. (1998) 'Genetic, Cultural or Socio-economic Vulnerability? Explaining Ethnic Inequalities in Health', *Sociology of Health and Illness* 20 (5): 710-30.

Nazroo, J. (2001) *Ethnicity, Class and Health*, London: Policy Studies Institute.

Nazroo, J. (2003) 'The Structuring of Ethnic Inequalities in Health: Economic Position, Racial Discrimination and Racism', *American Journal of Public Health* 93 (2): 277–84.

Nazroo, J. (2004) 'Ethnic Disparities in Aging Health: What Can We Learn from the United Kingdom?', in N. Anderson, R. Bulatao and B. Cohen (eds) *Critical Perspectives on Racial and Ethnic Differentials in Health in Late Life*, Washington, DC: National Academies Press.

Nazroo, J. Y. and Karlsen, S. (2003) 'Patterns of Identity among Ethnic Minority People: Diversity and Commonality', *Ethnic and Racial Studies* 26 (5): 902–30.

Neuborne, E. and Kerwin, K. (1999) 'Generation Y', *Business Week*, 15 February.

Neugarten, B. and Datan, N. (1973) 'Sociological Perspectives on the Life Cycle', in P. B. Baltes and K. W. Schaie (eds) *Life Span Development Psychology: Personality and Socialization*, San Diego: Academic.

Norberg, A., Melin, E. and Asplund, K. (2003) 'Reactions to Music, Touch and Object Presentation in the Final Stage of Dementia: An Exploratory Study', *International Journal of Nursing Studies* 40: 473–9.

Norman, A. (1985) *Triple Jeopardy: Growing Old in a Second Homeland*, London: Centre for Policy on Ageing.

Normann, H. K., Norberg, A. and Asplund, K. (2002) 'Confirmation and Lucidity During Conversations with a Woman with Severe Dementia', *Journal of Advanced Nursing* 39 (4): 370–6.

O'Boyle, C. A., McGee, H. and Joyce, C. R. B. (1994) 'Quality of Life: Assessing the Individual', in R. Fitzpatrick, (ed.), *Advances in Medical Sociology*, pp. 159–80, Greenwich, CT: JAI Press.

OECD (Organization for Economic Co-operation and Development) (1982) *Social Indicators*, Paris: OECD.

OECD (Organization for Economic Co-operation and Development) (2004a) *OECD Health Data 2004*, Table 9: Total expenditures on health, per capita US$ PPP; Table 10: Total expenditure on health, % GDP, retrieved April 2005 from: www.oecd.org/documentprint/0,2744,en_2649_34631_2085200_119656_119656_1_1_1,00.html.

OECD (Organization for Economic Co-operation and Development) (2004b) *Reforming Public Pensions: Sharing the Experiences of Transition and OECD Countries*, Paris: OECD.

OECD (Organization for Economic Co-operation and Development) (2004c) 'Ageing and Financial Markets', *Financial Market Trends* 86: 85–117.

OECD (Organization for Economic Co-operation and Development) (2005) *Solving the Pensions Puzzle: OECD Policy Brief, March 2005*, Paris: OECD.

Oldman, C. (2000) *Blurring the Boundaries: A Fresh Look at Housing Provision and Care for Older People*, Brighton: Pavillion.

Olshansky, S. J. and Carnes, B. A. (2001) *The Quest for Immortality: Science at the Frontiers of Aging*, New York: W. W. Norton and Co.

Olshansky, S. J., Carnes, B. and Cassel, C. (1990) 'In Search of Methuselah: Estimating the Upper Limits to Human Longevity', *Science* 250: 634–40.

Olshansky, S. J., Rudberg, M. A., Cassel, B. A. and Brady, J. A. (1991) 'Trading Off Longer Life for Worsening Health: The Expansion of Morbidity Hypothesis', *Journal of Aging and Health* 312: 194–216.

Olshansky, S. J., Hayflick, L. and Carnes, B. A. (2002) 'Position Statement on Human Aging', *Journal of Gerontology: Biological Science* 57A (8): B292–7.

Olshansky, S. J., Hayflick, L. and Perls, T. (2004) 'Anti-aging Medicine: The Hype and the Reality – Part I', *Journals of Gerontology Series A - Biological Sciences and Medical Sciences* 59: 513–4.

Onpoint (2004) 'Generation X Definition', www.onpoint-marketing.com/generation-x.htm.

Office for National Statistics (ONS) (1984) *Birth Statistics 1837-1983 - Historical Series*, Series FM1, Vol. 13, London: HMSO.

Office for National Statistics (ONS) (2000) *People Aged 65 and Over*, London: Office for National Statistics.

Office for National Statistics (ONS) (2003) *Entitled But Not Claiming? Pensioners, the MIG and Pension Credit*, London: Office for National Statistics.

Office for National Statistics (ONS) (2004a) *Population Trends 117*, London: The Stationery Office.

Office for National Statistics (ONS) (2004b) *Birth Statistics 2003*, Series FM1, Vol. 32, London: The Stationery Office.

Office for National Statistics (ONS) (2005a) in *Health Statistics Quarterly* No. 26, Table 3.1, p. 49 London: Palgrave.

Office for National Statistics (ONS) (2005b) *Birth Statistics: Historical Series 1838-2003*, FM1. www.statistics.gov.uk/.

Office of Population Censuses and Surveys (OPCS) (2002) *Marriage, Divorce and Adoption Statistics*, London: HMSO.

O'Rand, A. M. (1999) 'Risk, Rationality and Modernity: Social Policy and the Aging Self', in K. W. Schaie, and J. Hendricks, (eds) *The Evolution of the Aging Self: The Societal Impact of the Aging Process*, pp. 225-50, New York: Springer.

O'Rand, A. M. (2000) 'Risk, Rationality, and Modernity: Social Policy and the Aging Self', in K. W. Schaie (ed.), *Social Structures and Aging*, New York: Springer Publishing Company.

O'Rand, A. M., and Shuey, K. M. (2004) *Old and New Pension Risks for Workers*, prepared for Maxwell Policy Research Symposium on Changing Demographics, Stagnant Social Policies, Syracuse University.

Owen, D. (1994) 'Spatial Variations in Ethnic Minority Groups Populations in Great Britain', *Population Trends* 78: 23-33.

Packer, T. (2000) 'Does Person-centred Care Exist?', *Journal of Dementia Care* 8 (3): 19-21.

Palmer, G., Carr, J. and Kenway, P. (2004) *Monitoring Poverty and Social Exclusion 2004*, London: New Policy Institute.

Parfit, D. (1984) *Reasons and Persons*, Oxford: Clarendon Press.

Parsons, D. (1996) 'Retirement Age and Retirement Income: The Role of the Firm', in E. A. Hanushek, and N. J. Maritato (eds) *Assessing Knowledge of Retirement Behavior*, pp. 149-94. Washington, DC: National Academy Press.

Peace, S. and Holland, C. (eds) (2001) *Inclusive Housing in an Ageing Society: Innovative Approaches*, Bristol: The Policy Press.

Peace, S., Kellaher, L. and Willcocks, D. (1997) *Re-evaluating Residential Care*, Buckingham: Open University Press.

Peace, S., Holland, C. and Kellaher, L. (2006) *Environment and Identity in Later Life*, Maidenhead: Open University Press/McGraw-Hill Education.

Pellman, J. (1992) 'Widowhood in Elderly Women: Exploring its Relationship to Community Integration, Hassles, Stress, Social Support, and Social Support Seeking', *International Journal of Aging and Human Development* 35: 253-64.

Pensions Commission (2004a) 'Macro-theory and Macro Modelling', in *Pensions: Challenges and Choices. The First Report of the Pensions Commission. Appendices*, London: The Stationery Office.

Pensions Commission (2004b) *Pensions: Challenges and Choices. The First Report of the Pensions Commission*, London: The Stationery Office.

Pensions Policy Institute (PPI) (2003a) *The Pensions Landscape*, London: PPI.

Pensions Policy Institute (PPI) (2003b) *The Under-pensioned: Ethnic Minorities*, London: PPI.

Perenboom, R. J., van Herten, L. M., Boshuizen, H. C. and van den Bos, G. A. (2004) 'Trends in Disability Free Life Expectancy', *Disability and Rehabilitation* 26 (7): 377-86.

Perren, K., Arber, S. and Davidson, K. (2003) 'Men's Organizational Affiliation in Later Life: The Influence of Social Class and Marital Status on Informal Group Membership', *Ageing and Society* 23: 69-82.

Perrin, T. and May, H. (1999) *Wellbeing in Dementia: An Occupational Approach for Therapists and Carers*, London: Churchill Livingstone.

Phillips, J., Bernard, M., Biggs, S. and Kingston, P. (2001) 'Retirement Communities in Britain: A 'Third Way' for the Third Age?', in S. M. Peace and C. A. Holland (eds) *Inclusive Housing in an Ageing Society: Innovative Approaches*, Bristol: The Policy Press.

Phillipson, C. (1982) *Capitalism and the Construction of Old Age*, London: Macmillan.

Phillipson, C. (1998) *Reconstructing Old Age*, London: Sage.

Phillipson, C. (2002) 'Ageism and Globalization: Citizenship and Social Rights in Transnational Settings', in L. Andersson (ed.), *Cultural Gerontology*, Westport, CT: Auburn House.

Phillipson, C. and Scharf, T. (2004) *The Impact of Government Policy on Social Exclusion among Older People*, London: Office of Deputy Prime Minister/Social Exclusion Unit.

Phillipson, C., Alhaq, E., Ullah, S. and Ogg, J. (2001a) 'Bangladeshi Families in Bethnal Green: Older People, Ethnicity and Social Exclusion', in A. M. Warnes, L. Warren and M. Nolan (eds) *Care Services in Later Life: Transformations and Critiques*, London: Jessica Kingsley.

Phillipson, C., Bernard, M., Phillips, J. and Ogg, J. (2001b) *The Family and Community Life of Older People: Social Support and Social Networks in Three Urban Areas*, London: Routledge.

Pierson, P. (2001) *The New Politics of the Welfare State*, Oxford: Oxford University Press.

Pilcher, J. (1998) *Women of Their Time : Generation, Gender Issues and Feminism*, Aldershot: Ashgate.

Post, S. (2000) *The Moral Challenge of Alzheimer's Disease: Ethical Issues from Diagnosis to Dying*, London: Johns Hopkins University Press.

Poulain, M. and Perrin, N. (2002) 'The Demographic Characteristics of Immigrant Populations in Belgium', in W. Haug, P. Compton and Y. Courbage (eds) *The Demographic Characteristics of Immigrant Populations*, Strasbourg: Council of Europe Publishing.

Prince, M. (2000) 'The Epidemiology of Alzheimer's Disease', in J. O'Brien, D. Ames and A. Burns (eds) *Dementia*, London: Arnold.

Putney, N. M. and Bengtson, V. L. (2001) 'Families and Intergenerational Relations at Midlife', in M. E. Lachman (ed.), *Handbook of Midlife Development*, New York: Wiley.

Qin, D. (2004) 'Toward a Critical Feminist Perspective of Culture and Self', *Feminism and Psychology* 14 (2): 297–312.

Qureshi, H. (1994) 'Impact on Families: Young Adults with Learning Disability who show Challenging Behaviour', in C. Kiernan, (ed.), *Research to Practice? Implications of Research on the Challenging Behaviour of People with Learning Disability*, pp. 89–115. Clevedon: British Institute of Learning Disability.

Qureshi, H. (1996) 'Obligations and Support within Families', in A. Walker (ed.), *The New Generational Contract*. pp. 100–19, London: UCL Press.

Qureshi, H. and Simons, K. (1987) 'Caring for Elderly People', in J. Brannen and G. Wilson (eds) *Give and Take in Families*, London: Allen and Unwin.

Qureshi, H. and Walker, A. (1989) *The Caring Relationship: Elderly People and their Families*, Houndmills: Macmillan.

Radley, A. and Green, R. (1987) 'Illness as Adjustment: A Methodology and Conceptual Framework', *Sociology of Health and Illness* 9: 179–207.

Raging Grannies of Seattle (2003) *Raging Grannies Website*, www.raginggrannies.com/ (accessed 21 April 2005).

Raikhel, E. (2000) 'Cults of the Undying: Meditations on Quality of Life', *Scientific American* 283: 98–102.

Randel, J., German, T. and Ewing, D. (eds) (1999) *The Ageing and Development Report: Poverty, Independence and the World's Older People*, London: Earthscan.

Rapley, M. (2003) *Quality of Life Research: A Critical Introduction*, London: Sage Publications.

Rattan, S. I. S. (2004) 'Aging, Anti-aging, and Hormesis', *Mechanisms of Ageing and Development* 125: 285–9.

Ravenstein, E. G. (1885) 'The Laws of Migration', *Journal of the Royal Statistical Society* 48: 167–235.

Redford, A. (1926) *Labour Migration in England, 1800-50.* Manchester: Manchester University Press.

Rein, M. and Schmähl, W. (eds) (2004) *Rethinking the Welfare State: The Political Economy of Pension Reform,* Cheltenham: Edward Elgar Publishing.

Ridsdale, B. C. (2004) *CMIR (Continuous Mortality Investigation Reports) 21,* accessed 28 September 2004.

Riesman, D. (1950) *The Lonely Crowd: A Study of the Changing American Character,* New Haven, CT: Yale University Press.

Riggs, A. (1997) *Phantoms, Ghosts and Shadows: Missing Women in Widowers' Lives,* Aging Beyond 2000: One World One Future, the 16th Congress of the International Association of Gerontology, Adelaide, Australia.

Riley, M. (1983) 'Introduction: A Mosaic of Knowledge', in M. Riley, B. Hess and K. Bond (eds) *Aging in Society - Selected Reviews of Recent Research,* London: Lawrence Erlbaum.

Riley, M. W. and Riley, J. W. (1994) 'Structural Lag', in M. Riley, R. Kahn, and A. Foner, *Age and Structural Lag,* pp. 15–36, New York: Wiley and Sons.

Riley, M., Kahn, R. and Foner, A. (1994) *Age and Structural Lag: Society's Failure to Provide Meaningful Opportunities in Work, Family and Leisure,* New York: Wiley and Sons.

Robert, L. L. (2004) 'The Three Avenues of Gerontology: From Basic Research to Clinical Gerontology and Anti-aging Medicine. Another French Paradox', *Journals of Gerontology Series A - Biological Sciences and Medical Sciences* 59: 540–2.

Robertson, A. (1999) 'Beyond Apocalyptic Demography: Toward a Moral Economy of Interdependence', in M. Minkler and C. L. Estes (eds) *Critical Gerontology: Perspectives from Political and Moral Economy,* Amityville, NY: Baywood Publishing.

Robine, J. M., Mathers, C. and Brooard, N. (1996) 'Trends and Differentials in Disability Free Life Expectancy, Concepts, Methods and Findings', in G. Caselli and A. D. Lopez (eds) *Health and Mortality among Elderly Populations,* Oxford: Clarendon Press.

Rojek, C. and Turner, C. (2000) 'Decorative Sociology: Towards a Critique of the Cultural Turn', *Sociological Review* 48: 629–48.

Rose, N. (1998) *Inventing Our Selves,* Cambridge: Cambridge University Press.

Rose, S. (1997) *Lifelines: Biology, Freedom, Determinism,* Harmondsworth: Penguin Books.

Rosel, N. (1988) 'Clarification and Application of Erik Erikson's Eighth Stage of Man', *International Journal of Aging and Human Development* 27: 11–23.

Rosenbaum, J. (1984) *Career Mobility in a Corporate Hierarchy,* New York: Academic Press.

Rosenfeld, D. (2003) *The Changing of the Guard: Lesbian and Gay Elders, Identity and Social Change,* Philadelphia: Temple University Press.

Rubinstein, R. L. (1986) 'The Construction of a Day by Elderly Widowers', *International Journal of Aging and Human Development* 23: 161–73.

Rugg, J. (1999) *Hartrigg Oaks: The Early Development of a Continuing Care Retirement Community,* unpublished report, York: Centre for Housing Policy, University of York.

Runciman, W. G. (1966) *Relative Deprivation and Social Justice,* London: Routledge and Kegan Paul.

Ruta, D. A., Garratt, A. M., Leng, M., Russell, I. T. and MacDonald, L. M. (1994) 'A New Approach to the Measurement of Quality of Life: The Patient-Generated Index', *Medical Care* 32 (11): 1109–26.

Ryder, N. B. (1965) 'The Cohort as a Concept in the Study of Social Change', *American Sociological Review,* 30: 843–61.

Sabat, S. (2001) *The Experience of Alzheimer's Disease: Life through a Tangled Veil,* Oxford: Blackwell.

Sage Crossroads (2004) 'Is Aging a Disease', broadcast date 22 January, 11 am EST, video archive, www.sage-crossroads.net/public/webcasts/11/index.cfm.

Sampson, R. J. and Laub, J. H. (1993) *Crime in the Making: Pathways and Turning Points Through Life,* Cambridge, MA: Harvard University Press.

Saunders, P. (1990) *Social Class and Stratification*, London: Routledge.

Schaie, K. W. (1965) 'A General Model for the Study of Developmental Change', *Psychological Bulletin* 64: 92–107.

Scharf, T., Phillipson, C., Smith, A. E. and Kingston, P. (2002) *Growing Older in Socially Deprived Areas: Social Exclusion in Later Life*, London: Help the Aged.

Scharf, T., Phillipson, C. and Smith, E. (2004) 'Poverty and Social Exclusion: Growing Older in Deprived Urban Neighbourhoods', in A. Walker and C. Hagan Hennessy (eds) *Growing Older: Quality of Life in Old Age*, Maidenhead: Open University Press.

Schlesinger, M. and Kroncbrusch, K. (1994) 'Intergenerational Tensions and Conflict: Attitudes and Perceptions about Social Justice and Age-related Needs', in V. L. Bengtson and R. A. Harootyan (eds) *Intergenerational Linkages: Hidden Connections in American Society*, New York: Springer Publishing Company.

Schoeni, R. F., Freedman, V. A. and Wallace, R. (2001) 'Persistent, Consistent, Widespread and Robust? Another Look at Recent Trends in Old Age Disability', *Journal of Gerontology – B Psychological and Social Sciences* 56 (4): S206–18.

Schultz, J. H. (2001) 'Productive Aging: An Economist's View', in N. Morrow-Howell, J. Hinterlong, and M. Sherraden, (eds) *Productive Ageing: Concepts and Challenges*, pp. 145–74, Baltimore: Johns Hopkins.

Scientific American (2004) *The Science of Staying Young*, special edition, www.sciam.com/special/toc.cfm?issueid=23&sc=I100390.

Scott, J. (1999) 'Family Change: Revolution or Backlash in Attitudes?' in S. McRae, (ed.), *Changing Britain. Families and Households in the 1990s*, Oxford: Oxford University Press.

Settersten, R. A. (1999) *Lives in Time and Place*, Amityville, NY: Baywood.

Shaw, C. (1999) '1996–based Population Projections by Legal Marital Status for England and Wales', *Population Trends* 95: 23–32.

Shaw, C. (2000) '1998–based National Population Projections for the United Kingdom and Constituent Countries', *Population Trends* 99: 4–12.

Shaw, C. (2004) '2002–based National Population Projections for the United Kingdom and Constituent Countries', *Population Trends* 117: 6–15.

Shegog, R. F. A. (ed.) (1981) *The Impending Crisis of Old Age*, Oxford: Nuffield Provincial Hospitals Trust/Oxford University Press.

Shilling, C. (1993) *The Body and Social Theory*, London: Sage.

Shostak, S. (2002) *Becoming Immortal: Combining Cloning and Stem-cell Therapy*, Albany: State University of New York.

Sidorenko, A. and Walker, A. (2004) 'The Madrid International Plan of Action on Ageing: From Conception to Implementation', *Ageing and Society* 24: 147–67.

Silverstein, M. and Parrott, T. M. (1997) 'Attitudes Toward Public Support of the Elderly: Does Early Involvement with Grandparents Moderate Generational Tensions?', *Research on Aging* 19: 108–32.

Silverstein, M., Angelleli, J. J. and Parrott, T. M. (2001) 'Changing Attitudes toward Aging Policy in the United States during the 1980s and 1990s: A Cohort Analysis', *Journal of Gerontology: Social Sciences* 56B: S36–S43.

Silverstein, M., Conroy, S. J., Wang, H., Giarrusso, R. and Bengtson, V. L. (2002) 'Reciprocity in Parent-child Relations over the Adult Life Course', *Journal of Gerontology: Social Sciences* 57B: S3–S13.

Simpson, P. A., Greller, M. M. and Stroh, L. K. (2002) 'Variations in Human Capital Investment Activity by Age', *Journal of Vocational Behavior* 61 (1): 109–38.

Sinfield, A. (1981) *What Unemployment Means*, Oxford: Martin Robertson.

Sinfield, A. (2000) 'Tax Benefits in Non-state Pensions', *European Journal of Social Security* 2 (2): 137–68.

Sinnott, J. D. (1998) *The Development of Logic in Adulthood: Postformal Thought and its Applications*, New York: Plenum Press.

Sixsmith, A., Sixsmith, J., Green, S. and Kennedy, V. (2004) *ENABLE-AGE Survey Study T1, National Report United Kingdom,* the ENABLE-AGE Project, the ENABLE-AGE Consortium, the University of Liverpool.

Skidmore, P. and Huber, J. (2003) 'Ageing, Values and the Baby Boomers', *Generations Review* 13 (4): 16–19.

Slattery, L. (1999) 'Generation X to Generation Next', *Egoist,* http://members.tripod.com/barneygrant/GenxLS.htm.

Smith, B. (1968) 'Competence and Socialization', in J.A. Clausen, (ed.), *Socialization and Society,* Boston: Little Brown.

Smith, D. (1977) *Racial Disadvantage in Britain,* Harmondsworth: Penguin.

Smith, J. and Gerstorf, D. (2004) 'Ageing Differently: Potential and Limits', in S. O. Daatland and S. Biggs (eds) *Ageing and Diversity,* Bristol: The Policy Press.

Snyder, L. (1999) *Speaking Our Minds: Personal Reflections from Individuals with Alzheimer's,* Basingstoke: W. H. Freeman.

Speck, P. W. (1988) *Being There – Pastoral Care in Times of Illness,* London: SPCK.

Speck, P. W., Bennett, K., Coleman, P. G. and Mills, M. (2005) 'Bereavement', in A. Walker and C. Hennessy (eds) *Growing Older: Approaches to Quality of Life in Context,* Maidenhead: Open University Press.

Spector, A., Thorgrimsen, L., Woods, B., Royan, L., Davies, S., Butterworth, M. and Orrell, M. (2003) 'Efficacy of an Evidence-based Cognitive Stimulation Therapy Programme for People with Dementia: Randomised Controlled Trial', *British Journal of Psychiatry* 183: 248–54.

Sprangers, M. A. G. and Schwartz, C. E. (1999) 'Integrating Response Shift into Health-related Quality of Life Research: A Theoretical Model', *Social Science and Medicine* 48: 1507–15.

Standard and Poor's (2003) *Global Stock Markets Fact Book,* New York: Standard and Poor's.

StatBase (2002) 'Population: Age, Sex and Legal Marital Status, 1971 Onwards', *Population Trends* 109, accessed 20 September 2004.

Sterin, G. J. (2002) 'Essay on a Word: A Lived Experience of Alzheimer's Disease', *Dementia: The International Journal of Social Research and Practice* 1 (1): 7–10.

Stiglitz, J. E. (2002) *Globalization and its Discontents,* New York: W.W. Norton.

Stiglitz, J. (2003) *The Roaring Nineties,* London: Penguin.

Summerfield, C. and Babb, P. (eds) (2004) *Social Trends 34: A Portrait of British Society,* London: The Stationery Office.

Taylor, M. (2003) 'The Reformulation of Social Policy in Chile, 1973–2001', *Global Social Policy* 3 (1): 21–44.

Taylor, M., Berthoud, R. and Jenkins, S. (2004) *Low Income and Multiple Disadvantage 1991–2001,* analysis of the British Household Panel Survey, a Report for the Social Exclusion Unit in the Breaking the Cycle Series, London: ODPM.

Taylor-Gooby, P. (2004) *New Risks, New Welfare,* Oxford: Oxford University Press.

Taylor-Gooby, P. (2005) 'Uncertainty, Trust and Pensions: The Case of the Current UK Reforms', *Social Policy and Administration* 39: 217–32.

Teri, L., Logsdon, R. G., Uomoto, J. and McCurry, S. M. (1997) 'Behavioural Treatment of Depression in Dementia Patients: A Controlled Clinical Trial', *Journal of Gerontology Psychological Sciences* 52: 159–66.

Thane, P. (1978) 'The Muddled History of Retiring at 60 and 65', *New Society* 3: 234–6.

Thane, P. (2000) *Old Age in English History: Past Experiences, Present Issues,* Oxford: Oxford University Press.

Thomas, B. (1972) *Migration and Urban Development,* London: Methuen.

Thompson, J. B. (2000) 'The Globalization of Communication', in D. Held and A. McGrew (eds) *The Global Transformations Reader,* Cambridge: Polity Press.

Tinker, A., Wright, F. and Zelig, H. (1995) *Difficult to Let Sheltered Housing,* London: HMSO.

Tinker, A., Wright, F., McCreadie, M., Askham, J., Hancock, R. and Holmans, A. (1999) *Alternative Models of Care for Older People: Royal Commission on Long Term Care Research Vol. 2. Cm 4192-II/2,* London: Stationery Office.

Titmuss, R. (1958) *Essays on 'The Welfare State',* London: Unwin.

Titmuss, R. and Titmuss, K. (1942) *Parents Revolt: A Study of the Declining Birth-Rate in Acquisitive Societies,* London: Secker and Warburg.

Tornstam, L. (1996) 'Gerotranscendence: A Theory about Maturing into Old Age', *Journal of Aging and Identity* 1 (1): 37–50.

Torres, S. (2004) 'Late-in-life Immigrants in Sweden: Who Are They and What Do They Need?', in A. M. Warnes, M. Casado-Díaz and U. Lundh (eds) *Older Migrants in Europe: Sources, Case Studies and a Guide to Research*, Sheffield: Sheffield Institute for Studies on Ageing.

Townsend, P. (1957) *The Family Life of Old People*, London: Routledge and Kegan.

Townsend, P. (1962) *The Last Refuge*, London: Routledge.

Townsend, P. (1970) *The Concept of Poverty*, London: Heinemann.

Townsend, P. (1979) *Poverty in the United Kingdom*, Harmondsworth: Penguin.

Townsend, P. (1981) 'The Structured Dependency of the Elderly: Creation of Social Policy in the Twentieth Century', *Ageing and Society* 1: 5–28.

Townsend, P. and Davidson, N. (1992) *Inequalities in Health*, Harmondsworth: Penguin.

TSO (The Stationery Office) (2004) *Pensions: Challenges and Crises*, the First Report of the Pensions Commission, London: The Stationery Office.

Tulgan, B. (1996) *Managing Generation X*, Santa Monica, CA: Merritt Publishing.

Turner, B. S. (1984) *The Body and Society: Explorations in Social Theory*, Oxford: Blackwell.

Turner, B. S. (1998) 'Ageing and Generational Conflicts: A Reply to Sarah Irwin', *British Journal of Sociology* 49: 299–304.

Turner, L. (2004) 'Biotechnology, Bioethics and Anti-aging Interventions', *Trends in Biotechnology* 22 (5): 219–21.

Twigg, J. (1998) 'Informal Care of Older People', in M. Bernard and J. Phillips (eds) *The Social Policy of Old Age*, London: CPA.

Twigg, J. (1999) 'The Spatial Ordering of Care: Public and Private in Bathing Support at Home', *Sociology of Health and Illness* 21 (4): 381–400.

Uhlenberg, P. (1995) 'Demographic Influences on Intergenerational Relationships', in V. L., Bengtson, K. W. Schaie and L. Burton (eds) *Adult Intergenerational Relations: Effects of Societal Change*, New York: Springer.

Uhlenberg, P. (2004) 'Historical Forces Shaping Grandparent–Grandchild Relationships: Demography and Beyond', in M. Silverstein and K. W. Schaie (eds) *Annual Review of Gerontology and Geriatrics, Vol. 24: Focus on Intergenerational Relations Across Time and Place*, New York: Springer.

Ungerson, C. (1983) 'Why Do Women Care?', in J. Finch and D. Groves (eds) *A Labour of Love*, London: Routledge and Kegan Paul.

Urry, J. (2000) *Sociology Beyond Societies*, London: Routledge.

van den Hoonaard, D. K. (2002) 'Attitudes of Older Widows and Widowers in New Brunswick, Canada towards New Partnerships', *Ageing International* 27 (4): 79–92.

van Tassel, D. and Stearns, P. N. (1986) *Old Age in a Bureaucratic Society: The Elderly, the Experts, and the State in American History*, Westport, CT: Greenwood Press.

Vaupel, J. W., Baudisch, A., Dolling, M., Roach, D. A. and Gampe, J. (2004) 'The Case for Negative Senescence', *Theoretical Population Biology* 65: 339–51.

Victor, C. R. (2005) *The Social Context of Ageing*, London: Routledge.

Victor, C., Scambler, S., Shah, S., Cook, D., Harris, T., Rink, E. and de Wilde, S. (2002) 'Has Loneliness amongst Older People Increased? An Investigation into Variations between Cohorts', *Ageing and Society* 22: 585–97.

Vincent, J. A. (1999) *Politics, Power and Old Age*, Buckingham: Open University Press.

Vincent, J. A. (2003a) *Old Age*, London: Routledge.

Vincent, J. A. (2003b) 'New Forms of Global Political Economy and Ageing Societies', paper presented at the European Association Conference, Ageing in Europe: Challenges for Globalization for Ageing Societies, Murcia, Spain.

Voas, D. and Crockett, A. (2005) 'Religion in Britain: Neither Believing nor Belonging', *Sociology* 39: 11–28.

Vogel, G. (1999) 'Breakthrough of the Year: Capturing the Promise of Youth', *Science* 286: 2238–39.

Volicer, I., Collard, A., Hurley, A., Bishop, C., Kern, D. and Karon, S. (1994) 'Impact of Special Care Unit for Patients with Advanced Alzheimer's Disease on Patients' Discomfort and Costs', *Journal of the American Geriatric Society* 42 (6): 597–603.

Wadsworth, M. (1991) *The Imprint of Time: Childhood, History, and Adult Life*, Oxford: Clarendon Press.

Waite, L. J., Bachrach, C., Hindin, H., Thomson, E. and Thornton, A. (eds) (2000) *The Ties That Bind: Perspectives on Marriage and Cohabitation,* New York: Aldine de Gruyter.

Walker, A. (1980) 'The Social Creation of Poverty and Dependency in Old Age', *Journal of Social Policy* 9 (1): 45–75.

Walker, A. (1981) 'Towards a Political Economy of Old Age', *Ageing and Society* 1: 73–94.

Walker, A. (1982) 'Dependency and Old Age', *Social Policy and Administration* 16: 115–35.

Walker, A. (1986) 'Pensions and the Production of Poverty in Old Age', in C. Phillipson and A. Walker (eds) *Ageing and Social Policy. A Critical Assessment,* Aldershot: Gower Publishing.

Walker, A. (ed.) (2005) *Understanding Quality of Life in Old Age,* Maidenhead: Open University Press.

Walker, A. and Deacon, B. (2003) 'Economic Globalization and Policies on Aging', *Journal of Societal and Social Policy* 2 (2): 1–18.

Walker, A. and Hennessy, C. H. (2004) *Growing Older: Quality of Life in Old Age,* Maidenhead: Open University Press.

Wallace, P. (2001) *Agequake,* Norwood, MA: Nicholas Brealey.

Wanless, D. (2002) *Securing Our Future Health: Taking a Long Term View,* London: HM Treasury.

Warnes, A. M. (1983) 'Variations in the Propensity among Older Persons to Migrate: Evidence and Implications', *Journal of Applied Gerontology* 2: 20–7.

Warnes, A. M. (1992) 'Migration and the Life Course', in A. G. Champion and A. Fielding (eds) *Migration Processes and Patterns: Volume I, Research Progress and Prospects,* London: Belhaven.

Warnes, A. M. (1996) 'Migrations among Older People', *Reviews in Clinical Gerontology* 6: 101–14.

Warnes, A. M. (2004) 'Older Foreign Migrants in Europe: Multiple Pathways and Welfare Positions', in S. O. Daatland and S. Biggs (eds) *Ageing and Diversity,* Bristol: The Policy Press.

Warnes, A. M. and Ford, R. (1995) 'Housing Aspirations and Migration in Later Life: Development During the 1980s', *Papers in Regional Science: The Journal of the RSAI* 74: 361–87.

Warnes, A. M., Friedrich, K., Kellaher, L. and Torres, S. (2004) 'The Diversity and Welfare of Older Migrants in Europe', *Ageing and Society* 24: 307–26.

Warren, T. (2003) 'A Privileged Pole? Diversity in Women's Pay, Pensions and Wealth in Britain', *Gender, Work and Organization* 10: 605–28.

Webber, A. (1990) *Life Later On: Older People and the Church,* London: SPCK.

Weeks, J., Heaphey, B. and Donovan, C. (2001) *Same-Sex Intimacies: Families of Choice and Other Life Experiments,* London: Routledge.

Wenger, C. (1984) *The Supportive Network,* London: George Allen and Unwin.

Westergaard, J. (1995) *Who Gets What?,* Oxford: Polity Press.

Westerhof, G. J., Dittmann-Kohli, F. and Bode, C. (2003) 'The Aging Paradox: Toward Personal Meaning in Gerontological Theory', in S. Biggs, A. Lowenstein, and J., Hendricks, (eds) *The Need for Theory: Critical Approaches to Social Gerontology,* pp. 127–43, Amityville, NY: Baywood Publishing Company.

White, A. (2002) *Social Focus in Brief: Ethnicity 2002,* London: Office for National Statistics.

Whiteford, P. (2004) 'Introduction: Learning from Pension Reform Experiences', in *Reforming Public Pensions: Sharing the Experiences of Transition and OECD Countries,* Paris: OECD.

Wilkinson, P. B., Snowball, S. and Smith, K. (2002) 'General Hospitals Must Take a Lead in Improving Dementia Care in the NHS', *British Medical Journal* 324: 548.

Wilkinson, R. (1996) *Unhealthy Societies – The Afflictions of Inequality,* London: Routledge.

Willcocks, D., Peace, S. and Kellaher, L. (1987) *Private Lives in Public Places,* London: Tavistock Publications.

Williams, A. and Nussbaum, J. F. (2001) *Intergenerational Communication Across the Life Span*, Mahwah, NJ: Lawrence Earlbaum.

Williams, B. (1973) *Problems of the Self: Philosophical Papers 1956-1972*, Cambridge: Cambridge University Press.

Williams, R. (1990) *A Protestant Legacy: Attitudes to Illness and Death Among Older Aberdonians*, Oxford: Clarendon Press.

Williamson, J. B., McNamara, T. K. and Howling, S. A. (2003) 'Generational Equity, Generational Interdependence, and the Framing of the Debate over Social Security Reform', *Journal of Sociology and Social Welfare* 30: 3-13.

Wilshier, P. (1989) 'Justice in an Ageing World', *Sunday Times*, 9 July.

Winder, R. (2004) *Bloody Foreigners: The Story of Immigration to Britain*, London: Little, Brown.

World Bank (1994) *Averting the Old Age Crisis*, Oxford: Oxford University Press.

World Health Organization (WHO) (2001) *Health and Ageing: A Discussion Paper*, Geneva: WHO.

World Health Organization (WHO) (2002) *Towards a Common Language for Functioning, Disability and Health*, Geneva: WHO.

World Health Organization (WHO) (2003) *International Statistical Classification of Diseases and Related Health Problems*, 10th revision version for 2003, Ch. 5, 'Mental and Behavioural Disorders', www3.who.int/icd/vol1htm2003/fr-icd.htm accessed 8 Sept 2005.

Wright, F. (2004) 'Old and Cold: Older People and Policies Failing to Address Fuel Poverty', *Social Policy and Administration* 38 (5): 488-503.

Wurtzel, E. (1994) *Prozac Nation: Young and Depressed in America*, Boston: Houghton Mifflin.

Yeates, N. (2001) *Globalization and Social Policy*, London: Sage.

Zinnbauer, B. J., Pargament, K. I. and Scott, A. B. (1999) 'The Emerging Meanings of Religiousness and Spirituality: Problems and Prospects', *Journal of Personality* 67: 889-919.

Index

This index is in word by word order. Page numbers in *italics* indicate diagrams. Authors of works referred to in detail are included.